The Economic Consequences of Government Deficits

**Economic Policy
Conference Series**

Cosponsored by
The Center for the Study of American
  Business and The Institute for Banking
  and Financial Markets, Washington
  University, St. Louis, Missouri

Previously published books in the series:
Meyer, Laurence H., *The Supply-Side
  Effects of Economic Policy*
Meyer, Laurence H., *Improving Money
  Stock Control: Problems, Solutions and
  Consequences*

The Economic Consequences of Government Deficits

edited by
Laurence H. Meyer
Washington University

Kluwer–Nijhoff Publishing
a member of the Kluwer Academic Publishers Group
Boston—The Hague—Dordrecht—Lancaster

Distributors for North America:
Kluwer Boston, Inc.
190 Old Derby Street
Hingham, MA 02043, U.S.A.

Distributors Outside North America:
Kluwer Academic Publishers Group
Distribution Centre
P. O. Box 322
3300AH Dordrecht, The Netherlands

Library of Congress Cataloging in Publication Data
Main entry under title:

The Economic consequences of government deficits.

(Economic policy conference series)
Proceedings of a conference co-sponsored by the Center for
the Study of American Business and the Institute for Banking
and Financial Markets at Washington University, St. Louis,
Mo., Oct. 29–30, 1982.
1. Deficit financing—United States—Congresses.
2. Finance—United States—Congresses. 3. United States—
Economic conditions—1971–   —Congresses. I. Meyer,
Laurence H. II. Washington University (Saint Louis, Mo.).
Center for the Study of American Business. III. Washington
University (Saint Louis, Mo.). Institute for Banking and
Financial Markets. IV. Series.
HJ257.2.E24   1983   339.5′23′0973   83-4381
ISBN 0-89838-143-6

Printed in the United States of America

Contents

Preface

On October 29 and 30, 1982, the Center for the Study of American Business and the Institute for Banking and Financial Markets at Washington University cosponsored a conference on "The Economic Consequences of Government Deficits." This was the sixth annual Economic Policy Conference sponsored by the Center, and the first it has cosponsored with the Institute. This book contains the papers and comments delivered at that conference.

Recent and prospective large federal deficits have prompted a thorough reconsideration of the political sources and economic consequences of government deficits. The papers in Part I focus on the implications of deficits for monetary growth and inflation, and the papers in Part II consider the effect of deficits on interest rates and capital formation. The papers in Part III deal with the political sources and remedies for the explosive growth in government spending and increased reliance on deficits.

The papers in Part I by Alan S. Blinder, Professor of Economics at Princeton University, and Preston J. Miller, Assistant Vice President and Research Advisor at the Federal Reserve Bank of Minneapolis, discuss the relation between monetary growth and deficits and present evidence on the effects of deficits on inflation and output. A deficit is said to be monetized when the Federal Reserve purchases bonds to aid the Treasury in financing the deficit. Such monetization increases bank reserves and, hence, the money supply. A major focus of the papers in Part I is on the extent to which the Fed tends to monetize deficits and on the consequences of monetized relative to nonmonetized deficits. While Miller and Blinder agree that exclusive reliance on bond financing of deficits is likely to be destabilizing, they reach different conclusions about the effects of deficits on output and inflation.

Preston Miller's paper, "Examining the Proposition that Federal Budget Deficits Matter," outlines a variety of reasons why deficits may affect output, inflation and interest rates, and presents evidence that the effects of deficits may be much larger than both conventional economic wisdom and previous empirical evidence suggest. When Miller indicates that deficits matter, he means that the rule which policy authorities follow in regard to fiscal policy and deficits matters.

Miller also argues that "a higher deficit policy requires faster monetary growth." It may not be feasible, even temporarily, to finance deficits by issuing bonds alone. An increase in bonds without an increase in money may cause real interest payments to grow without limit and may therefore force the government into insolvency. In his empirical work, Miller estimates equations in which average output growth, inflation and interest rates over four postwar subperiods depend on average growth rates in government debt and total reserves. By dealing with averages over these subperiods, Miller hopes to pick up the effects of different deficit policies on inflation, output and interest rates. He finds that periods characterized by higher deficits also are associated with lower real growth, higher inflation, and higher nominal and real interest rates. Miller concludes that both economic theory and his empirical evidence support the conclusion that deficits matter, if we interpret deficits to mean deficit policy, validating the concern that politicians have been expressing about deficits.

While Professor Jerome L. Stein of Brown University is in general agreement with Miller's conclusions, his discussion develops these results from an alternative analytical framework. He supports Miller's conclusion that deficits lead to higher monetary growth with empirical evidence based on an equation relating monetary growth to the high employment deficit. He also draws on the recent literature examining the stability of models under alternative regimes in which deficits are financed by money issue or bond issue to demonstrate that monetized deficits both raise inflation and lower steady state output per capita.

In "On the Monetization of Deficits," Alan S. Blinder considers two issues regarding the monetization of deficits: the effects of monetization on output and inflation and the factors affecting the degree to which deficits are monetized. Blinder uses the Granger causality tests to investigate whether monetized and nonmonetized deficits help to predict growth in nominal and real GNP and inflation. Blinder finds that while both monetized and nonmonetized deficits help to predict nominal income growth, neither monetized or nonmonetized deficits have much effect on real GNP growth.

Blinder then turns to an analysis of the monetization decision. He offers a game–theoretic framework to explain why the central bank may choose not to monetize deficits and may even respond to increases in the deficit by lowering reserves. His empirical investigation of the link between deficits and bank reserves finds the link to be more systematic than he expected on the basis of previous evidence. The evidence suggests, however, that monetization of deficits has been very minor.

In his discussion of the Blinder paper, Scott E. Hein, senior economist at the Federal Reserve Bank of St. Louis, argues that Blinder's results bear on the effects and determinants of monetary policy and do not effectively deal with monetization decision. The problem, according to Hein, is Blinder's use of adjusted bank reserves as a measure of the Fed's monetization of deficits. Monetization is only one of several factors affecting adjusted bank reserves. Bank reserves, as a consequence, are a useful summary measure of monetary policy actions rather than of monetization.

The papers in Part II consider the effect of deficit-financed fiscal policy on interest rates and capital formation. In "Asset Substitutability and the Impact of Federal Deficits," V. Vance Roley, Assistant Vice President and Economist, Federal Reserve Bank of Kansas City, presents evidence that the effect of deficits on corporate bond and equity yields, and hence on capital formation, is substantially affected by the maturity class in which the deficits are financed. To study this issue, Roley integrates a disaggregate financial sector—including demands for corporate bonds, equities, and four maturity classes of government securities—into an otherwise conventional, large scale macroeconometric model.

Roley simulates the financial market impact of increases in different maturity classes of government debt. He finds that while increases in short term government securities raise corporate bond and equity yields only slightly, increases in long-term government securities have a more substantial effect, particularly on the corporate bond rate. Roley then simulates the effect of an increase in government expenditures financed by the issue of the three longer-maturity classes of government securities. While the results suggest there is some stimulus to income over the first four quarters, the multiplier is less than one after one year. These results are fairly pessimistic and suggest that increases in government expenditures financed by government securities, exclusive of Treasury bills, will be offset significantly, although not completely, by a decline in private expenditures.

In his discussion of the Roley paper, Frederic S. Mishkin, Professor of Economics, University of Chicago and Research Associate at the National Bureau of Economic Research, is critical of the specification of rate of return variables in the asset demand functions in Roley's model. As does most other econometric work on asset demands, Roley employs yields to maturity as measures of rates of return. Mishkin notes that the theoretical analysis underlying portfolio models suggests that holding period yields are the more appropriate measure of relevant rates of return. This misspecification of the rate of return variables in Roley's asset demand functions may account for an important finding in Roley's paper—the low degree of substitutability among various assets.

In "Investment versus Savings Incentives: The Size of the Bang for the Buck and the Potential for Self Financing Business Tax Cuts," Alan J. Auerbach and Laurence J. Kotlikoff, Associate Professors of Economics at Harvard and Yale Universities, respectively, examine the effect of government policies to stimulate investment. They consider two types of policies which differ insofar as they treat newly produced capital differently from old capital. The authors refer to policies which distinguish new capital from old as investment policies and those that do not as savings policies. Auerbach and Kotlikoff use a life-cycle simulation model to consider three issues: (1) the net impact on capital accumulation of deficit-financed investment and savings incentives; (2) the potential for business tax cuts to be "self-financing;" and (3) the consequences of a gradual phasing in of such incentives.

In analyzing the net impact on capital formation of deficit financed business tax cuts, Auerbach and Kotlikoff examine whether the "crowding in" of new capital formation arising from business tax cuts exceeds the "crowding out" produced from deficits associated with these policies. They conclude that investment incentives, even those which are deficit financed, significantly increase capital formation. Deficit-financed savings incentives, on the other hand, "typically reduce the economy's rate of capital formation in the long run."

The underlying explanation of the relative efficiency of investment as opposed to savings incentives is that investment incentives involve a wealth redistribution from the old to the young, while savings incentives yield the opposite redistribution. Since the old in life-cycle models have higher marginal propensities to consume out of lifetime resources than the young, a wealth redistribution from the old to the young reduces current consumption, permitting the crowding in of current investment.

Auerbach and Kotlikoff find that if tax cuts are restricted to new capital, they not only stimulate investment, but they may also be self-financing. However, they warn that a gradual phasing in of such business tax cuts can actually reduce rather than stimulate short-term investment.

Franco Modigliani, Professor of Economics and Finance and Institute Professor at the Massachusetts Institute of Technology, highlights the "unexpected and paradoxical results" Auerbach and Kotlikoff derive from the life-cycle model that Modigliani himself had been largely responsible for developing. While Modigliani confirms that the life-cycle model does indeed generate the results for savings and investment incentives reported by Auerbach and Kotlikoff, he is far less enthusiastic about the use of investment incentives, arguing that the redistribution they induce from the old to the young is "the most cruel form of redistribution, because the old, in contrast to the young, have no opportunity to recoup." Instead, if there is a case for increased capital accumulation, Modigliani urges that it be achieved "at the expense of the young who will benefit from it"—for example, by reducing capital income taxation and making up the revenue by raising taxes on wages.

The two papers in Part III focus on the political (especially legislative) causes of deficits and alternative institutional and constitutional mechanisms to resolve or ameliorate the problem of deficits. Peter H. Aranson, Professor of Economics and Special Research Administrator at the Law and Economics Center at Emory University, presents a "reconstructed" theory of representative democracy in his paper, "Public Deficits in Normative Economics and Positive Political Theory." Aranson considers alternative models of the manner in which the preferences of the electorate are converted into public policies. In the first traditional model, the political process effectively serves the public interest. However, this model is inadequate, according to Aranson, because it fails to take into account the possibility of "fiscal illusion" on the part of the electorate—i.e., because benefits are concentrated while costs are disbursed, benefits tend to be more readily perceived than costs.

Aranson's reconstructed theory of representative democracy emphasizes the influence of special interest groups. In the reconstructed view, deficits become the vehicle for facilitating the interest group process. Deficits are used to foster "public pursuit of private interests" and to transfer the burden to future generations who have not organized and cannot vote. Aranson is skeptical about the benefits of a constitutional amendment to restrict deficits because "it tries to ameliorate the symptom without affecting its cause." He prefers institutional reform to change the incentives that are the source of the problem.

On the other hand, Alvin Rabushka, Senior Fellow at Hoover Institution, Stanford University, advocates a constitutional amendment "to require a balanced federal budget and limit the growth in federal receipts to the rate of growth in national income." This amendment was considered by the Senate in the summer of 1982 (Senate Joint Resolution 58). The explanation for chronic deficits, according to Rabushka, is the conflict between budget objectives and the budget process. The Congress as a whole is concerned with checking government spending. Each Congressman, in contrast, faces pressure to increase spending to provide visible benefits to his or her constituents. "The collective need to control spending is no match for the pressures each member faces to increase it." Rabushka argues that the resulting "bias toward more spending" is an "institutional defect" that cannot be overcome by "electing the right people" or by institutional reform. He concludes his paper with a thorough review of the provisions in Senate Joint Resolution 58.

In his comments on the Aranson and Rabushka papers, Roger G. Noll, Institute Professor of Social Sciences at California Institute of Technology, is sharply critical of the analytical foundation of Aranson and Rabushka's conclusions about the size of government and the bias towards deficits. Noll argues that the economic theory of policy, as applied to government, does not yield any firm results on these issues. The theory simply does not tell us that government is too big or too prone to run deficits. Noll also argues that a balanced budget amendment is not likely to be a binding constraint. In most cases, Congress is likely to adopt economic scenarios that promise budget balance even when such an outcome is unlikely. When economic conditions are so weak that a large deficit seems certain, Congress is likely to vote for a deficit rather than cut expenditures or raise taxes.

In his discussion of the Aranson and Rabushka papers, Kenneth A. Shepsle, Professor of Policial Science and Research Associate at the Center for the Study of American Business at Washington University, likens government revenues and debt-financing opportunities to a "common pool." Because the benefits from grazing on the budgetary common are divorced from the costs of grazing, there is little incentive to economize on the use of the common resource. Shepsle notes that this analogy is the framework used to explain chronic deficits in both the Aranson and Rabushka papers. Shepsle then considers alternative solutions, including the constitutional amendment. He suggests that a variety of forms of adaptive behavior could fully offset any effect of the constitutional amendment. He uses the example of off-budget outlays and increased use of regulation to accomplish public purposes. To solve the problem, incentives must be changed, and Shepsle believes that potential exists for resolving the problem by institutional reforms.

In his luncheon talk, "Dealing With Deficits and the Rise in Federal Spending," Murray L. Weidenbaum, former Chairman of the Council of Economic Advisors, now Mallinckrodt Distinguished University Professor and Director of the Center for the Study of American Business at Washington University, examines the changes made by the Reagan Administration in government outlays and makes some recommendations for further cuts in government spending. Dr. Weidenbaum first shows that the differences between the Reagan Administration's projected budgets for 1982–1986 and Carter's budget estimates for that period are not as great as frequently reported. Weidenbaum points out that the modest size of the net spending cuts in relation to the 1981 tax cuts accounts for the high estimates of the budget deficit for the next several years.

Several areas of the budget "appear to be promising candidates for further pruning," according to Weidenbaum. The first is entitlement programs, such as social security, which comprise the largest category of the budget. Weidenbaum also maintains that future increases in real dollar outlays for defense, ranging between five and nine percent annually, may present potential capacity problems for the US economy, and he recommends an intensive analysis of the military budget, comparable to the tough-minded attitude taken toward many civilian spending activities of the government.

Acknowledgments

I would like to thank Ken Chilton, Associate Director of the Center for the Study of American Business, and Jess Yawitz, Director of the Institute for Banking and Financial Markets, for their help in organizing the conference. Gloria Lucy of the Center Staff coordinated the arrangements for the conference and Ron Penoyer, also of the Center Staff, helped with readying the manuscript for publication.

I THE IMPACT OF DEFICITS ON MONETARY GROWTH AND INFLATION

1 EXAMINING THE PROPOSITION THAT FEDERAL BUDGET DEFICITS MATTER

Preston J. Miller*

While politicians generally express much concern over large and persistent federal budget deficits, economists generally do not. This difference of views was very evident, for example, in the recent congressional debate over the proposed balanced budget amendment to the US Constitution. Although economists commonly counseled against the amendment, the Senate passed it anyway.[1]

Elected federal officials have a valid political reason to worry about deficits: according to opinion polls, voters worry about them. But another reason is that persistent deficits result in an escalation of net interest expense on the debt. The need to service the burgeoning debt subsequently limits future policy options.[2] Contrary to what many economists seem to think, there are also valid economic reasons to worry about deficits; large and persistent federal budget deficits do matter. The purpose of this paper is to defend that proposition. I develop my argument by confronting five basic questions asked of any economic proposition:

- What does the proposition really claim?

*The views expressed herein are those of the author and not necessarily those of the Federal Reserve Bank of Minneapolis or the Federal Reserve System.

3

- What features should a theory have in order to address the validity of the proposition?
- What are the positive economic implications of an acceptable theory?
- What are its normative implications?
- How well do the implications of the theory agree with actual experience?

Differences in economists' opinions on the deficits matter proposition can be reduced to differences in answers to these questions. While this paper focuses on my answers, the discussion expands beyond that focus where differences of opinion seem to be sharpest.

A General Model of Deficits

To begin, I posit a general model[3] to serve as a frame of reference for the basic questions. The state of the economy at time t, X_t, is described by the rate of real output, Y_t; the aggregate price level, P_t; and the nominal interest rate on one-period bonds, R_t:

$$X_t \equiv \begin{pmatrix} Y_t \\ P_t \\ R_t \end{pmatrix} \qquad (1.1)$$

The state of the economy depends on people's forecasts of two federal government policies: budget policy, which is identified by a path of total outside federal debt, $(D_t, D_{t+1}, \dots)$; and monetary policy, which is identified by a path of outside money, the value of D purchased by the monetary authority, $(M_t, M_{t+1}, \dots)$. We define the policy vector as

$$Z_t \equiv \begin{pmatrix} D_t \\ M_t \end{pmatrix} \qquad (1.2)$$

The policy rule is specified as

$$Z_t = a + bt + c(L)X_{t-1} + d(L)Z_{t-1} + \varepsilon_t \qquad (1.3)$$

where a, b, c, and d are coefficient matrices; ε is a white-noise stochastic process; and L is the lag operator. In longhand, we have

$$D_t = a_1 + b_1 t + \sum_{j=1}^{\infty} c_{11}(j)Y_{t-j} + \sum_{j=1}^{\infty} c_{12}(j)P_{t-j} \tag{1.3a}$$
$$+ \sum_{j=1}^{\infty} c_{13}(j)R_{t-j} + \sum_{j=1}^{\infty} d_{11}(j)D_{t-j}$$
$$+ \sum_{j=1}^{\infty} d_{12}(j)M_{t-j} + \varepsilon_{1t}$$

$$M_t = a_2 + b_2 t + \sum_{j=1}^{\infty} c_{21}(j)Y_{t-j} + \sum_{j=1}^{\infty} c_{22}(j)P_{t-j} \tag{1.3b}$$
$$+ \sum_{j=1}^{\infty} c_{23}(j)R_{t-j} + \sum_{j=1}^{\infty} d_{21}(j)D_{t-j}$$
$$+ \sum_{j=1}^{\infty} d_{22}(j)M_{t-j} + \varepsilon_{2t}$$

It is assumed that the economic process can be written as

$$X_t = f + gt + h(L)X_{t-1} + i(L)Z_{t-1} + k(L^{-1})\bar{Z}_t + \mu_t \tag{1.4}$$

where f, g, h, i and k are coefficient matrices; μ is a white-noise process which may be contemporaneously correlated with ε; $\bar{Z}_t$ is individuals' forecast of Z_t conditional on information at time t, which is assumed to consist of all lagged values of all variables; and $L^{-j}\bar{Z}_t \equiv \bar{Z}_{t+j}$.

The economic process (equation 1.4) builds in the implication derived from standard microeconomic theory that individuals' decisions depend on their forecasts of policies. It is assumed here that those forecasts are rational expectations subject to equations 1.3 and 1.4; that is, $\bar{Z}_{t+j} \equiv E_t Z_{t+j}$. In longhand, the system can be written

$$Y_t = f_1 + g_1 t + \sum_{j=1}^{\infty} h_{11}(j)Y_{t-j} + \sum_{j=1}^{\infty} h_{12}(j)P_{t-j} \tag{1.4a}$$
$$+ \sum_{j=1}^{\infty} h_{13}(j)R_{t-j} + \sum_{j=1}^{\infty} i_{11}(j)D_{t-j}$$
$$+ \sum_{j=1}^{\infty} i_{12}(j)M_{t-j} + \sum_{j=0}^{\infty} k_{11}(j)E_t D_{t+j}$$
$$+ \sum_{j=0}^{\infty} k_{12}(j)E_t M_{t+j} + \mu_{1t}$$

$$P_t = f_2 + g_2 t + \sum_{j=1}^{\infty} h_{21}(j)Y_{t-j} + \sum_{j=1}^{\infty} h_{22}(j)P_{t-j} \tag{1.4b}$$
$$+ \sum_{j=1}^{\infty} h_{23}(j)R_{t-j} + \sum_{j=1}^{\infty} i_{21}(j)D_{t-j}$$

$$+ \sum_{j=1}^{\infty} i_{22}(j)M_{t-j} + \sum_{j=0}^{\infty} k_{21}(j)E_tD_{t+j}$$

$$+ \sum_{j=0}^{\infty} k_{22}(j)E_tM_{t+j} + \mu_{2t}$$

$$R_t = f_3 + g_3t + \sum_{j=1}^{\infty} h_{31}(j)Y_{t-j} + \sum_{j=1}^{\infty} h_{32}(j)P_{t-j} \qquad (1.4c)$$

$$+ \sum_{j=1}^{\infty} h_{33}(j)R_{t-j} + \sum_{j=1}^{\infty} i_{31}(j)D_{t-j}$$

$$+ \sum_{j=1}^{\infty} i_{32}(j)M_{t-j} + \sum_{j=0}^{\infty} k_{31}(j)E_tD_{t+j}$$

$$+ \sum_{j=0}^{\infty} k_{32}(j)E_tM_{t+j} + \mu_{3t}$$

The economic process (equation 1.4) is not in estimable form, since it includes expectations terms. Those terms are functions of lagged values of all variables and are determined by equations 1.3 and 1.4. Replacing the expectations terms with these functions yields

$$X_t = \alpha + \beta t + \zeta(L)X_{t-1} + \delta(L)Z_{t-1} + \mu_t \qquad (1.5)$$

where α, β, ζ, and δ are coefficient matrices of dimensions 3×1, 3×1, 3×3, and 3×2, respectively. [In longhand, the system is like equations 1.4a–c, with $\alpha = f$, $\beta = g$, $\zeta = h$, $\delta = i$, and $0 = k$.]

The Deficits Matter Proposition

The questions raised in this section relate to the forms of restrictions which theory places on the policy rule equation 1.3 and the economic process (equation 1.4), and to some preliminary statistical tests of the restrictions.

What Does Deficits Matter Mean?

The proposition that deficits matter means that the economic process is not invariant to a change in the deficit policy rule. In terms of our model, the proposition is that the coefficients α, β, ζ, and δ of equation 1.5 are not invariant to a change in the coefficients α_1, b_1, $c_{1.}$, and $d_{1.}$ of equation 1.3a.

Examination of the system reveals two necessary conditions for this proposition to be true. One is that people care about future deficits; that is, not all $k_{.1}(j) = 0$. The other is that people's forecasts of deficits are not merely adaptive; they incorporate information about the policy rule equation 1.3a.

Economists who are skeptical about deficits mattering might ask why people should care about future deficits. One response is that future deficits are properly viewed as shorthand for future federal tax and expenditure policies, and these policies affect individual budget sets. These skeptics might rebut that, if all feasible deficit policies imply that the present value of real government expenditures equals the present value of real tax receipts, then deficits per se have no independent effect on the economy. That is, if deficits shift taxes over time and leave the present value of taxes unchanged, then a change in the pattern of deficits need not change individuals' budget sets (Barro, 1974). If these skeptics are right, then deficits matter only if people suffer from wealth illusion (Barth and Morrell, 1982; Seater, 1982). A response to this line of reasoning is that equality between present values of expenditures and tax receipts need not be an equilibrium condition in models of valued fiat money and debt (Sargent, 1982; Wallace, 1980). An ongoing deficit policy is therefore feasible. Since in these models the government can collect seignorage on its money and bonds, a higher deficit today need not imply a higher surplus in the future. When the government's deficit policy can affect the present value of its privately held real debt, then that policy certainly affects individual budget sets.

Examination of the system also reveals a fundamental misinterpretation of the deficits matter proposition. Contrary to what many people seem to think, this proposition does not refer to the relationships between realized deficits and other economic variables. A regression of X on D, for example, has little to say about the proposition. Even if deficit policies matter, the true coefficients in δ_1 of equation 1.5 can be anything. If a single deficit policy is in effect over the sample period, then the true δ_1 will be composed of complicated expressions in the coefficients of both equations 1.3 and 1.4. If more than one deficit policy is in effect over the sample period, the true δ_1 will have different values under different policies, so that estimates of δ_1 will confound the effects of deficits under given policies with the effects of different deficit policies. For the same reasons, the dynamic responses of the system to a deficit impulse have little to say about the proposition. Determining how the system of equations 1.3 and 1.5 evolves given a drawing of ε_{1t} requires the assumption that the coefficients in equations 1.3 and 1.5 remain invariant.

It should be emphasized that theories which indicate deficits matter relate to very simple economies and very simple policy experiments. The experiments consist of changing only a_1 or b_1 in the policy rule equation 1.3a, assuming the policies are immediately known and understood—E_t is conditioned on the new policy—and examining the changes in steady-state outcomes, $E_t[\Delta X_{t+n}]$ as $n \rightarrow \infty$. The theories provide information on k_1, and the contention is that this knowledge often permits the determination of the signs of changes in steady-state outcomes.

What Features Must a Theory Have to Determine Whether Deficits Matter?

An acceptable theory of deficit policies must be dynamic, explicitly micro-based, and capable of explaining valued fiat money and debt. These three features are minimum requirements.

Dynamic. The theory must be dynamic, because the economic consequences of a given deficit depend on the intended means of servicing the resulting debt, and debt servicing is a dynamic concept. The government can service its debt in essentially four ways: by applying the return on capital spending financed by the debt issue, by raising taxes, by printing money, and by issuing new bonds. In general, these different ways of servicing debt imply different streams of money and debt over time (different policy rules, equations 1.3a and 1.3b) and thus, different economic effects (different equation 1.4).

The government's first two options imply that the present value of additional real expenditures is matched by the present value of additional receipts. However, since these options also imply different equilibrium paths for Y, P, and R for a given increase in the deficit, they must imply different deficit policy rules equation 1.3a. In the case of spending on capital account, the government debt is backed by the return on investment, just as private debt is. If the government investment earns the market rate of return, the investment and debt issue need have no effect on equilibrium output, Y; prices, P; or interest rates, R (Wallace, 1981).

In the case of spending on current account, the government debt is backed by higher taxes in the future. Although the debt does not change the present value of taxes, it does change their distribution over time. The change in distribution of taxes may or may not have an effect on the economy [on equation 1.4], depending on assumptions about individual utility functions and markets (which determine k_1).[4] Aside from this consideration, an increase in the present value of government current expenditures matched by an increase in the present value of taxes will tend to drive out some private capital investment and thereby raise the real rate of return on capital. In general, output and prices will also change.

Any combination of the other two options, money creation and new bond issue, need not imply equality between the present values of expenditures and receipts (Miller, 1982b; Sargent, 1982). The path of nominal debt (equation 1.3a) will be higher under either of these options or some combination of the two than it will be under either of the first two options. Even if money creation alone is used to produce the same real debt path as could be achieved by explicit taxation, the policy rules (equations 1.3a and 1.3b) are very different under these two options and can be expected to have different economic effects. These differences occur because the incidences of the inflation tax and explicit taxes generally are very different.

Micro-based. An acceptable theory of deficit policies also must be explicitly micro-based. There are three reasons for this. First, only a theory of individual optimizing behavior can solve the problem of the noninvariance of the economic process (equation 1.5) with respect to a change in policy rules (equation 1.3). It does this in our model by allowing statistical identification of the coefficients in k.

Second, a micro-based theory is necessary to investigate the existence of equilibria under different deficit policies. Because the existence of equilibria with valued fiat money tends to be tenuous, this investigation is very important (Wallace, 1980). No equilibrium with valued fiat money exists under a given deficit policy, for example, when the maximal taxation of real money and bond holdings does not permit budget balance in a real sense. That is, no equilibrium exists when the inflation tax applied to real money holdings and the depreciation in bond values applied to real bond holdings do not provide the government with enough resources to finance its real expenditures net of real explicit taxes. Since the inflation and depreciation tax bases are the private demands for real fiat money and bonds, taxing at too high a rate easily can drive tax revenue to zero by reducing the asset demands to zero.

Third, a micro-based theory is required to examine the welfare effects of alternative deficit policies. Deficit policies are properly subjects of public finance theory. Relevant questions concern the relative efficiency and incidence of alternative inflation and depreciation taxes to finance given deficits. The desirability of alternative tax policies generally cannot be evaluated by examining only their effects on aggregate economic variables.

Able to Explain Valued Fiat Debt. Finally, an acceptable theory of deficit policies must explain valued fiat debt, both interest bearing and noninterest bearing. An ongoing deficit policy, one for which the present value of taxes is less than the present value of expenditures in real terms, is possible only if fiat debt has value. And different explanations for why the debt has value generally imply different effects of deficit policies (equation 1.3a) on the economy (equation 1.4).

A crucial issue in this area is why valued fiat money and bonds coexist. Fiat bonds are promises to pay sums of fiat money at specific dates in the future. Since bonds have value for every state of the world in which money has value and since in these states bonds pay a certain, positive rate of return over the investment period while money does not, why do people hold both money and bonds? (I first saw this question posed in Wallace, 1979.) The answer one gives to this question can have very different implications about the effects of deficit policies on the economy.

Suppose that money and bonds are issued in the same denominations and that the government in no way restricts or regulates the use of either instrument. The two then will become perfect substitutes, and arbitrage will guarantee that they will both be held only if they pay the same rate of return. If an n-period bond pays a positive interest rate while money does not, for instance, a trader can profit by breaking the bond into n one-period bonds, each paying a positive rate of return. The one-period bonds then will dominate money.

If money and bonds are perfect substitutes, it follows that monetary policy is irrelevant ($k_2 = 0$) and deficits are directly inflationary. Deficits determine the growth of total debt. Monetary policy determines the distribution of debt between two perfect substitutes.

In the real world, however, money and bonds are both held and their rates of return differ. Two explanations have been offered for this fact. One is that imperfect substitutability is due to real transaction costs (Bryant and Wallace, 1979). According to this explanation, bonds are issued in large denominations, and real resources are absorbed when the private sector breaks bonds down into smaller denominations. One implication of this explanation is that the interest rate on bonds is a real rate and reflects the real cost of breaking down large denomination bonds. Another implication is that bond financing is inefficient. Resources could be preserved if all deficit financing were done by money creation. Deficits would remain inflationary but would be less inflationary if the debt were monetized.

Another explanation for the imperfect substitutability of money and bonds—the one I adopt here—is that the government has imposed restrictions on the use of bonds to reduce their liquidity (Bryant and Wallace, 1980; Miller, 1982a). Banks are prohibited, for example, from buying government bonds and issuing bearer notes backed by the bonds. These restrictions result in money circulating as a medium of exchange, while bonds compete with private capital as a store of value. A rationale for the restrictions is that they allow the government to finance a wider range of deficit paths and to finance given deficits more efficiently. By providing two distinct debt instruments paying different returns, the restrictions allow the government to tax-discriminate in financing deficits. This explanation for the imperfect substitutability of money and bonds can generate some common monetarist propositions: prices proportional to money, a Fisher effect on interest rates, and expansiveness of open market purchases (Miller, 1982a). Unlike common monetarist doctrine, however, this explanation implies deficit policy (equation 1.3a) and monetary policy (equation 1.3b) must be coordinated because there are restrictions across the coefficients of equations 1.3a and 1.3b.

What Are the Positive Economic Implications of This Restrictions Theory?

The theory which assumes government restrictions on bonds implies that the economic effects of alternative deficit policies come about by changes in inflation and real interest rates. Some economists argue that when bonds are close substitutes for capital, deficits need not be inflationary. Here I argue that when the close substitution is due to government restrictions on the liquidity of bonds, deficits still can lead to more inflation in three ways: monetary accommodation, crowding out, and private monetization of government debt.

Monetarists commonly acknowledge that deficits lead to more inflation when the Federal Reserve accommodates by purchasing some of the debt. They tend to view the Fed's accommodation either as a lack of resolve or as shortsightedness (Friedman, 1981a; Hein, 1981; Weintraub, 1981). Theory, however, suggests that the Fed may have no choice.

Again, a key implication of theories of deficits with restrictions on bonds is that fiscal and monetary policies must be coordinated (Sargent and Wallace, 1981; Miller, 1982a,b). If the allocation of goods in the economy is efficient initially, it is not feasible to finance a larger deficit—even temporarily—by bond issue alone. In such a situation, an increase in bonds without an increase in money will cause real interest payments on bonds to grow without limit and will force the government into insolvency. Monetary accommodation, then, is necessary at some point to prevent the insolvency.

This theoretical result has an intuitive interpretation. If the Federal Reserve sticks to a predetermined path of money, then the federal government is denied the option of creating money to finance deficits above some limit. Additional debt issue becomes like that of state and local governments: it must be backed by higher revenue in the future. Trying to service the debt by issuing new debt only causes interest on the debt and, thus, total debt to snowball.

Crowding out is another way deficits lead to greater inflation. Different degrees of monetary accommodation are feasible for a given increase in deficits. Less monetary accommodation necessitates the selling of bonds on the open market to private investors, and in general more private capital is driven out of the market. Bonds compete with private capital in individual portfolios. When there are decreasing returns to capital, the substitution of government current expenditures for private capital expenditures raises the rate of real interest and lowers the rate of real economic growth (Friedman, 1981b; Miller, 1982c). With a given path of money, this results in a higher price path.

Deficits can lead to more inflation when individuals are encouraged to circumvent the restrictions on bonds and, in effect, to *privately monetize* government debt. Suppose the restrictions can be broken down in successive steps at only successively higher costs. The profit from breaking down the restrictions is the arbitrage revenue less these costs. The arbitrage revenue is the income which can be earned by substituting bond holdings for money holdings, for example, private notes backed by government bonds for government fiat money. This revenue then is related directly to the difference in returns on money and bonds: the nominal interest rate. A policy of higher deficits raises interest rates, causing the private sector to seek alternative ways to circumvent the restrictions on bonds. This makes bonds more liquid by making them closer substitutes for money. Their greater liquidity implies more inflation for given deficits and money growth.

Casual observation suggests that this third way deficits lead to inflation is more than a theoretical possibility. In recent years in the United States there have developed demand deposit accounts at money market mutual funds which are backed by Treasury securities and deep-discount insured bank certificates of deposit that are backed by Treasury securities, issued in denominations of as little as $250, and assured of purchase by a broker (Sloane, 1982). In Brazil, which has run high deficits for years, the average turnover on government debt is now less than three days (Sargent, 1982).

The effects of deficit financing on real interest rates depend on the magnitude of crowding out and the curvature of the aggregate production function. The higher is the inflation tax associated with a given deficit policy, the less is the need to raise real revenue through bond issue and the less is the crowding out of private capital. The increase in real interest rates which results from a given amount of crowding out, meanwhile, depends on how much the marginal productivity of capital rises as the capital stock is reduced.

What Does This Theory Suggest About How Policies Should Be Coordinated?

What theory suggests about how monetary and fiscal policies should be coordinated depends on both political and economic considerations. The political consideration concerns the nature of the policy game being played by the Fed, on the one hand, and the Treasury and Congress, on the other. If the game is cooperative, then the result that monetary and fiscal policies must be coordinated obviously suggests that some accommodation is desirable. In such a game, if the monetary and fiscal policy authorities jointly decide to raise the path of deficits, for example, then they should also decide to raise the path of money to some degree.

If the policy game is not cooperative, however, then the political consideration on the desirability of accommodation depends on which of the players has the last move. If budget policy is firmly set, so that the Fed always has the last move, then desirability is irrelevant; the Fed has no choice but to accommodate. If, in contrast, budget policy is not firmly set, then a nonaccommodative monetary policy may make sense. The Fed can then control the size of deficits which can be financed by placing an unconditional limit on the amount of bonds it will purchase (Miller, 1982b).

The economic consideration for policy coordination is a function of the optimal tax structure. Inflation is a distorting tax, as are all the taxes in the Treasury's arsenal. Generally, the optimal tax structure for a given level of expenditures spreads the burden over many taxes. If the Fed attempts to minimize the inflation tax for a given deficit policy, too little of the inflation tax may be used. When there are decreasing returns to capital in production, for instance, the minimal inflation rate which allows a given deficit stream to be financed could result in an overaccumulation of capital. Welfare for all could be improved by increasing inflation, reducing capital accumulation, and thereby increasing the rate of return on capital (Miller, 1982c).

What Does US Experience Suggest About the Effects of Deficit Policies?

Macroeconometric studies of the United States generally find that federal budget deficits hurt the economy little, if at all. Large macroeconometric models suggest, in fact, that policies which permanently raise budget deficits, policies such as a reduction in tax rates or a liberalization of eligibility rules for transfer payments, actually raise the path of real output while having only slight effects on inflation and interest rates (Miller and Rolnick, 1980; US Congress, CBO 1982b, pp. 79–84). The effect on inflation comes entirely from a movement along a (flat) Phillips curve; the effect on interest rates reflects an increased demand for money stemming from a higher level of nominal income. Vector autoregressive models estimated over US postwar data generally suggest weak relationships between deficits and major economic indicators (Miller, 1982d), as do studies which estimate those relationships individually (Hein, 1981; Perry, 1978; Weintraub, 1981). Altogether, these findings seem so overwhelming that Beryl Sprinkel, Under Secretary of the Treasury for Monetary Affairs, has claimed that he knows of no evidence that deficits matter for either inflation or interest rates.[5]

The evidence, however, is not as overwhelming as it first appears. Whether deficits matter in the sense of this paper cannot be determined by standard macroeconometric studies, because those studies do not distinguish between a change in deficits and a change in deficit policies. Those studies attempt to estimate δ_1 in equation 1.5 under the assumption that equation 1.3 is fixed over the sample period. In order for their estimation techniques to be valid, they must assume that 1.5 is stationary, and according to the model (equations 1.3–1.5), that assumption is itself valid only if 1.3 is unchanged.

Studies done in the standard way thus offer very little evidence about whether deficit policies matter. If the stationarity assumption is valid, then they offer no evidence about the effects of a change in deficit policies. If the assumption is not valid, then neither are the estimates. An acceptable attempt to determine the effects of deficit policies can be divided into two parts. The first is to test for a change in policies equation 1.3 and see whether or not the relationships in 1.5 change. The second is to quantify how much these relationships change. The first part is decidedly easier than the second.

Testing for Changes.   I approach the first part of the task by estimating a vector autoregression (VAR), a version of equation 1.5, testing for a break in the budget policy rule 1.3a, and then reestimating the VAR separately over each subperiod beginning and ending with the break in policy (Miller, 1982d). I qualitatively assess the significance of the differences between the two subperiod models by comparing impulse response functions, decompositions of variance, within-sample fits, and out-of-sample predictions conditioned on identical information. By these measures, the estimated relationships among the economic variables in 1.5 are dramatically different under the different budget policies 1.3a.

The VARs contain five quarterly time series: real GNP (RGNP), GNP deflator (GNPD), 90 day Treasury bill rate (RTB), bank reserves (TR), and federal debt (DEBT). The measure of bank reserves is the St. Louis Federal Reserve Bank's total reserves, adjusted for seasonal factors and changes in reserve requirements. It is intended as a measure of outside money.[6] The measure of federal debt is constructed by adding the accumulated, quarterly NIA deficit (not annualized) to the total public debt net of government account holdings in 1948. It is intended as a measure of outside federal debt. In the regressions, all series except the bill rate are logged.

This limited set of variables is intended to be the smallest system able to capture major channels of policy influence: monetary and fiscal policies together determine the inflation rate and the interest rate, which in turn affect real output by their impact on the rate of investment. Monetary and fiscal policies are represented as feedback rules which determine the current levels of bank reserves and federal debt, respectively, as functions of lagged values of all the variables in the system.

Each variable in the system is regressed on a constant and on m lags of all five variables. Thus, the system—a merging of equations 1.3 and 1.5—can be written as

$$X_t = C + \sum_{i=1}^{m} A_i X_{t-1} + \mu_t \tag{1.6}$$

where

$$X \equiv \begin{pmatrix} \ln(\text{RGNP}) \\ \ln(\text{GNPD}) \\ \text{RTB} \\ \ln(\text{DEBT}) \\ \ln(\text{TR}) \end{pmatrix} \tag{1.7}$$

$$\mu \equiv \begin{pmatrix} \mu_1 \\ \cdot \\ \cdot \\ \mu_5 \end{pmatrix} \tag{1.8}$$

and C and A_i are 5×1 and 5×5 matrices of coefficients, respectively, and $m =$ lag length. The coefficients in the matrices C and A_i are estimated by

Table 1–1.   Stability of the DEBT Equation

Lag Lengths	Marginal Significance Levels
1	.0000
2	.0129
3	.0176
4	.0049
5	.0019
6	.0002
7	.0020
8	.0702

OLS, and $E\mu\mu' = \Sigma$ is estimated by the variance-covariance matrix of residuals.

In the test for a break in the budget policy rule, the entire postwar period is divided into two subperiods: from 1948:1 to 1966:4 and from 1967:1 to 1981:4. The test statistic is distributed as $F(n,k)$, where n is the number of regressors and k is the number of degrees of freedom in the subperiod regressions (the number of observations minus $2n$). The marginal significance level indicates the probability that the residuals from the subperiod regressions were drawn from the same distribution.

Table 1–1 reports the marginal significance levels (to four significant digits) for the DEBT equation in the VARs for lag lengths $m = 1$ through 8. For all lag lengths except 8, structural stability can be rejected at a 95 percent confidence level.

The next two tables illustrate some of the more dramatic differences in the VARs estimated over different time periods. The VARs have lag length $m = 3$. The model estimated over the full postwar period (1948:1–1981:4) is denoted VAR(F); the model estimated over the first subperiod (1948:1–1966:4) is denoted VAR(I); and the model estimated over the second subperiod (1967:1–1981:4) is denoted VAR(II).

Table 1–2 reports part of the decomposition of variance for the GNP deflator according to the three different models. The part is the proportion of the standard error of forecast in the deflator which is attributable to innovations in DEBT and TR. According to the decompositions of variance, monetary policy is less important in explaining movements in inflation when each subperiod is viewed separately than when the data are pooled. Fiscal policy is more important in explaining inflation in the second subperiod than in the first.

Table 1–3 shows the deterministic forecasts of the VARs for the eight-quarter horizon beginning with 1982:1. The forecasts were made by using the estimated coefficients of each model with actual data for 1981:2–1981:4.

The differences among the models in predicting NIA debt and real GNP are striking. Comparison of the debt forecasts suggests that the current level of debt is much higher than would have been predicted based on the experience through 1966. A similar, though not quite as strong statement can be made about the forecasts of total reserves. Thus, VAR(I) interprets recent policy as being very expansionary. Since VAR(I) also implies that an innovation in policy variables of given magnitude has an impact on real GNP greater than that in either VAR(F) or VAR(II), it predicts a much higher path of real GNP than does either of those models.

Measuring the Changes. In the second part of the empirical task it is difficult to quantify the effects of different deficit policies. There seem to be two valid ways to approach the problem. One is to estimate a structural model. However, structural here means that the model must be constructed from an explicit theory of individual behavior and must include estimation of parameters in individual objective functions. That is because, as Lucas and Sargent (1979) have so convincingly argued, neither aggregate nor individual excess demand functions can be expected to remain invariant to a change in policies which impinge on individual budget constraints. The econometric challenge of this approach is to identify the parameters of individual objective functions and budget constraints and then determine analytically how the demand functions change when policies change.[7]

The other valid approach to quantification is to directly examine the effects of different deficit policies that have actually been used. The challenge here is to identify breaks in the policy rule and then examine how the economic system behaved on average over the periods before and after the breaks.

Table 1–2. Percentages of the Standard Errors of the Three Models' GNPD Forecasts Due to Innovations in DEBT and TR

	VAR(F)		VAR(I)		VAR(II)	
Step	DEBT	TR	DEBT	TR	DEBT	TR
2	0.24	1.72	0.48	1.77	0.09	6.40
5	0.52	28.57	0.57	19.15	5.98	18.88
10	1.16	57.67	0.48	25.74	23.07	21.61
15	6.55	68.37	1.70	26.39	32.58	19.76
20	12.13	70.47	3.43	25.43	28.50	17.04

While these two approaches seem valid for examining the deficits matter proposition, neither is likely to provide decisive results soon. The first approach appears to exceed current research capabilities. It requires the formulation and estimation of general equilibrium models with endogenous roles for money and bonds. While models of this type now are being constructed, they are probably still too simple to confront the data (Kareken and Wallace, 1980). Most, for example, abstract from business cycle movements and focus on steady states. Moreover, the identification and estimation problems associated with models that have a sizable number of equations are likely to be very severe (Hansen and Sargent, 1980).

Although the second, direct approach is less demanding, it is also more limited, because of an inadequate number of observations. Under this approach, an observation covers a period of time for which a single deficit policy has been in place. Thus, one observation is likely to be measured in units of ten years or more.[8] To get enough observations to be able to directly estimate the effects of different deficit policies, therefore, one must go way back in time or go across countries. In either case, the observations are likely to be contaminated by important differences in economic structure.

The method used here to estimate the effect of deficits is a crude application of the second approach. I conjecture that differences in economic performance over substantial periods of time can largely be explained by differences in federal monetary and budget policies. The method is crude for at least two reasons: first, no attempt is made to estimate policy rules and test statistically for breaks in the rules; and second, the number of observations is so small that the estimates must be considered very unreliable. Despite the crudeness of the method, however, the results suggest the view that deficits matter should not be rejected without further study.

My method is to estimate a reduced-form model of the average performance of the five variables in the VAR over equal subperiods of postwar data. I add an equation for the real Treasury bill rate, which is defined by an identity. The average performance measure for real GNP, the GNP deflator, debt, and total reserves is the average annual growth rate $[g(\cdot)]$, while the measure for the bill rate and the real bill rate is the average level over the subperiod. There are four subperiods of 8½ years each. The year 1948 is the base. Values of variables for 1982 are taken from the Congressional Budget Office's baseline forecast made in the spring of 1982 (US, Congress, CBO, 1982a). The estimated model is presented in table 1–4. There are four observations and thus only one degree of freedom. R-squared adjusted for degrees of freedom is reported after each equation, and t-statistics are reported in parentheses under each coefficient. The actual values and the model's predicted values of each variable over the sample period are given in

Table 1-3. The Three Models' Forecasts

	RGNP (bils. of 1972 $)			*GNPD (1972 = 100.0)*		
	VAR(F)	*VAR(I)*	*VAR(II)*	*VAR(F)*	*VAR(I)*	*VAR(II)*
Actual						
1981:4	1,497.6	1,497.6	1,497.6	200.0	200.0	200.0
Forecast						
1982:1	1,490.5	2,214.8	1,493.1	204.1	210.3	203.7
2	1,497.5	2,915.5	1,493.1	208.3	224.9	208.1
3	1,509.1	3,375.8	1,506.0	212.6	232.2	211.9
4	1,515.2	3,439.1	1,531.6	216.7	227.8	215.2
1983:1	1,522.0	3,312.4	1,548.6	221.0	220.0	218.7
2	1,532.4	3,155.8	1.569.2	225.5	212.7	222.3
3	1,543.4	3,047.5	1,589.5	230.3	207.7	225.8
4	1,552.5	3,005.6	1,609.6	235.1	204.2	229.5

table 1–5. The predictions are generated by using the model in table 1–4 with the actual values of the independent variables.

Finally, the model is used to forecast the next four year period, assuming that the NIA deficit is $150 billion per year and that the growth in total reserves is four percent per year. The deficit assumptions are in the range of the estimates in the Congressional Budget Office's 1982 midyear update (US, Congress, CBO, 1982a). The total reserves assumption is taken to be roughly consistent with the Federal Reserve's stated objectives. An implicit

Table 1-4. A Reduced-Form Model

Equations (and t-Statistics)					$\bar{R}^2$
g(RGNP) = 3.83	−	.18g(DEBT)	+	.05g(TR)	.972
(36.53)		(−10.19)		(1.59)	
g(GNPD) = 1.97	+	.56g(DEBT)	+	.13g(TR)	.953
(4.16)		(7.26)		(0.89)	
RTB = 2.02	+	.70g(DEBT)	+	.33g(TR)	.994
(9.08)		(19.07)		(4.69)	
Real R ≡ RTB	−	g(GNPD)			
= .05	+	.13g(DEBT)	+	.20g(TR)	.260
(0.08)		(1.17)		(0.90)	

RTB (percent)			DEBT (bils. of $)			TR (bils. of $)		
VAR(F)	VAR(I)	VAR(II)	VAR(F)	VAR(I)	VAR(II)	VAR(F)	VAR(I)	VAR(II)
12.0	12.0	12.0	641.0	641.0	641.0	46.6	46.6	46.6
11.5	9.6	11.6	671.0	582.7	670.4	47.7	41.4	47.2
12.6	10.4	12.6	703.0	485.6	701.4	48.6	38.1	47.9
12.7	13.7	12.3	733.9	400.8	734.4	49.2	39.6	48.4
12.2	16.7	11.8	764.6	344.9	768.8	49.8	41.1	49.0
12.2	17.4	11.8	796.3	313.7	803.4	50.7	42.8	49.6
12.6	16.0	12.0	828.2	298.3	837.4	51.5	44.3	50.2
12.9	14.0	12.2	859.1	292.7	869.8	52.3	45.7	50.8
13.1	12.5	12.5	889.6	292.5	900.0	53.1	47.1	51.4

assumption is that the experience of the next four years will be representative of the entire 8½ year period.

According to this model, budget deficits matter (See table 1.5). Higher deficits, which result in faster growth of government debt over a period of time, result in lower real growth, higher inflation, higher nominal interest rates, and higher real interest rates. Except for the effect of deficits on real interest rates, all relationships are highly statistically significant. The small effect of deficits on real interest rates may indicate that in the aggregate there are only slightly decreasing returns to capital in production. The model assigns little explanatory power to monetary policy, except with regard to nominal interest rates. The statistical explanation for why relatively more weight is given to budget policy than to monetary policy is apparent. The accelerating growth in total debt comes much closer to matching the accelerating deterioration in the dependent variables.

The model's predictions for the next four years are very pessimistic. That is hardly surprising considering the large weight the model gives to deficits. If NIA deficits average $150 billion per year over the next four years, the annual average growth in outside debt over this period will be nearly twice that of the preceding 8½ year period.

Summary: Deficits Do Matter

Theory suggests that deficits matter, if we interpret deficits to mean deficit policy and if we recognize that in a fiat money economy the present values of

Table 1–5. Predictions of a Reduced-Form Model

| | Average Annual Growth Rates (%) | | | | | | Average Levels (%) | | | | | | Average Annual Growth Rates (%) | |
| | RGNP | | | GNPD | | | RTB | | | REAL R | | | DEBT | TR |
Period	Act.	Pred.	Error	Act.	Pred.	Error	Act.	Pred.	Error	Act.	Pred.	Error	Actual	Actual
1948–1956 1/2	3.9	3.9	0.0	2.2	1.8	0.4	1.7	1.8	−0.1	−0.5	0.0	−0.5	−0.1	−0.3
1956 1/2–1965	3.8	3.9	−0.1	1.8	2.2	−0.4	2.9	2.7	0.2	1.1	0.5	0.6	0.1	1.8
1965–1973 1/2	3.6	3.6	0.0	4.7	4.5	0.2	6.0	6.1	−0.1	1.3	1.6	−0.3	3.2	5.6
1973 1/2–1982	2.2	2.2	0.0	7.8	7.8	0.0	9.7	9.7	0.0	1.9	1.9	0.0	9.9	2.3
													Assumed	
1982–1986		0.8			12.6			16.0			3.4		18.1	4.0

real government expenditures and receipts need not be identically equal. In such an economy, deficits determine the growth of outside debt: money and bonds. If the demands for these two instruments are separate, then fiscal and monetary policies must be coordinated. A higher deficit policy requires faster money growth.

Separateness of demands for the two instruments is not natural. Government restrictions on the use of bonds cause them to be imperfect substitutes for money. Larger deficits increase private incentives to circumvent the restrictions. As the private sector breaks down the restrictions, bonds become more liquid, so more inflation results from the same monetary and budget policies.

Empirical evidence on the effects of federal budget deficits is not conclusive. However, this paper shows that the data are not inconsistent with the view that deficit policies do matter in the way theory suggests.

Notes

1.   According to the *New York Times* (Roberts, 1982), on July 29 Senator John Chafee of Rhode Island in a floor speech "pointed out that more than 200 prominent economists had signed a letter denying the basic premise of the amendment: 'that deficits are bad and that balanced budgets are good.'"

2.   See, for example, the US Senate Budget Committee's report on the "First Concurrent Resolution on the Budget" for fiscal year 1983, which points out that

> net interest payments have grown rapidly in recent years. For the three years ending in FY 1982, net interest has grown at an average annual rate of 26 percent per year. Even after adjustment for the effects of inflation, net interest payments have grown by an average of 16 percent per year. The rapid growth in real interest payments is reflected in the sharply rising share of the Federal budget that is absorbed by interest, which has risen from less than 8 percent before 1979 to 11.6 percent of 1982 outlays. To the extent that interest costs for financing the Federal deficits rise in real terms, resources absorbed by interest requirements will "crowd out" other government program objectives. (US Congress, Senate 1982, p. 36)

3.   This model is loosely motivated by Miller, 1982a, Sargent, 1982, and Sargent and Wallace, 1981.

4.   If a complete set of contingent markets exists and people care appropriately about the welfare of future generations, then changing the distribution of taxes over time will not affect equilibrium output, prices, or interest rates (Barro, 1974). If, however, either complete markets do not exist or people do not care adequately about the welfare of future generations, then changing the distribution of taxes over time will affect equilibrium outcomes (Sargent, 1982).

5.   In congressional testimony (U.S. Congress, House, 1981), Sprinkel said, "But that still leaves the first question as to whether deficits cause inflation. The evidence is very clear that they do not" (p. 469). Then to Representative D'Amours' statement, "And when you eliminate deficits, you have declining interest rates," Sprinkel responded, "I would appreciate it if you could show me the evidence on it, because I have looked and I can't find it" (p. 474).

6. I use this measure of outside money instead of the Board of Governors' series on the monetary base and total reserves or the St. Louis Fed's series on the monetary base because it is the only series that has data back to 1948.

7. In general, all coefficients in equation 1.4 change when policies change. In my formulation, however, those coefficients remain invariant, but all coefficients in equation 1.5 change.

8. In the last section, one break in the deficit policy rule is found for the whole postwar period.

References

Barro, R.J. "Are Government Bonds Net Wealth?" *Journal of Political Economy* 82 (November/December 1974), 1095–117.

Barth, J.R., and S.O. Morrell. "A Primer on Budget Deficits." Federal Reserve Bank of Atlanta. *Economic Review* 67 (August 1982), 6–17.

Bryant, J., and N. Wallace. "The Inefficiency of Interest-Bearing National Debt." *Journal of Political Economy* 87 (April 1979), 365–81.

Bryant, J., and N. Wallace. "A Suggestion for Further Simplifying the Theory of Money." Research Department Staff Report 62, Federal Reserve Bank of Minneapolis, 1980.

Friedman, M. "A Memorandum to the Fed." *Wall Street Journal* (January 30, 1981a).

Friedman, M. "Deficits and Inflation." *Newsweek* (February 23, 1981b), 70.

Hansen, L.P., and T.J. Sargent. "Formulating and Estimating Dynamic Linear Rational Expectations Models." *Journal of Economic Dynamics and Control* 2 (February 1980), 7–46.

Hein, S.E. "Deficits and Inflation." Federal Reserve Bank of St. Louis *Review* 63 (March 1981), 3–10.

Kareken, J.H., and N. Wallace, eds. *Models of Monetary Economies.* Minneapolis: Federal Reserve Bank of Minneapolis, 1980.

Lucas, R.E., Jr., and T.J. Sargent. "After Keynesian Macroeconomics." *Federal Reserve Bank of Minneapolis Quarterly Review* 3 (Spring 1979), 1–16.

Miller, P.J. "Fiscal Policy in a Monetarist Model." Research Department Staff Report 67, Federal Reserve Bank of Minneapolis, 1982a.

Miller, P.J. "A Monetarist Approach to Federal Budget Control." Research Department Working Paper 210, Federal Reserve Bank of Minneapolis, 1982b.

Miller, P.J. "Optimal Crowding Out in a Monetarist Model." Research Department Working Paper 212, Federal Reserve Bank of Minneapolis, 1982c.

Miller, P.J. "A Time Series Analysis of Federal Budget Policy." Research Department Working Paper 213, Federal Reserve Bank of Minneapolis, 1982d.

Miller, P.J., and A.J. Rolnick. "The CBO's Policy Analysis: An Unquestionable Misuse of a Questionable Theory." *Journal of Monetary Economics* 6 (April 1980), 171–98.

Perry, G.L. "Slowing the Wage-Price Spiral: The Macroeconomic View." *Brookings Papers on Economic Activity* 2 (1978), 259–91.

Roberts, S.V. "Budget Deficits: A 'Solution' Raises New Questions." *New York Times* (August 3, 1982), 10.

Sargent, T.J. "Consumption, Loans, and Currency: II." Unpublished paper, March 1982.

Sargent, T.J., and N. Wallace. "Some Unpleasant Monetarist Arithmetic." *Federal Reserve Bank of Minneapolis Quarterly Review* 5 (Fall 1981), 1–17.

Seater, J. "Are Future Taxes Discounted?" *Journal of Money, Credit and Banking* 14 (August 1982), 376–89.

Sloane, L. "Your Money: Zero Coupon, Insured CD.'s." *New York Times* (September 4, 1982), 20.

US Congress. Congressional Budget Office (CBO). "The Economic and Budget Outlook: An Update." A report to the Senate and House committees on the budget, September 1982a.

US Congress. "Balancing the Federal Budget and Limiting Federal Spending: Constitutional and Statutory Approaches," September 1982b.

US Congress. House. Committee on Banking, Finance, and Urban Affairs. "Conduct of Monetary Policy: Hearings Before the Committee on Banking, Finance and Urban Affairs, House of Representatives, July 14, 21, 22, and 23, 1981." 97th Cong., 1st sess., 1981.

US Congress. Senate. Committee on the Budget. "First Concurrent Resolution on the Budget, FY 1983: Report to Accompany S. Con. Res. 92." 97th Cong., 2d sess., 1982. S. Rept. 97–385.

Wallace, N. "Significant Rate-of-Return Dominance: A Proposed Explanation in Terms of Legal Restrictions." Unpublished paper, October 1979.

Wallace, N. "The Overlapping Generations Model of Fiat Money." In *Models of Monetary Economies*. J.H. Kareken and N. Wallace, Eds. Minneapolis: Federal Reserve Bank of Minneapolis, 1980, 49–82.

Wallace, N. "A Modigliani-Miller Theorem for Open-Market Operations." *American Economic Review* 71 (June 1981), 267–74.

Weintraub, R.E. "Deficits: Their Impact on Inflation and Growth." Staff study prepared for the use of the Subcommittee on Monetary and Fiscal Policy of the Joint Economic Committee, Congress of the United States. 97th Cong., 1st sess., July 1981.

DISCUSSION
Jerome L. Stein

There are two major themes to Preston Miller's paper. First: deficit policy matters because a deficit policy requires faster money growth. Second: higher deficits result in lower real growth, higher inflation, higher nominal and real rates of interest. It is a pleasure to report that I am in agreement with his themes, subject to certain qualifications. My discussion shows how his results can be obtained in a way different than that presented in his paper.

There are three distinct views concerning debt policy; the first and third are not far from Miller's view. The second point of view is fundamentally different.

The first view stresses that there is a real cost to the deficit policy associated with a rise in government purchases because it consists of transferring resources from the private to the public sector. This cost to the private sector exists regardless of how the government purchases are financed. From the graceful style, the reader will recognize Keynes as the writer of the following passage.

> It is common to speak as though, when a government pays its way by inflation, the people of the country avoid taxation. We have seen that this is not so. What is raised by printing notes is just as much taken from the public as is a beer-duty or an income tax. What a government spends the public pays for. There is no such thing

as an uncovered deficit. But in some countries it seems possible to please and content the public, for a time at least, by giving them, in return for the taxes they pay, finely engraved acknowledgements on water marked paper. The income tax receipts, which we in England receive from the Surveyor, we throw into the wastepaper basket; in Germany they call them bank notes and put them into their pocket books; in France they are termed Rentes and are locked up in the family safe. (Keynes, 1923, p. 62).

The second point of view, called the balanced budget view, is that a rise in government purchases of goods generates an increase in real output and a rise in tax revenues sufficient to produce a balanced budget. Central to this view is that a balanced budget is a condition of equilibrium. This is analogous to the view that a rise in real investment generates an equal amount of planned real savings. Contrary to the first point of view, the balanced budget view states that output rises by more than the value of goods initially sacrificed to finance the government expenditures. The following quotation lucidly describes the second point of view. The senior author is James Tobin.

Nothing in the analysis of this paper supports the claim that expansionary fiscal effects on aggregate demand are only transitory. To investigate the question, the main section of this paper focussed on the pure logic of aggregate demand. Supply constraints were assumed away—there is always labor available to produce the output demanded. In this situation, an increase in government expenditure either leads to a new long-run equilibrium with higher real income or, in unstable cases, to an explosive increase in income and interest rate. We do not stress the latter possibility . . . since the economy would sooner or later hit a full employment ceiling . . .

In section 6 we considered the long-run effects of fiscal expansion in an economy with full employment and flexible prices . . . . The new long-run equilibrium, after a permanent increase of government expenditures, has larger real income and capital stock but lower price level and interest rate. But such equilibria are stable, if at all, only if price expectations adapt fairly quickly to price experience. (Tobin and Buiter, 1976, pp. 302–03).

A more recent point of view is consistent with that of Keynes and Miller but contrary to that expressed by Tobin. The trajectories of the economic variables are examined in a growing economy, in the stable case when government expenditures are financed by changes in the money stock.

It is shown that government budget balance is not a condition for equilibrium . . . . A rise in real government purchases per capita has the following effects. There will be a positive impact upon output per capita but steady state output per capita and the capital intensity will decline, and there will be a rise in the inflation tax on real balances and steady state rate of inflation (Infante and Stein, 1980, p. 259).

Whereas Tobin and Buiter claim that in the steady state: (1a) the budget is in balance; (2a) output and capital rise; and (3a) the price level declines, Infante and Stein claim that: (1b) there will be permanent deficits and a higher rate of monetary expansion; (2b) output and capital per capita will decline; and (3b) the rate of inflation will rise. Miller's theme is close to that of Infante and Stein but inconsistent with that of Tobin and Buiter. I now show how Miller's results can be obtained in a different way than was presented in his paper.

Deficits, Money Growth and Inflation

Miller's first point is that a deficit policy leads to higher money growth. I agree with that view when deficit policy is measured by the high employment deficit $F^H(t)$, which is a control variable, rather than by the actual deficit $F(t)$, which is an induced variable.[1]

Denote the total nominal government deficit at time t by $F(t)$. It is financed by the change in the stock of high powered money $H(t)$ plus the value of new bonds issued by the government. The deficit determines the sum of the changes in the stocks of high powered money and bonds. Assume that the bonds are perpetuities paying one dollar per year, and sold at the market price $1/\rho(t+1)$, the reciprocal of the interest rate in period $t+1$. Equation 1.1 describes the financing of the deficit in discrete time.

$$F(t) = [H(t+1) - H(t)] + \frac{1}{\rho(t+1)} [B(t+1) - B(t)] \qquad (1.1)$$

Consider the following policy described by equations 1.2 and 1.3. Fraction $\alpha(t)$ of the high employment deficit $F^H(t)$ is financed by high powered money, and fraction $\beta(t)$ of the difference between the actual $F(t)$ and high employment deficit $F^H(t)$ is financed by high-powered money. The sum of equations 1.2 and 1.3 is equation 1.1.

$$H(t+1) - H(t) = \alpha(t)F^H(t) + \beta(t)[F(t) - F^H(t)] \qquad (1.2)$$

$$\frac{B(t+1) - B(t)}{\rho(t+1)} = [1 - \alpha(t)]F^H(t) + [1 - \beta(t)][F(t) - F^H(t)] \qquad (1.3)$$

The monetary authority must determine what fraction $\alpha(t)$ of the high employment deficit $F^H(t)$, and what fraction $\beta(t)$ of the deviation of the actual deficit from the high employment deficit $[F(t) - F^H(t)]$ to finance with high powered money. The more anxious is the monetary authority to stabilize nominal interest rates, the larger will be the fractions $\alpha(t)$ and $\beta(t)$. The values of these coefficients represent the control policies effected through open market operations by the monetary authority. They will vary with the preferences of the party in power and economic conditions, e.g., the balance of payments.

The money multiplier $\lambda(t) \equiv M(t)/H(t)$ is the ratio of the money stock $M(t)$ to the stock of high powered money $H(t)$. The percentage change in the stock of money can be approximated by the percentage change in high powered money plus the percentage change in the money multiplier. This is equation 1.4, where $\mu(t + 1)$ is the percentage change in the money stock.

$$\mu(t + 1) = \frac{M(t + 1) - M(t)}{M(t)}$$

$$= \lambda(t) \frac{[H(t + 1) - H(t)]}{M(t)} + \frac{[\lambda(t + 1) - \lambda(t)]}{\lambda(t)} \qquad (1.4)$$

Substitute equation 1.2 into 1.4 and derive equation 1.5 for the growth of the money stock $\mu(t + 1)$.

$$\mu(t + 1) = \lambda(t) \left[\alpha(t) \frac{F^H(t)}{M(t)} + \beta(t) \frac{(F(t) - F^H(t))}{M(t)} \right]$$

$$+ \frac{[\lambda(t + 1) - \lambda(t)]}{\lambda(t)}. \qquad (1.5)$$

The money multiplier $\lambda(t)$ varies procyclically: it rises during expansions and declines during contractions. The variation in the money multiplier, which is a function of the deposit-currency and deposit-reserve ratios, is the chief contributor to specific cycles in the rate of change of the money stock. Moreover, the main source of variation in the money multiplier has been the deposit-currency ratio (Cagan, 1965, table 4, p. 26, 29).

Similarly, the actual deficit tends to rise above the high employment deficit during contractions and decline below the high employment deficit during expansions. When these two characteristics are combined, equation 1.6 states that the percentage change in the money multiplier is negatively associated with the difference between the actual and high employment deficit. Both sides of equation 1.6 are induced by the business cycle.

$$\frac{\lambda(t+1) - \lambda(t)}{\lambda(t)} = -\gamma(t) \frac{[F(t) - F^H(t)]}{M(t)} \qquad (1.6)$$

Substitute equation 1.6 into 1.5 and derive equation 1.7 for the rate of monetary expansion from year t to year $t+1$ denoted by $\mu(t+1)$. It is a function of (i) the ratio of the high employment deficit to the money stock $F^H(t)/M(t)$ in year t and (ii) the deviation of the actual from the high employment deficit relative to the money stock $[F(t) - F^H(t)]/M(t)$ in year t. The first determinant is based upon the fiscal policies pursued $F^H(t)$ and a control law $\alpha(t)$. The second determinant depends upon the state of the economy $(F(t) - F^H(t))$ or $(\lambda(t+1) - \lambda(t))$ and a control law $\beta(t)$.

$$\mu(t+1) = \alpha(t)\lambda(t) \frac{F^H(t)}{M(t)} + [\beta(t)\lambda(t) - \gamma(t)] \frac{[F(t) - F^H(t)]}{M(t)} . \qquad (1.7)$$

A regression of the rate of monetary expansion $\mu(t+1)$ on the ratio of the high employment deficit to the money stock $F^H(t)/M(t)$ in year t, and the corresponding ratio of the actual deficit $F(t)/M(t)$, where t ranges from 1957 through 1979 is equation 1.8.

$$\mu(t+1) = 4.25 + 0.365 \ F^H(t)/M(t) + 0.00 \ F(t)/M(t)$$
$$(t=) \quad (11) \quad (3.9) \qquad\qquad (0.0) \qquad\qquad (1.8)$$

$$R^2 = 0.63$$
$$SE = 1.42$$
$$DW = 1.6$$

The coefficient of the high employment deficit is significant at the one percent level, but the coefficient of the actual deficit is zero. The two induced effects $F(t) - F^H(t)$ and $\lambda(t+1) - \lambda(t)$ effectively cancel each other. In a recession (expansion), the induced growth (decline) in the actual deficit is offset by a decline in the money multiplier. What remains is the effect of the high employment deficit.

Table 1–6 is a compact summary of why I agree with Miller's first point within the context of my analysis. The mean ratio of the high employment deficit to the money stock $F^H(t)/M(t)$ increased by seven percentage points, from -2.24 to 4.72 percent per annum, from the 1957–66 period to the 1967–79 period. On average, there were high employment surpluses

Table 1–6. Average high employment deficit to the money stock, compound annual rates of monetary expansion μ and of inflation π, average nominal rate of interest ρ, 1957–80.

Period	Mean $F^H(t)/M(t)$	Period	μ	π	ρ
1957–66	−2.24	1956–67	2.7	2.1	4.34
1967–79	4.72	1968–80	6.3	6.6	7.77
change	6.96		3.6	4.5	3.43

Source: Stein (1982), p. 212. A deficit is positive and a surplus is negative in column 1.

(denoted by a negative sign) during the 1957–66 period and high employment deficits during 1967–79. As a consequence, the compound rate of monetary expansion μ rose from 2.7% p.a. during the 1956–67 to 6.3% p.a. during the 1968–80 period. The compound annual rate of inflation rose from 2.1% p.a. during the first period to 6.6% p.a. during the second period. The average Aaa corporate bond yield ρ rose from 4.34% p.a. during 1956–67 to 7.77% p.a. during the 1967–80 period.

Two conclusions are drawn from this analysis. First: a credible change in monetary policy must be accompanied by a change in the autonomous component of fiscal policy, the high employment deficit. Second: long range predictions of the rate of inflation and nominal rates of interest which are not long range predictions of the rate of monetary expansion and of the high employment deficit have no scientific validity. Hence, I am in basic agreement with Miller's first point.

Deficit Policy, Output per Capita, the Capital Intensity and rate of Inflation

I also agree with a modification of Miller's second point. A rise in real government purchases, which are not used as investment and are financed by money, will lower steady state output per capita and raise the rate of inflation. First, I show why the balanced budgets view expressed by Tobin and others requires very restrictive assumptions for its validity. Second, I sketch the proof for the third point of view (cited in the introduction) that there are adverse long run effects of a rise in real government purchases upon the capital intensity and rate of inflation.

The Balanced Budget View is Only Valid under
Very Restrictive Assumptions [2]

The view that budget balance is a condition for equilibrium requires a very restrictive and unrealistic assumption concerning the price level. It rests upon the following line of reasoning. Equation 1.9 is the IS-LM solution for nominal income (per capita) $Y = py$, where y is real output (per capita), p is the price level, M is the money stock (per capita) and B is the number of bonds (per capita) each paying \$1 per year of interest in perpetuity. Parameter G is nominal government purchases per capita and T is the tax rate.

$$Y = py = F(M, B{:}G, T) \qquad (1.9)$$

The crucial equation for the balanced budget view is 1.10 or 1.10a which states that the price level p is an algebraic function of output y. Equation 1.10 states that the price level is positively correlated with output; equation 1.10a fixes the price level $p = 1$. It makes no difference to the argument which equation is used.

$$p = P(y); \quad \infty > p' > 0 \qquad (1.10)$$

$$p = 1 \qquad (1.10\text{a})$$

Therefore, the equilibrium level of output y is described by equation 1.11.

$$P(y)y = F(M, B{:}G, T) \qquad (1.11)$$

The total budget deficit is financed by new high powered money plus bonds. There are two regimes: (i) an "M" regime where deficits and surpluses are financed by money ($\alpha = 1$) and (ii) a "B" regime where deficits and surpluses are financed by bonds ($\alpha = 0$). Equations 1.12 and 1.13 describe the rates of change of money and bonds in general. The deficit is: $G + B$, government expenditures G plus interest on the debt B less taxes $T(y + B)$ on personal income $y + B$. The nominal rate of interest is ρ.

$$DM = \alpha[G + B - T(Y + B)] \qquad D \equiv d/dt \qquad (1.12)$$

$$\frac{DB}{p} = (1 - \alpha)[G + B - T(Y + B)] \qquad (1.13)$$

Equation 1.11 states that real output y can only be constant (i.e., in equilibrium) if the stocks of money and bonds are constant. Equations 1.12 and 1.13 state that the stocks of money and bonds will only be constant if the budget is in balance. Therefore, budget balance is alleged to be a condition for equilibrium. I define this as the budget balance view.

Price equation 1.10 or 1.10a is responsible for this result. If a more general price equation is used, where there can be inflation or deflation in the steady state, then it has been proved by Christ (1979), Infante and Stein (1980) and Stein (1982, ch.5) that budget balance is not a condition for equilibrium. One such equation is 1.14 where the rate of inflation $\pi(t) = D\ln p(t)$ is equal to the anticipated rate of inflation π^* plus a function of the gap between actual output (per capita) $y(t)$ and capacity output (per capita) $f(k(t))$. The latter depends upon the capital intensity $k(t)$ and is evaluated at the equilibrium rate of unemployment.

$$\pi(t) = \pi^* + \lambda[y(t) - f(k(t))] \qquad (1.14)$$

In the medium run model of Christ, where the capital intensity is predetermined, the economy converges to capacity output $f(k(t))$ regardless of the level of government expenditure or taxes. A rise in the high employment deficit permanently increases the growth of the money stock and rates of inflation with no effect upon the steady-state level of output. This is fundamentally different from the balanced budget view.

The experience since 1968 has convinced many economists, but not all, that price equation 1.10 does not describe the economy. Prices and output, relative to their trends, are not positively correlated. Therefore, the balanced budget view is an implication of a model which is inconsistent with the empirical data.

A second deficiency of the balanced budget view is that, given what we know of the world, a B-regime (i.e., bond financed fiscal policy) characterized by $\alpha = 0$ in equations 1.12 and 1.13 is unstable. Consider a medium run model of a B-regime where: (i) the capital intensity is constant and (ii) the money stock is changing at a constant rate. The following theorem was proved by Christ (1979, p. 533) in a model with price equation 1.14 and by Infante and Stein (1976, p. 492) in their criticism of the Keynesian model with equation 1.10.

Theorem 1: If a parametric rise in the money stock per capita (in a B-regime) raises the steady-state level of nominal income, $dy/dM > 0$, then the B-regime is unstable. This theorem is also true in a general growth model, as proved by Kazuo Mino and the author. Very few economists believe that dy/dM is negative. Consequently, if dy/dM is positive, the B-regime is unstable.[3]

A very simple example of the instability of a B-regime will serve to show the deficiencies of the balanced budget view. Consider the Keynesian fiscalist model below, in nominal terms.

$$Y = C + I + G \qquad\qquad (1.15)$$

$$C = c_1(1 - \tau)(Y + B) + c_2 M \qquad\qquad (1.15a)$$

$$I = aY + v \qquad\qquad (1.15b)$$

Equation 1.15 is the goods market equilibrium. Consumption C in 1.15a is a function of disposable income $(1 - t)(Y + B)$ and exogenous money M. Parameter τ is the tax rate. Investment function 1.15b just depends upon income and is interest inelastic. Government purchases are G. This is the prototype Keynesian fiscalist model with a vertical IS curve.

The level of nominal income is equation 1.16.

$$Y(t) = \frac{c_1(1 - \tau)B(t) + c_2 M_0 + v + G}{1 - c_2(1 - \tau) - a} \qquad\qquad (1.16)$$

The quantity of bonds varies with the government deficit according to equation 1.17, where $\rho(t)$ is the nominal rate of interest.

$$\frac{DB(t)}{\rho(t)} = G + B(t) - \tau(Y(t) + B(t)) \qquad\qquad (1.17)$$

The stability condition is equation 1.18.

$$\frac{\tau c_1(1 - \tau)}{1 - c_1(1 - \tau) - a} > (1 - \tau) \qquad\qquad (1.18)$$

System 1.16–1.17 is stable if and only if:

$$c_1 + a > 1 \qquad\qquad (1.19)$$

Only if the marginal propensity to spend $(c_1 + a)$ exceeds unity can this system be stable. In particular, if investment is exogenous $I = v$ with a zero marginal propensity to invest $(a = 0)$, then stability requires that the marginal propensity to consume exceeds unity. This discussion can be summarized as Theorem 2: The fiscalist model of a B-regime will only be stable if the marginal propensity to spend exceeds unity.

Carl Christ drew the following inferences from Theorem 1 concerning the method of financing deficits and the rule for the expansion of the stock of money.

> The policy that is unstable . . . resembles a policy that has been advocated by some of the monetarists, that is, fix government purchases and tax-transfer schedules, make the money stock grow at a constant moderate rate, and allow any variation in deficits or surpluses to be covered by issuing or retiring government debt. (1979, p. 534).

Since we believe that a parametric rise in the stock of money leads to a higher price level, a B-regime (i.e., a constant rate of monetary expansion rule) is unstable.

The Short and Long Run Effects of a Deficit Policy

Miller's second point concerning the relation between deficits, growth and inflation is consistent with recently published work, subject to two qualifications.[4] First, the deficits referred to must be autonomous (e.g., high employment deficits) not those induced by deviation between actual and capacity output. Second, the M-regime must be used to finance the marginal deficits rather than the unstable B-regime.

Christ's 1979 paper, to my mind, is the best analysis in every respect of the implications of the budget constraint and of deficits, when the capital intensity is predetermined. However, variations in the capital intensity cannot be ignored in the analysis because the stock of real capital has grown more rapidly than the stocks of money and debt (e.g., from 1950–70). Moreover, any useful model must use a price equation where inflation or deflation can exist in the steady state. Equation 1.14 is acceptable but 1.10 is not acceptable.

The IS growth model (Infante and Stein, 1980; Stein, 1982, ch. 5) satisfies these requirements, and its implications agree with Miller's conclusions. A very brief sketch of this analysis is presented here. Let the full employment FE curve in Figure 1–1 describe output per worker $y(t)$ when it is equal to capacity output per worker $f(k(t))$, where $k(t)$ is the capital intensity at the equilibrium rate of unemployment and f is the production function. Below this curve, output is below capacity, and above this curve output exceeds capacity.

$$y(t) = f(k(t)) \qquad FE \qquad (1.20)$$

In the steady state capital must grow at the same rate n as does effective labor. The curve $I(g) = n$ is the locus of $y(t)$ and $k(t)$ such that capital and

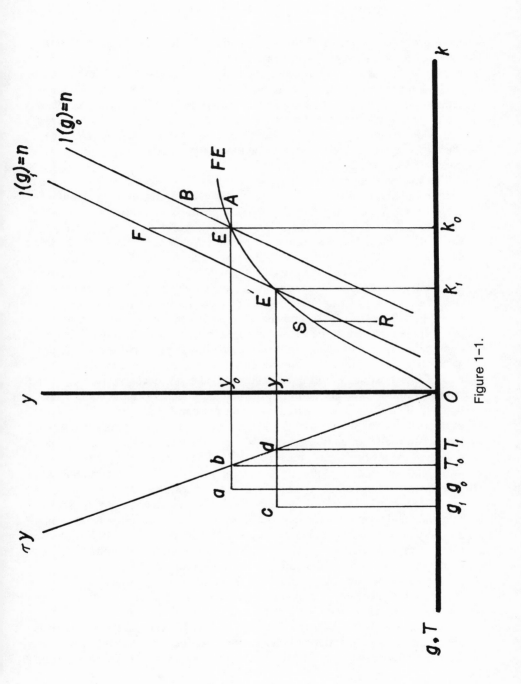

Figure 1-1.

labor grow at rate n. It is positively sloped for the following reason. Say that capital and labor are growing at rate n at point E. Then the capital intensity rises by EA. The rise in the capital intensity, given $y(t)$, is associated with a decline in the marginal product of capital relative to the real rate of interest. At point A, the growth of capital is less than n. For capital to grow at rate n, the marginal product would have to rise relative to the real rate of interest. This would occur if the level of output per worker increased by AB. Hence the $I(g) = n$ curve is positively sloped. Stability requires that the $I(g) = n$ curve be steeper than the FE curve.

The tax revenue function $\tau y(t)$ in real per capita terms is drawn in the second quadrant. Initially, when real government purchases per capita are g, the steady state is at point E. Capital intensity is k_0, output y_0 is equal to capacity output $f(k_0)$, and capital is growing at rate n. Real tax revenues per capita $T_0 = \tau y_0$ is less than real government purchases per capita g_0. Deficit $ab = T_0 g_0$ determines the rate of monetary expansion and rate of inflation.

Suppose that the economy were at point R and there is a rise in real government purchases per capita to g_1 to reduce the Okun gap RS. There is a positive impact effect upon aggregate demand, described by the Keynesian multiplier. Price flexibility and the endogenous money growth (M-regime) are sufficient to return the economy to capacity output at point S; but the demand management policy, in the form of a higher g, accelerates the return. When output is equal to the current capacity output S, there is a higher real rate of interest than would have occurred had there been no rise in g. The reason is that at capacity output S, the higher g must crowd out some private demand. The rise in g lowers real balances per capita and raises the real rate of interest. If capital is to grow at rate n at the higher real rate of interest, the marginal product of capital must be higher. This means that, at any capital intensity, the level of output must be higher. The curve describing the growth of capital at rate n shifts up from $I(g_0) = n$ to $I(g_1) = n$. Some real investment is crowded out by the rise in real government purchases, which is exactly Keynes' description quoted above. Consequently, there is a lower rate of capital formation associated with every level of real output and capital intensity. The economy converges to point E' rather than to point E. There is a lower capital intensity $(k_1 < k_0)$ and a lower output per capita $(y_1 < y_0)$ than would have been attained if g were not increased.

At the new steady-state point E', there is a larger budget deficit $cd > ab$. Not only are there larger real government expenditures $(g_1 > g_0)$, but there are lower tax revenues $(T_1 < T_2)$.

Contrary to Tobin, (1) real output is lower, (2) the capital intensity is lower and (3) a budget deficit is permanently produced. The budget balance view does not characterize the models which contains price equation 1.14 in an essential way. (4) The inflation tax on real balances is the real per capita deficit *cd* which is financed by money. This tax is raised from *ab* to *cd* as a result of the rise in real government purchases.

I have shown that Preston Miller's basic conclusions can be obtained using a different method of analysis. I am pleased to conclude that, in a broad sense, we share the same point of view.

Notes

1. This section is drawn from Stein (1982), pp. 42–46, 210–12.
2. This is based upon Stein (1982), pp. 170–83.
3. Tobin's model of the balanced budget view implies that in a B-regime velocity is reduced by a rise in real government purchases. See Tobin (1976), equations 46 and 48.
4. This is based upon Stein (1982), pp. 183–200.

References

Cagan, P. *Determinants and Effects of Changes in the Stock of Money 1875–1960*. New York: National Bureau of Economic Research, 1965.

Christ, C.F. "On Fiscal and Monetary Policies and the Government Budget Constraint," *American Economic Review* 69 (September 1979), 526–538.

Infante, E.F. and J.L. Stein, "Money Financed Fiscal Policy in a Growing Economy," *Journal of Political Economy* 88 (1980).

Keynes, J.M. *A Tract on Monetary Reform*. London: MacMillan, 1923.

Stein, J.L. *Monetarist, Keynesian and New Classical Economics*. Basil Blackwell, Oxford and New York University Press, 1982.

Tobin, J. and W. Buiter "Long-run Effects of Fiscal and Monetary Policy on Aggregate Demand." In: *Monetarism*. J.L. Stein, Ed. Amsterdam: North–Holland, 1976.

2 ON THE MONETIZATION OF DEFICITS

Alan S. Blinder

A government deficit is said to be monetized when the central bank purchases the bonds the government issues to cover its deficit. Because of the central bank's balance sheet identity, such purchases increase bank reserves unless offset by other transactions. By contrast, new government debt purchased by private parties does not increase bank reserves. Because of this difference, whether or not a deficit is monetized is often thought to have important macroeconomic ramifications. And there is considerable evidence that this supposition is correct.

This paper is organized around two questions: Does monetization matter? What factors determine how much monetization the Federal Reserve will undertake? Both of these questions have been asked before, and my answers will be less than startling. I intend simply to bring a bit more evidence to bear on the issues and to add a few new thoughts to the discussion.

I thank Leonard Nakamura for research assistance, the National Science Foundation for research support, and Scott Hein, Dwight Jaffee, Michael Levy, Jorge de Macedo, Hyman Minsky, Franco Modigliani, Joseph Stiglitz, John Taylor, and Burton Zwick for helpful comments and suggestions on an earlier draft.

The initial section takes up the first question, for a given budget deficit, will nominal or real variables behave differently depending on whether the new bonds are purchased by the central bank or by the public? Notice that this is basically the same as asking, Do open-market operations matter? Virtually all macro models give an affirmative answer. But some recent theoretical developments, which I review, suggest that the issue is a good deal more complicated than indicated by simple models like the quantity theory or IS-LM. After sorting out some theoretical issues that arise in a dynamic context, I present some new time series evidence which supports the old idea that monetization does matter.

The second section addresses the issue, How does the Fed decide how much of each deficit to monetize? First, some normative rules dictating how the Fed should make this decision are presented and briefly evaluated. Then a game-theoretic argument is offered to explain why a central bank with discretionary authority may choose not to monetize deficits at all and may instead do the opposite, i.e., contract bank reserves as the government raises its deficit. Finally, I offer some empirical evidence suggesting that there is a systematic link between budget deficits and growth in reserves. This relationship suggests that the Federal Reserve monetizes deficits less when inflation is high and when government purchases are growing rapidly.

Does Monetization Matter?

Elementary macro models, including both the quantity theory and IS-LM, suggest that budget deficits have a greater effect on aggregate demand if they are monetized. This difference is extreme under the crude quantity theory. Obviously, if $Py = MV$ and V is a constant, then deficits increase nominal demand if and only if they are monetized.[1] A slightly more sophisticated quantity theory, which recognizes that nonmonetized deficits raise velocity by raising interest rates, allows for an effect of deficits on aggregate demand. But the supposition that the effect of money is greater is maintained.

Essentially the same conclusion emerges from the fix-price IS-LM model. Figure 2–1 shows an initial IS-LM equilibrium at point A. Higher government spending or a cut in taxes raises the IS curve to I_1S_1. If the deficit is not monetized, the LM curve is unchanged and equilibrium moves to point B; output rises. But if the deficit is monetized, the LM curve shifts as well (to L_1M_1) and output increases even more (point C).

This is all very simple, but it leaves out much. Among the important omissions are: (1) wealth effects on the IS and/or LM curves and the resulting dynamics that are implied by the government budget constraint; (2)

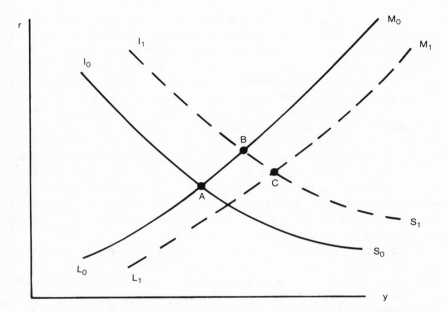

Figure 2–1. Monetized and Nonmonetized Deficits in IS-LM Analysis

changes on the supply side of the economy as higher or lower interest rates affect investment; and (3) expectational effects set up by the government's financing decision (which, among other things, intervene between the real interest rate and the nominal interest rate). The next three subsections take up each of these in turn.

Wealth Effects and the Government Budget Constraint

The government budget constraint states that any excess of total expenditures over total receipts must be financed by selling bonds either to the Federal Reserve (and hence creating high powered money) or to the public:

$$dH/dt + dB/dt = G + rB - T(Y) \qquad (2.1)$$

where H is high powered money, B is publicly held bonds (here taken to have zero maturity), G is nominal government purchases, r is the nominal interest rate, and T is nominal receipts, written as a function of nominal income.

As Solow and I (1973) showed almost a decade ago, if there are wealth effects on the *IS* and *LM* curves, then the dynamics set up by equation 2.1 lead to results that seem paradoxical from the viewpoint of static macro models. In particular, if the model remains stable under bond financing of deficits (which is by no means a sure thing), then the long run effects of a deficit on aggregate demand are greater if it is not monetized.

How can this be true in view of Figure 2.1? Suppose we add wealth effects to the analysis and assume that government bonds are net wealth.[2] Start with the case of bond financing (point *B*). The additional wealth represented by the new bonds augments consumer spending and pushes the *IS* curve further to the right. At the same time, however, the *LM* curve shifts leftward if there is a wealth effect on the demand for money.[3] The net result of these two wealth effects is clearly to increase *r*. But the net effect on *Y* seems to be ambiguous. However, Solow and I showed that in a stable system the net impact of the two wealth effects must increase income.

The dynamic adjustment proceeds as follows. Each injection of bonds increases income, and the process continues (in a stable system) until the induced tax receipts bring the budget into balance. The dynamics are similar under money financing, except that each dollar of newly created money has an additional liquidity effect on the *LM* curve which makes *Y* rise even faster.

Why, then, do bond financed deficits have larger effects in the long run? The reason, loosely speaking, is that bond financed deficits "last longer." More precisely, bond financed deficits raise the government's interest expenses whereas money financed deficits reduce them. Thus, while each $1 billion bond issue expands *Y* by less than a $1 billion issue of high powered money, the total amount of new paper assets that must be created before the deficit is closed is greater under bond financing.

How do we know that the new result is that *Y* expands more under bond financing? Set equation 2.1 equal to zero and take the (long run) total derivative with respect to *G*, including the wealth effects of the creation of new paper assets. Under bond financing, a rise in *G* leads to a rise in *B* so:

$$dY/dG = (1/T'(Y)) (1 + d(rB)/dG) \qquad (2.2)$$

Under money financing, a rise in *G* leaves *B* unchanged but raises *M*, so:

$$dY/dG = (1/T'(Y)) (1 + B(dr/dG)) \qquad (2.3)$$

In equation 2.2, both *r* and *B* are driven up by the increase in *B*. In 2.3, *r* is driven down by the increase in *M*. It follows that the multiplier in 2.2 exceeds the multiplier in 2.3. Of course, all this assumes that the economy is stable under both methods of financing, a matter to which I will return. It also ignores expectations, the behavior of prices, and changes in the capital stock.

Capital Accumulation and the Long Run

The original paper by Solow and myself allowed for capital accumulation and showed that, apart from modifications in the stability conditions, this wrinkle did not affect the basic results. However, the model we used maintained the (inappropriate) assumption of a fixed price level. Subsequent work fortunately established very similar conclusions in models which deal more satisfactorily with the price level.[4]

If the labor force and technology are more or less exogenous, then the long run effects of monetization depend on how the capital stock reacts. Neoclassical growth models lead to the supposition that money financing of deficits is better for capital formation than bond financing,[5] but adding even a minimal amount of complexity to standard macro models introduces enough ambiguity so that even this intuitive conclusion cannot be derived.

The ambiguities arise from the interaction of wealth effects and interest elasticities, neither one of which can be ignored without assuming away the problem. Consider, as an example, the following simple IS-LM model augmented to include wealth effects:

$$y = c(y - t(y), a) + i(r - \pi, K) + g \qquad (2.4)$$

$$M/P = L(r, y, a) \qquad (2.5)$$

$$a = K + M/P + B/P \qquad (2.6)$$

$$dM/dt + dB/dt = P(g - t(y)) + rB \qquad (2.7)$$

$$(1/P)(dP/dt) = \pi + h(y - F(K)) \qquad (2.8)$$

$$dK/dt = i(r - \pi, K) \qquad (2.9)$$

Equations 2.4 and 2.5 are *IS* and *LM* curves augmented to include real wealth *a*, which is defined in 2.6. Here *r* denotes the nominal interest rate and π the expected rate of inflation. The difference between *M* and *H* is ignored. Equations 2.7–2.9 give the dynamics of the three state variables: *P*, *K*, and either *M* or *B*. Equation 2.7 is the government budget constraint, equation 2.8 is an expectational Phillips curve, and equation 2.9 updates the capital stock.

The signs of most of the short-run comparative static multipliers implicit in equations 2.4–2.6 can be determined with only the usual qualitative assumptions. An important exception, however, is dr/dM which, even ignoring possible effects of M on expected inflation (about which more later), has the sign of:

$$C_a L_y - (1 - L_a)[1 - C_y(1 - t')] \qquad (2.10)$$

an expression which is negative in the absence of wealth effects, but ambiguous in their presence. The economics behind this ambiguity is quite simple. Normally, an increase in M lowers interest rates by shifting the LM curve to the right. But the wealth effects of an injection of money shift the LM curve to the left and the IS curve to the right, thereby pushing up interest rates. These wealth effects could conceivably be strong enough to offset the original effect of M on the LM curve.

As might be surmised, this ambiguity is devastating to long-run analysis where primary attention focuses on the behavior of the capital stock. If we do not know in which direction M pushes r, then we certainly will not be able to tell in which direction it pushes K. In fact, none of the long-run comparative static derivatives (obtained from equations 2.4–2.6 and from equations 2.7–2.9 set equal to zero) are of determinate sign unless wealth effects are assumed away. But this is not a legitimate way out of the indeterminacy because Solow and I (1973) showed years ago that wealth effects are intimately involved in the stability conditions.[6]

The dynamic constraints across choices of policy mixes set up by the about the long-run consequences of the monetization decision. Econometric estimation and simulation of quantitative models seem to be the only ways out.

The Government Budget Constraint and Expectations

The dynamic constraints across choices of policy mixes set up by the government budget constraint bring expectational issues to the fore. The identity points out that today's deficit and monetization decisions have implications for the feasible set of fiscal-monetary combinations in future periods.

For example, suppose an expansionary fiscal policy today leads to a large deficit that is not monetized. Future government budgets will therefore inherit a larger burden of interest payments, so the same time paths of G, M, and tax rates will lead to larger deficits. What will the government do about this? That depends on its reaction function. For example, large deficits and high interest rates might induce greater monetary expansion in the future (the possibility emphasized by Sargent and Wallace (1981)). Alternatively, it might induce future tax increases (the case stressed by Barro (1974)), or cuts in government spending (the apparent hope of Reaganomics). Yet another possibility is that the government will simply finance the burgeoning deficits by issuing more and more bonds.[7] All of these are live options, and have different implications for the long run evolution of the economy. In fact, under rational expectations, they may have different implications for the state of the economy today.

As an example of a nonmonetized deficit, consider a tax cut financed by issuing new bonds. Such a tax cut today enlarges current and prospective future budget deficits, thereby requiring some combination of the following policy adjustments: (1) increases in future taxes; (2) decreases in future government expenditures; (3) increases in future money creation; and (4) increases in future issues of interest-bearing national debt. To the extent that the current decisions made by individuals and firms are influenced by their expectations about the future, each of these alternatives may have different implications for the effects of the tax cut today.

For example, if people believe that a tax cut financed by bonds simply reduces today's taxes and raises future taxes in order to pay the interest on the bonds, then consumption may not be affected. This is essentially Barro's (1974) argument.

Alternatively, people may believe that the policy will eventually lead to greater money creation. If so, the inflationary expectations thereby engendered may affect their current decisions in ways that are not captured by standard behavioral functions. This is essentially the point made by Sargent and Wallace (1981) in arguing that tight money may be inflationary. Still different reactions would be expected if people thought the current deficit would lead to lower government spending or to more bond issues in the future. The theoretical possibilities are numerous, limited only by the imagination of the theorist.[8]

Rational expectations interact with the government budget constraint in an obvious way. People's beliefs about the future consequences of current monetary and fiscal decisions are conditioned by their views of the policy rules that the authorities will follow. To the extent that these beliefs affect their current behavior, different perceived policy rules actually imply different short run policy multipliers under rational expectations. This is easily illustrated in the context of the preceding IS-LM model. Consider the short run multiplier dy/dg, allowing for a possible effect of g on inflationary expectations via the mechanisms just discussed. It follows directly from equations 2.4–2.6 that:

$$\frac{\partial y}{\partial g}\bigg|_{\pi \text{ const.}} = \frac{1}{1 - C_y(1 - t') + \dfrac{i_r}{L_r}L_y} \equiv \mu;$$

$$\text{and} \quad \frac{\partial y}{\partial \pi}\bigg|_{g \text{ const.}} = -i_r u \qquad (2.11)$$

and from the chain rule that:

$$dy/dg = \frac{\partial y}{\partial g}\bigg|_{\pi} + (d_\pi/dg)\left(\frac{\partial y}{\partial \pi}\bigg|_{g}\right) \qquad (2.12)$$

The first term is the standard (positive) government spending multiplier in IS-LM analysis. The second term is the product of a positive effect of inflationary expectations on output and an effect of g on π which depends on the factors enumerated above. If it is positive, as seems likely, then expectational effects make the short run multiplier larger. But it is conceivable that $d\pi/dg$ could be zero or even negative.

A key question for policy formulation is, how important are these expectational effects in practice? This seems to depend principally on how forward-looking current economic decisions really are. Take the tax cut example again. Under the pure permanent income hypothesis (*PIH*) only the present discounted value of lifetime after-tax income flows affects current consumption.[9] So expectations about future budget policy should have important effects on current consumption. But if shortsightedness, extremely high discount rates, or capital market imperfections effectively break many of the links between the future and the present, then current consumption may be rather insensitive to these expectations and rather sensitive to current income. Even under fully rational expectations and the pure *PIH*, consumption may depend largely on current income if the stochastic process generating income is highly serially correlated. These are issues about which knowledge is accumulating but much remains to be learned. The evidence to date does not lead to the conclusion that long-term expectations rule the roost.[10]

The other two places where expectations about future fiscal and monetary policies might have significant effects on current behavior are wage and price setting and investment. Investment, of course, is the quintessential example of an economic decision which is strongly conditioned by expectations about the future. Even Keynes knew this! But once again there are some real world considerations that interfere with the strictly neoclassical view of investment as the unconstrained solution to an intertemporal optimization problem. One is that capital rationing may interfere with a firm's ability to run current losses on the expectation of future profits. A second is that management may use ad hoc rules such as the payback period criterion in appraising investment projects. A third is the emerging "business school" view that managers are more shortsighted than they "should be" because they face the wrong incentives. A fourth is that there may be a strong accelerator element in investment spending, which ties the current investment decision much more tightly to the current state of the economy than neoclassical economics recognizes. As in the consumption example, each of these things diminishes the importance of the future to current decisionmaking and thereby renders expectational effects less important.

Wage and price setting is another important example. Ad hoc rules which adjust wages or prices in accordance with "the law of supply and demand," or which are mainly backward looking, render expectational effects rather unimportant. But rules which are based on forward looking considerations (such as expected future excess demand) make expectational effects crucial. Again, this is an area where we must learn much more before we can make any definitive judgments.[11]

A word on uncertainty seems appropriate before leaving this topic. It seems to me that people probably attach great uncertainty to their beliefs about what future government policies will be. If so, the means of their subjective probability distributions may have far less influence on their current decisions than the contemporary preoccupation with rational expectations would suggest. For example, how much influence does the two-week-ahead weather forecast have on your decision about whether or not to plan a picnic on a given date?

Similarly, the importance of expectations for macroeconomic aggregates is diminished by the likelihood that different people hold different expectations about what future government policies are likely to be.[12] If some people believe today's tax cuts signal higher future taxes, some believe they signal higher future money creation, and some believe they signal lower future government spending, then expectations about the future may have meager current effects in the aggregate. The conclusion seems to be that while we should not forget about expectational effects operating through the government budget constraint, neither should we get carried away by them. There is no reason to believe that they are the whole show.

New Time Series Evidence

The two preceding sections showed that capital accumulation and expectations considerably complicate theoretical discussion of the monetization issue. The former creates complexities that can be handled in principle, but not in practice. The latter opens up so many possibilities that it may be intractable even in principle. Can we let the data speak for themselves? This is hazardous in the absence of a reliable structural model embodying many of the effects just enumerated. What I offer in this section is far less ambitious: some simple time series evidence on whether or not knowledge of the monetization decision helps predict movements in nominal GNP, real GNP, and the price level.

The framework for such an analysis has been well established by Granger (1969) and Sims (1972), and will not be repeated here. Two points are worth making, however: (1) Granger-causation has nothing to do with causation in the usual sense. Since it is quite possible, especially once expectational influences are accounted for, that the effect might precede the cause, learning that X Granger-causes Y tells us nothing about whether or not Y moved because of X. It means that X adds to the ability to predict Y, no more and no less; and (2) Whether or not X contributes to the ability to predict Y may depend on what other information is considered. Thus, for example, it is perfectly possible that X might Granger-cause Y when some other variable, Z, is excluded from the regression, but fail to Granger-cause Y when Z is included. In this context, I will interpret the question "Does monetization matter?" as asking whether or not changes in bank reserves Granger-cause nominal GNP growth (or inflation) once we control for growth of the national debt.

Letting Y denote nominal GNP, R denote bank reserves, D denote the outstanding stock of government bonds (including the portion owned by the Fed), and Δ denote the first difference operator, regressions of the following form were run:

$$\Delta Y/Y = a(L)(\Delta Y/Y) + b(L)(\Delta R/R) + c(L)(\Delta D/D) \quad (2.13)$$

These were estimated on annual fiscal year data, with the maximum lag extending back either two or three years.[13]

Monetization does not matter, that is, fails to help predict growth in Y, if the b coefficients are jointly insignificant. Analogously, debt policy does not matter (given monetary policy) if the c coefficients are jointly insignificant. Notice that the crude quantity theory suggests a unitary long-run elasticity for bank reserves and a zero long-run elasticity for the nonmonetized debt, that is: $\Sigma a + \Sigma b = 1$ and $\Sigma c = 0$. These hypotheses are all testable by standard F tests.

In estimating equation 2.13, ΔD_t was defined as the increase in government indebtedness to the public during fiscal year t. Fiscal years rather than calendar years were used so as to get a more accurate measure of the deficit. Budget numbers in the national income and product accounts (NIPA) differ in several ways from those in the unified budget, and the deficit series I used differs further from the unified budget owing to the activities of off-budget agencies. This suggests a potentially large slippage between, say, quarterly NIPA deficit numbers and the true government borrowing requirement.

In order to use the fiscal year as the unit of time, quarterly data on adjusted bank reserves, R,[14] and nominal GNP, Y, were put on a fiscal year basis.[15] Results from estimating equation 2.13 by ordinary least squares over the period 1952–1981 appear as regressions in columns 1 and 2 in table 2–1. Roughly speaking, the regressions make it look as if only the first lag of each variable matters. But, in keeping with the spirit of this sort of work, the insignificant variables were not dropped.

The first question to be addressed is, once growth of national debt is controlled for, does growth of reserves help to predict nominal GNP growth? The point estimates certainly suggest an affirmative answer, since in each regression the lagged change in reserves has a large and significant coefficient. More formally, F test number 1, reported at the bottom of table 2.1, decisively rejects the null hypothesis that $\Delta R/R$ does not Granger-cause $\Delta Y/Y$.

A weaker hypothesis is that the sum of the b coefficients is zero, that is, that reserves have no long-run effect. Once again, the point estimates are unfavorable to this hypothesis since the estimated elasticity of Y with respect to R, controlling for D, is about .57. And, as can be seen in the table (F test number 2), the appropriate F test confirms that this elasticity is significantly different from zero. Thus monetization does matter.

We can, of course, turn the tables and ask whether growth in national debt helps to predict nominal GNP growth once we control for growth in bank reserves. Hard core monetarism suggests a negative answer. However, as can be seen in F-test number 3, the null hypothesis that all the c coefficients are zero is decisively rejected. Even the weaker hypothesis that, while deficits matter in the short run, they do not matter in the long run, to wit: $\Sigma c = 0$, is easily rejected by the data. Deficits certainly seem to matter.

What about the characteristic quantity-theory implication that the long-run elasticity of Y with respect to R is unity? As the table shows (in F test number 5), the null hypothesis that this elasticity is unity, i.e., that

Table 2-1.   Regressions for Nominal GNP Growth,
Fiscal Years 1952–1982

Variable	(1)	(2)
Constant	.068	.052
	(0.15)	(0.12)
$(\Delta Y/Y)_{t-1}$	−.536	−.515
	(.196)	(.187)
$(\Delta Y/Y)_{t-2}$	−.082	.093
	(.203)	(.125)
$(\Delta Y/Y)_{t-3}$	−.174	—
	(.133)	
$(\Delta R/R)_{t-1}$	.675	.715
	(.150)	(.146)
$(\Delta R/R)_{t-2}$	.186	.116
	(.212)	(.199)
$(\Delta R/R)_{t-3}$	.149	—
	(.197)	
$(\Delta D/D)_{t-1}$	.349	.328
	(.091)	(.080)
$(\Delta D/D)_{t-2}$	.125	.177
	(.114)	(.104)
$(\Delta D/D)_{t-3}$	.161	—
	(.108)	
R^2	.80	.78
DW	2.16	2.25
$\dfrac{\Sigma b_j}{1 - \Sigma a_j}$	.56	.58
$\dfrac{\Sigma c_j}{1 - \Sigma a_j}$	.35	.36
F Test for		
1) All $b_i = 0$	6.93**	9.18**
2) $\Sigma b_i = 0$	7.92*	9.96**
3) All $c_i = 0$	10.48**	14.58**
4) $\Sigma c_i = 0$	23.02**	24.33**
5) $\Sigma a + \Sigma b = 1$	12.14**	12.01**
6) $\Sigma a + \Sigma b = 1$ and $\Sigma c = 0$	12.01**	13.16**

Notes: Standard errors in parentheses. *denotes significant at 5% level. **denotes significant at 1% level.

$\Sigma a + \Sigma b = 1$, is clearly rejected. The quantity theory fares no better if it is extended to include the implication $\Sigma c = 0$ (F test number 6). The overall conclusion from these regressions is clear. Both monetized and nonmonetized deficits are significant predictors of subsequent GNP growth.

An obvious question is whether the debt and reserves variables used in table 2.1 are mainly predicting movements of prices or movements of real output. To address this question, table 2–2 reports the results from regressions analogous to equation 2.13, but using the GNP deflator in place of nominal GNP.

The results differ from those obtained with nominal GNP in a number of ways, and are far more favorable to the quantity-theoretic approach. Unfortunately, in contrast to the case of nominal GNP, some of the results depend on whether we use the regression with three lags (column 1) or the regression with two lags (column 2). First, the null hypothesis that growth in reserves does contribute to the explanation of inflation can be rejected in the equation using three lags—but only at the five percent level of significance, not at the one percent level. In the equation using two lags, it cannot be rejected at all. (See F test number 1 at the bottom of table 2.2) Second, in the two lag equation we cannot even reject the hypothesis that the long run elasticity of P with respect to R is zero—an hypothesis that almost no one would seriously entertain. However, we can easily reject it in the three lag equation. (See F test number 2.)

Fortunately, the other results do not depend on whether we use two or three lags of the variables. For example, growth in national debt helps to predict inflation (once growth in reserves are controlled for) at the five percent, but not the one percent, level. (F test number 3). However, the null hypothesis that the long-run elasticity of P with respect to D is zero cannot be rejected at al. (See F test number 1 at the bottom of table 2.2.) Second, in the two-lag equation we cannot even reject the hypothesis that the long-run

Table 2–3 reports the analogous regressions and F tests using real GNP in place of nominal GNP. Naturally, the explanatory power is much lower since we are using nominal reserves and nominal debt to explain a real variable. In general, very few significant effects are found. For example, the hypothesis that growth in reserves does not help predict real GNP growth can be rejected at the five percent level in the regression using two lags of each variable. But it cannot be rejected at the one percent level. It cannot be rejected at all in the regression using three lags of each variable. The hypothesis that growth in debt does not help predict real GNP growth cannot be rejected in either regression.

While the point estimates of the long-run elasticity of y with respect to R are sizeable and negative ($-.46$ and $-.35$ in the two versions), neither differs

Table 2–2. Regressions for Inflation, Fiscal Years 1952–1981

Variable	(1)	(2)
Constant	−.005	−.000
	(.006)	(.006)
$(\Delta P/P)_{t-1}$	.432	.508
	(.179)	(.173)
$(\Delta P/P)_{t-2}$	−.009	.318
	(.207)	(.182)
$(\Delta P/P)_{t-3}$	.209	—
	(.178)	
$(\Delta R/R)_{t-1}$	.219	.239
	(.096)	(.107)
$(\Delta R/R)_{t-2}$	−.009	−.099
	(.102)	(.100)
$(\Delta R/R)_{t-3}$	.189	—
	(.096)	
$(\Delta D/D)_{t-1}$	−.071	−.087
	(.077)	(.075)
$(\Delta D/D)_{t-2}$	.135	.182
	(.069)	(.063)
$(\Delta D/D)_{t-3}$	.086	—
	(.064)	
R^2	.87	.81
DW	1.50	1.54
$\dfrac{\Sigma b_j}{1 - \Sigma a_j}$	1.08	.81
$\dfrac{\Sigma c_j}{1 - \Sigma a_j}$	.79	.55
F Test for		
1) All $b_i = 0$	3.47*	2.82
2) $\Sigma b_i = 0$	6.55*	1.02
3) All $c_i = 0$	3.47*	4.23*
4) $\Sigma c_i = 0$	2.10	1.57
5) $\Sigma a + \Sigma b = 1$	.02	.04
6) $\Sigma a + \Sigma b = 1$ and $\Sigma c = 0$	3.25	1.08

Notes: Standard errors in parentheses. *denotes significant at 5% level.

Table 2-3. Regressions for Real GNP Growth, Fiscal Years 1952–1981

Variable	(1)	(2)
Constant	.033	.022
	(.015)	(.013)
$(\Delta y/y)_{t-1}$	−.019	.147
	(.209)	(.184)
$(\Delta y/y)_{t-2}$	.427	.296
	(.256)	(.213)
$(\Delta y/y)_{t-3}$	−.120	—
	(.227)	
$(\Delta R/R)_{t-1}$	.262	.258
	(.187)	(.188)
$(\Delta R/R)_{t-2}$	−.393	−.450
	(.169)	(.172)
$(\Delta R/R)_{t-3}$	−.198	—
	(.208)	
$(\Delta D/D)_{t-1}$	.374	.291
	(.152)	(.138)
$(\Delta D/D)_{t-2}$	−.203	−.218
	(.156)	(.124)
$(\Delta D/D)_{t-3}$	−.126	—
	(.135)	
R^2	.48	.36
DW	2.35	2.24
$\dfrac{\Sigma b_j}{1 - \Sigma a_j}$	−.46	−.35
$\dfrac{\Sigma c_j}{1 - \Sigma a_j}$	.06	.13
F Test for		
1) All $b_i = 0$	2.56	4.01*
2) $\Sigma b_i = 0$	1.11	0.64
3) All $c_i = 0$	2.57	2.35
4) $\Sigma c_i = 0$	0.11	0.43

Notes: Standard errors in parentheses. *denotes significant at 5% level.

significantly from the quantity-theoretic value of zero (see F text number 2). The estimated long-run elasticity of y with respect to D is a small positive number (.06 and .13 in the two versions), but is nowhere near significant (see F test number 4).

In sum, neither growth in bank reserves nor growth in national debt carries much information that is useful in predicting future real GNP growth according to these equations. The fact that both variables were significant predictors of future growth in nominal GNP seems to stem mainly from their value in predicting inflation.

The Determinants of Monetization

There are two ways to finance a deficit. The government budget constraint creates a presumption that a blend of the two methods will normally be used, that is, it creates a presumption that some fraction of the deficit will be monetized. Let δ_t denote the nominal deficit in fiscal year t and write equation 2.1 as:

$$dH/dt + dB/dt = \delta_t \qquad (2.14)$$

Define β_t as the fraction of the deficit that is monetized and write equation 2.14 as:

$$dH/dt = \beta_t \delta_t \qquad (2.15)$$

This is nothing but an identity, it carries no behavioral implications, not even that β_t is typically positive. Our interest is in the factors determining β_t.

First note that high powered money is the sum of reserves plus currency, so:

$$dH/dt = dR/dt + dC/dt \qquad (2.16)$$

It is well known that the Fed supplies currency passively to meet demand so as to insulate the money stock, M, from short term gyrations in the currency ratio. Remembering that M is the sum of deposits plus currency, a linear money multiplier model would be: $M = mR + sC$, with m approximately equal to the reciprocal of the required reverse ratio, ρ, and s approximately equal to unity. If M is to be insulated from fluctuations in C,[16] then R will have to react to changes in C according to $dR/dC = -(s/m)$, which is approximately equal to $-\rho$. By equation 2.16 this means that H will have to react to C approximately according to $dH/dC = 1 - \rho$. Embodying this idea in equation 2.15 leads to:

$$dH/dt = \gamma_t \delta_t + (1 - \rho)(dC/dt) \qquad (2.16)$$

and then using equation 2.16 gives:

$$dR/dt = \gamma_t \delta_t - \rho(dC/dt) \qquad (2.17)$$

In this expression, the first term includes all the things in which we are interested while the second term represents the Fed's efforts to offset currency fluctuations. Nevertheless, this second term does offer an informal test of the reasonableness of the empirical results: the coefficient of dC/dt should resemble a weighted average of required reserve ratios.

Some Suggested Monetization Rules

Before estimating equation 2.17 let us consider some specific rules that have been suggested for the monetization decision.

Monetarism. The most famous and most widely discussed suggestion for a monetary rule can be attributed, more or less accurately, to Milton Friedman. Under Friedman's suggested regime, the Fed would keep the money supply growing at some constant rate regardless of budget policy and would refuse to deviate from the rule for cyclical reasons. Here I interpret this policy as a constant growth rule for bank reserves (or for the monetary base). Under such a rule the marginal monetization rate, γ_t in equation 2.17, would presumably be zero.

This is not the place to offer a comprehensive review of the pros and cons of the k-percent rule, but one new element that has entered the debate in recent years is worth mentioning. Some years ago, Solow and I (1973) showed that a policy of holding the money supply constant and financing all deficits by issuing bonds could destabilize the economy, whereas financing deficits by money creation probably led to a stable system. This finding, while derived in a very simple and special case with fixed prices, proved to be remarkably robust. Tobin and Buiter (1976) established a parallel result for a full employment economy with perfectly flexible prices. Pyle and Turnovsky (1976) and others showed that analogous results obtain in models intermediate between these two extremes, such as models with an expectations augmented Phillips curve.

Recently, McCallum (1981, 1982), Smith (1982), and Sargent and Wallace (1981) have reemphasized the importance of this result for the monetarist policy rule. Though using rather different models, each has made the same point: the system is liable to be dynamically unstable under a policy that holds both fiscal policy (defined in various ways by the different authors) and the money supply (or its growth rate) constant.

The mechanism behind these results is not hard to understand. Suppose some shock (such as an autonomous decline in demand in a Keynesian model) opens up a deficit in the government budget, and the monetarist regime is in force. Bonds will be issued to finance the deficit. With both interest rates and the number of bonds increasing, interest payments on the national debt will be increasing. But this increases the deficit still further, requiring even larger issues of bonds in subsequent periods, and the process repeats. If the real rate of interest exceeds the rate of population growth, then the real supply of bonds per capita will grow without limit. Consequently, unless bonds are totally irrelevant to other economic variables (as in the non-Ricardian view of Barro (1974)), the whole economy will explode.[17] So the stabilizing properties of the monetarist rule are open to serious question, to say the least. What about its longer run effects?

As a long-run defense against inflation, the monetarist rule seems to be very effective. Although academic scribblers can and have constructed examples of continuous inflation without growth in reserves, my feeling is that policymakers can justifiably treat these models as intellectual curiosa and proceed on the assumption that a maintained growth rate of reserves will eventually control the rate of inflation.

But what about capital formation and real economic growth? When a recession comes, the k-percent rule takes no remedial action. If there is an important accelerator aspect to investment spending, the slack demand will retard capital formation. At the same time, the issuance of new government bonds to finance the budget deficits that recession brings will push up interest rates. And this too will retard investment spending. The likely result is that rigid monetarism will not create a climate conducive to investment unless long-run predictability of the price level is a more important determinant of investment than I think it is.[18]

It seems to me that much of the current fuss over lack of fiscal-monetary coordination and the concommitant pressures for monetization derives from concern over the implications of the policy mix for investment. If so, then hard core monetarism, which eliminates the coordination issue by eliminating policy, does not look like a very good solution.

Bondism. As McCallum (1981) pointed out, a potentially better monetization rule was actually suggested by Friedman in his earlier "A Monetary and

Fiscal Framework for Economic Stability" (1948), but subsequently abandoned. For lack of a better name, Gary Smith (1982) suggested that we call the policy bondism because it treats bonds in much the same way as monetarism treats money.

Under the old Friedman policy, the marginal monetization rate would be unity, not zero. Specifically, Friedman suggested that government spending and tax rates be set according to allocative considerations so as to balance the budget on average, and that all deficits be financed by creation of money.[19] Both McCallum (1981, 1982) and Smith (1982) observed that this policy regime is equivalent to the money financing scenario in Blinder and Solow (1973), and hence probably leads to a stable system. On this score alone, it has much to recommend it over monetarism.

But there is more to the story. Consider what would happen when, for example, a deficiency of aggregate demand brought on a recession. Falling incomes would open up a budget deficit, and this would automatically induce the Fed to turn on the monetary spigot. The economy would get a strong anti-recessionary stimulus from monetary policy. Thus the old Friedman rule would seem to be a powerful stabilizer.

How does it score on the more long-run criteria? The fact that recessions would automatically engender easy money under the bondist policy augurs well for capital formation. So does the notion that cyclical disturbances would probably be considerably muted. The one potential worry is over inflation. The rule can conceivably lead to a lot of money creation in a hurry, with subsequent inflationary consequences. But if the fiscal part of the rule keeps the high employment budget balanced, and if the economy fluctuates around its high employment norm, this should not be a major worry. Monetary expansions should subsequently be reversed by monetary contractions.[20] If the rule is believed, even large injections of money should not raise the spectre of secular inflation.

While I have never been an advocate of rigid rules, it seems to me that all this adds up to a clear conclusion: the old Friedman rule ought to get more serious quantitative attention and the new Friedman rule ought to get less.

Game Theory and Monetization

We have seen that it has been suggested that the optimal marginal monetization rate is zero and that the optimal marginal monetization rate is one. These suggestions would seem to bracket the relevant alternatives. But such is not necessarily the case once we remember that stabilization policy in the United States is in the hands of two independent authorities, one in charge of fiscal policy and the other in charge of monetary policy, with neither one dominating the other.[21]

When the two policymakers are at loggerheads, a policy mix of tight money and loose fiscal policy frequently results, with deleterious effects on interest rates and investment.[22] What outcome does theory lead us to expect when fiscal and monetary policy are in different hands and the two parties have different ideas about what is best for the economy?

A natural way to conceptualize this situation is as a two person non-zero-sum game. And a natural candidate for what will emerge, it seems to me, is the Nash equilibrium. Why the Nash equilibrium? Both policymakers understand that they do not operate in a vacuum. Each presumably understands that he is facing an intelligent adversary with a decisionmaking problem qualitatively similar to his own. Furthermore, this is a repeated game; each policymaker has been here before and assumes that he will be here again. It seems natural that each would assume that the other will make the optimal response to whatever strategy he plays. If so, each will probably play his Nash strategy.

Let us see how the Nash equilibrium works out in a moderately realistic example. Using the payoff matrix in Figure 2–2, I assume that each policymaker has two available strategies: the government can raise or lower the deficit, and the central bank can raise or lower bank reserves. I also assume that they order the outcomes differently, but know each other's preference ordering. Specifically, the fiscal authority (whose preference ordering appears below the diagonal in each box) is assumed to favor expansionary policy. From its point of view, the case of a monetized deficit is best (rank 1) and the case where both play contractionary strategies is worst (rank 4). The monetary authority (whose ordering appears above the diagonal) wants to contract the economy to fight inflation, and so orders these alternatives in the opposite way. However, as between the two outcomes which combine expansion and contraction, I assume that the two players agree that society is better served by easy money and a tight budget rather than tight money and a loose budget.

This explains the entries in the payoff matrix (figure 2–2). Now where is the Nash equilibrium? The example is a case of the Prisoners' Dilemma since each player has a dominant strategy. Specifically, if the Fed raises bank reserves, the administration will plan for a higher deficit and the Fed will wind up with its least preferred outcome (the lower righthand box). So the Fed will reduce bank reserves. Knowing this, the administration's best strategy is to raise the deficit, so the outcome will be the lower lefthand box. Clearly, this is the only Nash equilibrium for this game. It also seems to be the most plausible outcome of uncoordinated but intelligent behavior. But

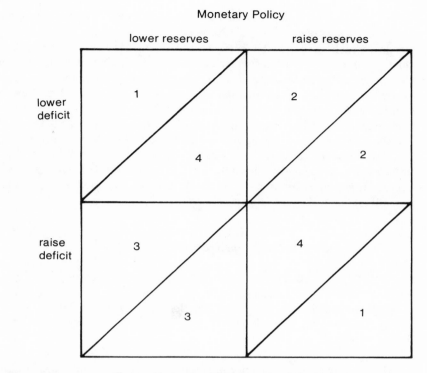

Figure 2-2   The Nash Equilibrium and Monetary/Fiscal Policy

notice two interesting aspects of this outcome. First, the deficit goes up and bank reserves go down; from the perspective of equation 2.17 the marginal monetization rate is negative.

Second, both the Fed and the fiscal authority agree that the upper righthand box—easy money plus tight fiscal policy—is superior to the Nash equilibrium. Under full monetary fiscal coordination, they might well select this policy mix. But, if they cannot reach an agreement, then the Nash equilibrium—a Parato-inferior outcome—is likely to arise. If this example is typical, then switching from a system of two uncoordinated policymakers to one with a single, unified policymaker might yield substantial gains. And there is good reason to think that it is typical, because it has long been known that there is no reason to expect Nash equilibria in two person non- zero- sum games to be Pareto optimal.

The problem, of course, is that achieving greater coordination is more easily said than done. The two authorities have reasons for disagreeing, reasons which may not be easily ironed out.[23] However, this example illustrates that full coordination (which is probably impossible in any event) may not be critical. What we need in this case is no more than an agreement to consult with one another enough to avoid outcomes that both parties view as inferior. Maybe this is not too much to ask.

However, things become far less clear if one policymaker lacks knowledge of either the preferences or the economic model of the other. Then there is no particular reason to think the Nash equilibrium will result, and other solutions become equally plausible. For example, each player may simply pursue his global optimum ignoring the decision of the other. There are other possibilities as well.[24]

Empirical Evidence on Monetization

Econometric study of the Fed's reaction function began some years ago and has generated some interesting papers. In recent years, several authors have investigated whether or not Federal deficits per se increase the growth of money (presumably via monetization). The evidence obtained so far is decidedly mixed.

Previous Literature.   The first papers to focus on the monetization issue, by Barro (1978) and Niskanen (1978), reached more or less the same conclusion: the size of the federal deficit has rather little to do with money growth.

Barro studied the period 1941–1976, using an equation he had developed elsewhere to divide money growth into anticipated and unanticipated components. He found that the federal deficit (NIPA basis), when added to his annual regression (which included a federal expenditure variable), obtained the "wrong" sign, suggesting that deficits actually deter money growth. However, when the expenditure variable was omitted, the coefficient of the deficit was correctly signed. In view of the literature that followed, it is also worth mentioning that the estimated coefficients of the deficit in Barro's regressions changed dramatically when the war years (1941–1945) were excluded from the sample.

Niskanen's specification looked more like a traditional reaction function. Using annual data covering 1948–1976, he sought to explain money growth by the lagged growth rates of real GNP and prices (reflecting stabilization objectives) and the federal deficit. His regression fit the data rather poorly but, unlike Barro's, yielded a correctly signed and statistically significant coefficient on the deficit. However, Niskanen found that the coefficient of the deficit became small and insignificant when he included a dummy variable for the years 1967–1976.

Hamburger and Zwick (1981) changed Barro's money growth and government spending variables to make them more comparable to his measure of the deficit and also to align them better in time. They also shortened the period to 1954–1976. Consistent with Barro, they obtained a coefficient of 1.09 (with a t-ratio of 2.2) on spending and a coefficient of −0.26 (with a t-ratio of 0.6) on the deficit. However, when they further shortened the period to 1961–1976 (leaving just sixteen observations) the results changed dramatically. The coefficient of the spending variable fell to 0.18 (and became insignificant) while the coefficient of the deficit rose to 0.92 (with a t-ratio of 1.9).

These results appear to tell us as much about the extreme sensitivity of the estimates to the choice of sample period as they do about whether or not the Fed monetizes deficits. However, in a very recent paper Hamburger and Zwick (1982) extend their results through 1981 with very little change in the estimates.

These studies lead to no firm conclusions about the determinants of monetization.[25] However, they do create a skeptical attitude about facile assertions that deficits induce faster money growth. More importantly, the studies teach us some valuable lessons about the formulation of an appropriate research strategy. Specifically: (1) Results are extremely sensitive to the choice of time period, suggesting that the Fed's behavior pattern may have changed over time. This led me to do considerable testing of the estimated relationships for temporal stability; and (2) Results are also rather sensitive to the particular time series that are used, suggesting a relationship that is far from robust. This led me to pay careful attention to the measurement of certain variables—especially money and the deficit—and their alignment in time.[26]

A First Look at the Data.   My point of departure is equation 2.17, which can be thought of as a modified version of the government budget constraint. Until we specify the nature of γ_t more fully, all this equation does is remind us that (a) monetization means creation of high powered money, not of any of the standard M's, and (b) currency changes ought to be controlled for in analyzing the determinants of changes in bank reserves.

Figure 2–3 plots the change in adjusted bank reserves against the increase in the outstanding stock of government interest bearing debt. As in the regressions in the first section, the fiscal year is the unit for measuring time.

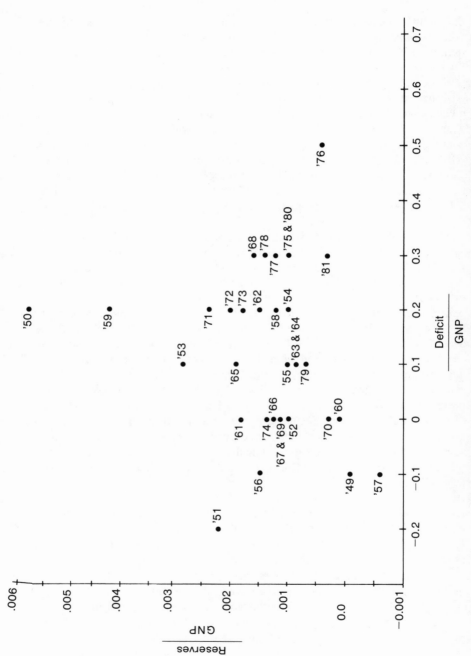

Figure 2-3 The Change Adjusted Bank Reserves and the Deficit, 1949–1981

The scatter diagram covers fiscal years 1949 through 1981. Though the measure of money is quite different from that used in earlier studies,[27] we see immediately that more subtle techniques will be required to unearth a relationship between deficits and growth in reserves. The eyeball, with its inability to do multiple regression analysis, is unable to discern any such relationship.

Regression one in table 2–4 takes the next step. It controls for changes in currency as suggested by equation 2.17, but maintains the null hypothesis that γ_t is constant through time.[28] Once again, there is no apparent relationship between the deficit and growth in reserves; the adjusted R^2 of the regression, for example, is $-.01$. Note, however, that the coefficient of changes in currency, while insignificant, turns out more or less as expected (perhaps a bit too high).

Breaking the sample into smaller subperiods, as suggested by the previous literature, does not improve the relationship between deficits and growth in reserves. The data show no obvious correlation between the two variables.

Regression Analysis. Of course, a lack of zero-order correlation does not necessarily imply that there is no relationship once other pertinent influences

Table 2–4. Determinants of Monetization[a]

	(1)	(2)	(3)	(4)	(5)	(6)
Time Period	1949–81	1949–81	1949–60	1961–81	1968–81	1954–81
Coefficient (s.e. of):						
Constant	.0014	.0010	.0005	.0013	.0006	.0006
	(.0003)	(.0003)	(.0005)	(.0003)	(.0008)	(.0002)
δ_t/Y_t	.013	.076	.151	.064	.070	.039
	(.015)	(.023)	(.061)	(.019)	(.022)	(.019)
$\pi_{t-1}(\delta_t/Y_t)$	—	−.862	−5.015	−.733	−.833	−.550
		(.303)	(2.262)	(.194)	(.226)	(.228)
$x_t(\delta_t/Y_t)$	—	−.455	−.645	−.398	−.367	−.230
		(.161)	(.297)	(.137)	(.154)	(.171)
$\Delta C_t/Y_t$	−.140	−.061	.093	−.099	.110	.153
	(.118)	(.107)	(.307)	(.108)	(.222)	(.089)
R^2	.05	.36	.58	.56	.67	.27
DW	1.78	1.78	2.94	2.16	2.53	2.60

[a]Dependent variable = change in adjusted bank reserves, divided by nominal GNP.

are controlled for. Among the variables that might be expected to influence γ_t, the fraction of the deficit that is monetized, are (a) the size of the deficit (if there is a nonlinear relationship); (b) the lagged dependent variable (if there is inertia in the Fed's behavior);[29] (c) interest rates (if the Fed wants to limit the extent to which deficits raise the rate of interest); (d) real output (or unemployment) and/or inflation (reflecting traditional stabilization motives); (e) the composition of federal spending (reflecting certain optimal public finance considerations raised by Barro (1979) in considering the choice between debt and taxes); and (f) growth in the money stock, if the Fed was pursuing a monetarist style money growth rule.

These variables were all tried, singly and in combination, as linear determinants of γ_t. With so many plausible hypotheses, and so little data, some data-mining was inevitable. My procedure was as follows. First, variables were tried one at a time, to see which had some explanatory power. Then other variables were added, to see which factors survived the inclusion of other variables (and hence had some claim to robustness). Finally, equations that had been estimated on the full sample (1949–1981) were estimated on subsamples to see which empirical relationships survived.

The explanatory variables that seemed to perform best on these criteria were the rate of inflation (lagged, to minimize least squares bias) and the rate of growth of real federal purchases (which is dominated by national defense purchases), henceforth denoted by x_t. Hence, I model the marginal monetization rate a: $\gamma_t = \gamma_0 + \gamma_1 \dot{p}_{t-1} + \gamma_2 x_t$.

Regression two in table 2.4 gives the result for the whole period. According to this regression, 7.6 percent of any deficit would be monetized if there were no inflation last year and real purchases were unchanged. Both inflation and growth of purchases tend to decrease the fraction of the deficit that is monetized. The coefficient of currency is reasonable. The explanatory power of the equation ($R^2 = .36$) is moderate, at best.[30]

Regressions three and four break the sample into two subperiods, 1949–1960 and 1961–1981. This break point was prompted both by the Hamburger-Zwick results and by the observation that several of the residuals for years prior to 1960 were quite large. Although Levy placed the break in his regression after 1969, a series of regressions confirmed that the 1960/1961 break created a local minimum in the combined sum of squared residuals of the two equations.

Substantial differences emerge between the two equations. The effect of inflation on the rate of monetization is only about one-seventh as large in the later period, suggesting a greater tolerance of inflation. The coefficient of currency is reasonable in the later period, but unreasonable in the earlier period. The Durbin-Watson statistic is also far better in the later period. In general, the equation performs much better in 1961–1981 than it does in 1949–1960.

It is tempting to conclude that a stable relationship has existed since 1961, but not before, which would help explain some of the earlier results. To test this notion further, the time period for the 1961–1981 regression was changed by alternatively adding or subtracting a year from the start of the sample. I found a remarkably stable relationship as the period was shortened to begin later than 1961. For example, the regression over 1968–1981 (which has only fourteen observations) is reported as regression five in table 2.4. Except for the currency coefficient, it looks amazingly similar to regression four. There was considerably less stability as the sample was lengthened by beginning earlier than 1961, however. As an illustration, regression six reports the results for the 1954–1981 period.

Two further tests for equation stability were performed. First, the equation for 1961–1981 was differenced, a procedure suggested by Plosser and Schwert (1978) as a test for specification error. The estimates changed little, which provides further support for the specification. (Changes were greater for the 1949–1960 regression, where we are a bit short on degrees of freedom.) Second, a Chow test was performed to look for evidence of a structural shift starting in 1973, the period of floating exchange rates. The F statistic for this test was nearly zero.

The implied marginal monetization rates for the two periods, based on regressions three and four in table 2–4, are as follows: for 1949–1960: $\gamma_t = .15 - 5.02\dot{p}_{t-1} - .65x_t$: for 1961–1981: $\gamma_t = .06 - 0.73\dot{p}_{t-1} - .40x_t$. The major difference is in the reaction to inflation. At the inflation rates near two percent ($= .02$) that were typical in the 1949–1960 period, the implied monetization rates are quite close (around four percent of the deficit). At higher inflation rates, the more recent rule leads to more monetization. For example, at ten percent inflation (and two percent growth in real purchases), the 1949–1960 rule would monetize -36% of the deficit, whereas the 1961–1981 rule would monetize -2%.

A more important point, however, is that no conceivable combination of the independent variables leads to very much monetization of deficits. Both estimated rules, for example, come much closer to the monetarist $\gamma_t = 0$ than to the bondist $\gamma_t = 1$. Negative monetization rates, such as suggested by the game-theoretic analysis in the second section seem more likely than high monetization rates. If deficits are mainly inflationary to the extent that they are monetized, then budget deficits should kindle little in the way of inflationary fears.

Other Results. The measure of the Federal deficit used in the empirical work violates elementary principles of inflation accounting because it fails to net out the decrease in the real value of the outstanding debt caused by inflation. Putting the same point somewhat differently, it fails to include the implicit receipts from the inflation tax. Should the deficit be corrected for inflation?

If we want to model the Fed as a rational government bureau free of inflation illusion, then it is hard to argue against making the correction. True, it is the entire (uncorrected) deficit that must be financed by selling bonds. But some of these new bonds merely replace existing bonds whose real values are eroded by inflation. Since we do not count rollover as part of the government's borrowing requirement, neither should we count the portion of the putative deficit that merely maintains the real value of the existing debt.

On the other hand, casual empiricism suggests that it is only a minority of economists and accountants who are free of this particular form of inflation illusion. If we are interested in describing how the Fed actually behaved, rather than how it should have behaved, then perhaps the uncorrected deficit is the appropriate variable to use.

In fact, when I ran regressions like those in table 2–4 using the inflation corrected deficit, the fits of the regressions deteriorated enormously. The adjusted R^2 for the new version of regression two actually became negative. In other words, whatever success we have in explaining monetization of the uncorrected deficit completely disappears when we seek to explain monetization of the corrected deficit. This leaves two possibilities. Either we have a passable mode of the monetization decision of a Federal Reserve which suffers from inflation illusion, or the Fed is free of inflation illusion but its behavior is unpredictable. I am personally inclined toward the former view, but the data admit of both interpretations.

A second issue is raised by Barrow's non-Ricardian equivalence theorem. I have tacitly accepted the view that taxes are something quite distinct from debt by taking debt and money as alternative ways of financing the excess of expenditures over tax receipts. But, if debt and taxes are equivalent, then the true decision is among current taxes, future taxes (i.e., debt), and money as alternative ways of financing government expenditures. On this view, expenditures, not the deficit, should be the independent variable in a regression explaining money creation.

To study this issue, I disaggregated the deficit into three additive components—outlays, tax receipts, and net off budget borrowing—and reran the regressions in order to test the following two constraints: (i) that outlays and the off budget deficit have the same coefficient; and (ii) that the coefficient of tax receipts is equal and opposite to that of outlays. Both constraints are imposed by the regressions in table 2–4, and the results strongly supported them. Not only did an F test fail (by a large margin) to reject them, but the point estimates conformed reasonably well to the constraints. By contrast, the non-Ricardian equivalence hypothesis would seem to call for a coefficient of zero on taxes, a restriction that was easily rejected.

As indicated earlier, other plausible righthand variables were tried, but did not contribute to the explanation of monetization. These included both nominal interest rates and unemployment, variables often thought to be stabilization targets of the Fed. The findings here are consistent with those of Levy (1981). If the Fed monetizes a larger fraction of small deficits than of large deficits, then the deficit itself should help explain γ_t. However, I had little success with either the deficit or its absolute value. If the Fed was targeting money growth, then it should have reduced reserves whenever M grew too rapidly. Tests of this hypothesis using (what we now call) $M1$ to measure money turned up no evidence in its favor. Whenever $M1$ had a significant effect on monetization, its coefficient had the wrong sign (from the point of view of this hypothesis). Finally, the lagged dependent variable was totally insignificant when added to the regression. This stands in stark contrast to the regressions using money growth as the dependent variable (See footnote 29).

There is still one further possibility. Perhaps the Fed really ignored deficits, but systematically reacted to either higher inflation or increased growth of real federal purchases by slowing the expansion of reserves. Then our regression, by forcing $\dot{p}_{t-1}$ and x_t to enter interactively with δ_t, might make the deficit appear to be a significant factor in the Fed's behavior when, in fact, it was not.

To examine this possibility, I reran regressions two, three, and four in table 2–3 replacing the interaction variables $x\delta$ and $\dot{p}\delta$ by x and $\dot{p}$ alone. For the 1961–1981 period this substitution caused the fit of the regression to deteriorate enormously; R^2 fell to .10 and all the righthand variables were insignificant. For the 1949–1981 period as a whole, the R^2 deteriorated only slightly, but the Durbin-Watson statistic fell to 1.18, giving strong evidence of misspecification. Only for the short 1949–1960 period did the simpler functional form work better.

Summary

Simple old-fashioned Keynesian macro models suggest that budget deficits always expand aggregate demand, but that their effects are stronger if they are monetized, that is, monetary policy does matter. The time series evidence on nominal GNP growth offered here, though incapable of giving structural information, is consistent with these ideas. Information on changes in bank reserves helps predict nominal GNP changes, even when changes in government debt are controlled for. Symmetrically, changes in outstanding debt are a significant predictor of nominal GNP changes even after controlling for changes in reserves.

If we focus on inflation rather than nominal GNP growth, however, more surprising results are obtained. Growth in government debt is a significant predictor of inflation, even after growth in bank reserves are controlled for. But, surprisingly enough, the evidence that bank reserves contributes anything to the prediction of inflation that is not already supplied by debt is decidedly mixed.

The received theory gives us far less guidance on long-run issues. Some ambiguities arise from interest elasticities and wealth effects. Others arise from complexities stemming from the reaction of expectations. A believable empirical model for addressing these issues is sorely needed, but has yet to be developed. If the coefficients of the time series regressions are interpreted as reduced-form multipliers, they imply that both monetized and nonmonetized deficits have sizable, though not always statistically significant, long-run effects on nominal GNP and prices. But this evidence is no more than suggestive, if that, given the nonstructural approach that has been followed. I regard the question as open.

While the Fed has not followed any rigid monetization rule, its postwar behavior comes far closer to the "new Friedman" monetarist rule (no monetization at the margin) than it does to the "old Friedman" bondist rule (complete monetization at the margin). But when inflation has been high, the Fed typically has reduced bank reserves despite government deficits, that is, monetization has been negative—an outcome predicted by the game-theoretic analysis of monetary and fiscal policy presented here.

In general, the empirical relationship between budget deficits and the creation or destruction of bank reserves seems far more stable and systematic than previous research would lead us to believe. However, the relationship appears to date only from 1961 or so.

This paper has focused on two empirical questions. The tentative answers suggested are, yes, monetization does matter—certainly for real variables, and maybe for nominal variables as well. And the Fed seems to look chiefly at the inflation rate and the growth rate of real government purchases in deciding what fraction of the deficit to monetize. I would like to close, however, by posing a theoretical question: Exactly why does the monetization decision matter?

The question is both deep and vexing. The usual story—that easy (tight) money creates a surplus (shortage) of the medium of exchange which, in turn, spurs (retards) economic activity—strains the credulity of many observers. Yet money creation does seem to have real effects in practice. Why?

One possibility, raised first by Tobin (1970) and recently by King and Plosser (1982), is that money simply reacts passively to real activity. On this view, money has no causal role; real activity simply pulls money along, creating a statistical correlation with no causal interpretation. I have some sympathy with this view. However most economists, and virtually all businessmen, seem to think they can identify periods in which tight money led to a downturn in economic activity.

A second possibility, which Joseph Stiglitz and I (1982) are developing in a forthcoming paper, is that creation of new bank reserves leads to an expansion of credit which loosens quantitative constraints that were previously binding. On this view, the statistical correlation between money and real economic activity is no accident, but it merely reflects their mutual connection to the same important phenomenon—the ebb and flow of credit.

Neither of these views has yet been fully worked out and subjected to empirical testing. It may be that neither will prove correct. But little progress can be made in resolving the theoretical issues pertaining to monetization until we have a more convincing story of why monetary policy has real effects in the first place.

Notes

1. The only possible slippage is between expansion of bank reserves (which is the direct consequence of monetization) and expansion of the money stock. In practice, the money multiplier is stable enough so that this is not a major worry.

2. As is well known, Barro (1974) has argued against this assumption. For a critique of Barro's argument, see Buiter and Tobin (1979). For an analysis of the dynamics of the government budget constraint under the assumption that Barro was right, see McCallum (1982).

3. The existence of a wealth effect on the demand for money, though often assumed (see, for example, Tobin (1982)), is by no means guaranteed. It could be absent, for example, under a strict transactionist point of view.

4. See, among others, Tobin and Buiter (1976), Pyle and Turnovsky (1976), and Turnovsky (1978).

5. See, for example, Diamond (1965) or Phelps and Shell (1969). The latter shows that it is just a suggestion, not a clean deduction.

6. If P is somehow fixed, as it was in the original Blinder-Solow article, then these difficulties do not arise. But such a model makes little sense for long-run analysis.

7. The stability of the economy under this last policy has been called into question. More on this later.

8. For a more detailed discussion of this issue, see Feldstein (1982).

9. Indeed, under the hypothesis advanced by Barro (1974)—that each generation has an operative bequest motive based on the next generation's lifetime utility—the period from now to the end of time is relevant.

10. See, for example, Blinder (1981), Hall and Mishkin (1982), Hayashi (1982), or Mankiw (1981). Bernanke (1981) is more optimistic about the PIH.

11. For an interesting discussion of forward looking versus backward looking wage contracts, and how we might distinguish between them empirically, see Taylor (1982).

12. Divergent expectations have been emphasized recently by, among others, Phelps (1981) and Frydman (1981).

13. Nothing in the Granger-Sims methodology, which is atheoretic, tells us in what form to enter the variables. The form of equation 2.13 is suggestive of a theoretical model in which asset stocks influence income flows, like the quantity theory. By contrast, in Keynesian models the flow of income depends on the stock of reserves, but on the flow of additions to the national debt (i.e., on the deficit). This motivated me to experiment with a reformulation of equation 2.13 in which $\Delta^2 D$ replaced ΔD. However, this alternative version had less explanatory power than equation 2.13 in almost every regression I ran.

14. The series comes from the Federal Reserve Bank of St.Louis, and is adjusted both for interbank shifts of deposits and changes in required reserves.

15. The transition quarter was omitted. In aggregating quarterly data into fiscal years, I used seasonally adjusted GNP data due to their presumed greater accuracy than the seasonally unadjusted data.

16. Insulating the rate of interest from currency shifts amounts to the same thing. It is the schedule relating money supply to r that is presumed to be insulated by the Fed.

17. In a complex system, many more things are going on than I can describe in a single paragraph. For example, income and prices are changing, with important consequences for the budget deficit. Yet the basic mechanism described here seems to come shining through in all the models.

18. Or unless inflation itself is sufficiently damaging to investment via, for example, the deterioration of the real value of depreciation allowances. This last factor has been stressed in a number of places by Feldstein. See, among others, Feldstein (1980).

19. There is no distinction between money and high-powered money under Friedman's plan, since part of his plan was the elimination of fractional reserve banking.

20. This statement is predicated on defining high employment as approximately the natural rate. With a Humphrey-Hawkins type definition of high employment, the old Friedman rule can lead to inflationary disaster.

21. In reality, things are more complicated still because the President and Congress often disagree over national economic policy. A model with three stabilization authorities may be better.

22. The opposite policy mix—tight budgets and easy money—while conceivable, seems to be rarely encountered.

23. For a full discussion of the reasons for these disagreements, and why it is not obvious what to do about them, see Blinder (1982).

24. In the simple example of figure 2–2, "going it alone" also leads to the Nash equilibrium. But this is not generally true. A fuller discussion of some alternatives appears in Blinder (1982).

25. McMillan and Beard (1982) study the same issue, reaching conclusions opposite from those of Hamburger and Zwick (1981). But Hamburger and Zwick (1982) argue that this is because McMillan and Beard fail to align the data correctly in time. A fifth study, far similar in spirit to my own, is that of Levy (1981). I will comment on Levy's work as I present my own results.

26. Hamburger and Zwick (1981, 1982) obtain stronger results when they use a better measure of the deficit, a measure which is similar to my own. They also stress the importance of properly aligning the data in time.

27. Except for Levy (1981). His dependent variable is similar to my own. The main difference is that he uses (quarterly) changes in the adjusted base, whereas I use (annual) changes in adjusted bank reserves. Viewed from the perspective of equation 2.17, Levy's choice imposes a coefficient of -1 on dC/dt. As will be seen below, the estimated coefficient is closer to zero.

28. To correct for potentially severe heteroskedasticity, all variables were divided by nominal GNP. Also, to allow for some trend provision of reserves even in the absence of deficits, a constant was added to the regression.

29. Barro (1978), Hamburger-Zwick (1981), and McMillan-Beard (1982) all found the lagged value of money (not reserves) to be important. Levy's (1981) study of changes in reserves also found a significant lagged dependent variable, but he worked with quarterly data.

30. Levy (1981) estimated a (constant) marginal monetization rate of 6.4 percent for the period 1952–1978, quite close to my estimate. The two equations cannot be compared in terms of goodness of fit because Levy did not make the correction for heteroskedasticity mentioned in note 28, used quarterly data, and got much of his explanatory power from the lagged dependent variable and seasonal dummies. I presume the fits are comparable, and so cannot agree with his conclusion that "any implication that the largest portion of monetary policy is random (should) be rejected" (p. 365).

References

Barro, R.J. "Are Government Bonds Net Wealth?" *Journal of Political Economy* (November/December 1974), 1095–1117.

Barro, R.J. "Comment from an Unreconstructed Ricardian." *Journal of Monetary Economics* (August 1978), 569–581.

Barro, R.J. "On the Determination of the Public Debt." *Journal of Political Economy* (October 1979), 940–971.

Bernanke, B.S. "Permanent Income, Liquidity, and Expenditure on Automobiles: Evidence from Panel Data." Mimeo, Stanford University, September 1981.

Blinder, A.S. "Issues in the Coordination of Monetary and Fiscal Policy." NBER Working Paper No. 982, September 1982 (forthcoming in a Federal Reserve Bank of Kansas City conference volume).

Blinder, A.S. "Temporary Income Taxes and Consumer Spending." *Journal of Political Economy* (February 1981), 26–53.

Blinder, A.S. and R.M. Solow, "Does Fiscal Policy Matter?" *Journal of Public Economics* (November 1973), 319–337.

Blinder, A.S. and J.E. Stiglitz, "Money, Credit Constraints, and Economic Activity." Paper presented at the December 1982 meetings of the American Economic Association.

Buiter, W.H. and J. Tobin. "Debt Neutrality: A Brief Review of Doctrine and Evidence." In: *Social Security versus Private Saving*. G.M. von Furstenburg (Ed.), Cambridge: Ballinger, 1979.

Diamond, P. "National Debt in a Neoclassical Model." *American Economic Review* (December 1965), 1126–1150.

Feldstein, M.S. "Fiscal Policies, Inflation, and Capital Formation." *American Economic Review* (September 1980), 636–650.

Feldstein, M.S. "Government Deficits and Aggregate Demand." *Journal of Monetary Economics* (January 1982), 1–20.

Friedman, M. "A Monetary and Fiscal Framework for Economic Stability." *American Economic Review* (June 1948), 245–264.

Frydman, R. "Individual Rationality, Decentralization and the Rational Expectations Hypothesis." Mimeo, New York University, November 1981.

Granger, C.W. "Investigating Causal Relations by Econometric Models and Cross-Spectral Methods." *Econometrica* (July 1969), 424–438.

Hall, R.E. and F.S. Mishkin. "The Sensitivity of Consumption to Transitory Income: Estimates from Panel Data on Households," *Econometrica* (1982), 461–482.

Hamburger, M.J. and B. Zwick, "Deficits, Money, and Inflation." *Journal of Monetary Economics* (January 1981), 141–150.

Hamburger, M.J. and Zwick, B. "Deficits, Money, and Inflation: Reply. *Journal of Monetary Economics* (September 1982), 279–283.

Hayashi, F. "The Effect of Liquidity Constraints on Consumption: A Cross-Sectional Analysis." NBER Working Paper No. 882, April 1982.

King, R.G. and C.I. Plosser, "The Behavior of Money, Credit and Prices in a Real Business Cycle." NBER Working Paper No. 853, February 1982.

Levy, M.D. "Factors Affecting Monetary Policy in an Era of Inflation." *Journal of Monetary Economics* (November 1981), 351–373.

Mankiw, N.G. "Hall's Consumption Hypothesis and Durable Goods." Mimeo, MIT, January 1981.

McCallum, B.T. "Monetarist Principles and the Money Stock Growth Rule." *American Economic Review* (May 1981), 134–138.

McCallum, B.T. "Are Bond-Financed Deficits Inflationary? A Ricardian Analysis." Mimeo, Carnegie-Mellon University, May 1982.

McMillan, W.D. and T.R. Beard. "Deficits, Money, and Inflation: Comment." *Journal of Monetary Economics,* (September 1982), 273–277.

Niskanen, W.A. "Deficits, Government Spending, and Inflation: What is the Evidence?" *Journal of Monetary Economics* (August 1978), 591–602.

Phelps, E.S. "The Trouble with 'Rational Expectations' and the Problem of Inflation Stabilization." Mimeo, Columbia University, October 1981.

Phelps, E.S. and K. Shell. "Public Debt, Taxation, and Capital Intensiveness." *Journal of Economic Theory,* (1969), 330–346.

Plosser C.I. and G.W. Schwert. "Money, Income and Sunspots: Measuring Economic Relationships and the Effects of Differencing." *Journal of Monetary Economics* (November 1978), 637–660.

Pyle D.H. and S.J. Turnovsky. "The Dynamics of Government Policy in an Inflationary Economy: An 'Intermediate Run' Analysis." *Journal of Money, Credit, and Banking* (November 1976), 411–437.

Sargent T.J. and N. Wallace. "Some Unpleasant Monetarist Arithmetic." *Federal Reserve Bank of Minneapolis Quarterly Review* (Fall 1981), 1–17.

Sims, C.A. "Money, Income, and Causality." *American Economic Review* (September 1972), 540–552.

Smith, G. "Monetarism, Bondism, and Inflation." *Journal of Money, Credit, and Banking* (May 1982), 278–286.

Taylor, J.B. "Rational Expectations and the Invisible Handshake." In: *Macroeconomics, Prices, and Quantities,* a volume in honor of Arthur Okun. J. Tobin (Ed.), 1982.

Tobin, J. "Money and Finance in the Macroeconomic Process." *Journal of Money, Credit, and Banking* (May 1982), 171–204.

Tobin, J. "Money and Income: Post Hoc Ergo Propter Hoc?" *Quarterly Journal of Economics* (May 1970), 301–317.

Tobin, J. and W. Buiter. "Long-Run Effects of Fiscal and Monetary Policy on Aggregate Demand," In: *Monetarism.* J.L. Stein (Ed.), Amsterdam North-Holland, 1976, 273–309.

Turnovsky, S.J. "Macroeconomic Dynamics and Growth in a Monetary Economy." *Journal of Money, Credit, and Banking* (February 1978), 1–26.

DISCUSSION
Scott E. Hein

The paper presented by Professor Blinder purports to address two questions: (1) Does monetization matter? and (2) what factors determine how much monetization the Federal Reserve will do? Professor Blinder suggests that others have addressed these issues before, and his aim is simply to bring a bit more evidence and thought to bear on these matters. I must disagree: I do not think these issues have been fully addressed before and, I do not think the present paper addresses them either. Blinder's paper, like the majority of the others cited, really investigates two much older and more familiar issues: (1) Does monetary policy (specifically money growth) matter? and (2) what factors determine the Federal Reserve's monetary policy? Instead of being carefully assessed, the issue of monetization simply disappears in the analysis presented.

I would like to thank Rob Hess for valuable research assistance and my colleagues R. Alton Gilbert, R.W. Hafer, Courtenay C. Stone, John A. Tatom and Daniel L. Thornton for helpful comments on this paper. I would also like to thank Sue Briggs and Linda Hoops for their help. The views expressed here are those of the author and not necessarily those of the Federal Reserve Bank of St. Louis.

Does Monetary Policy Matter?

If Professor Blinder had written a paper on "Money Creation and Deficits," I would have little critical to say about his analysis. Blinder does a very thorough job of reviewing the theoretical issues regarding the effectiveness of monetary policy actions and translating much of the analysis from math into more accessible prose. Interestingly, when the analytical dust settles, no qualitative theoretical statement about the effectiveness of monetary policy can be made.

Since theory is not much help, Blinder turns his attention to empirically estimating the effectiveness of monetary policy. It is somewhat amusing that he examines the effectiveness issue by estimating reduced-form equations similar to the Andersen-Jordan (1968) equation, precisely the type of analysis that he and others have criticized so thoroughly.[1] Because I happen to believe there is much to be learned from such results, I will not raise Blinder's own past objections to reduced-form estimation. It should be noted, however, that Blinder's empirical results support several well known monetarist propositions. For example, his evidence indicates that (1) a rise in steady-state adjusted bank reserve growth leads to roughly a proportional rise in nominal GNP growth and,[2] (2) unless associated with faster adjusted bank reserve growth, deficits do not result in greater inflation.

The Difference Between Monetization and The Growth of Adjusted Bank Reserves

I do not doubt Blinder's empirical results. His findings simply tell us that the growth of adjusted bank reserves is an important determinant of aggregate demand and inflation, and federal deficits are not. The problem with Blinder's paper is that he infers incorrectly from this result that monetization affects the economy. This inference is simply invalid.

Blinder's error occurs when he uses adjusted bank reserves as a measure of the Federal Reserve's monetization of federal debt. This is simply incorrect; there are important theoretical and empirical differences between the adjusted bank reserve series and some useful measure of monetization. The error is observable from the start. Blinder explicitly defines monetization as the central bank's purchase of government securities. This definition is inconsistent with the use of the adjusted bank reserves series. The adjusted bank reserve measure summarizes, in one number, all relevant Federal Reserve actions influencing bank deposits (see appendix). The Fed can increase adjusted bank reserves—providing a foundation for greater bank deposits—through a whole host of channels that have nothing to do with the issue of monetization. For example, *ceteris paribus,* the Fed can increase adjusted bank reserves by increasing discount window borrowings (loans to financial institutions), or by reducing reserve requirements (thus increasing RAM, an adjustment for reserve requirement changes used in the computation of adjusted bank reserves), or by the purchase of other assets. The relation between the growth in adjusted bank reserves and monetization is developed in more detail in the Appendix.

Monetization, as measured by changes in security holdings, is itself only one factor that enters into the determination of changes in the adjusted bank reserves. Thus, in a *ceteris paribus* analysis, the Fed's monetization of the federal debt will lead to an increase in adjusted bank reserves, thereby supporting a larger money stock. When Blinder finds that an increase in adjusted bank reserve growth is associated with an increase in nominal GNP growth, his results indicate nothing more than that an increase in adjusted bank reserve growth, regardless of the source, stimulates aggregate demand. In this regard, float, discount window borrowing, a reserve requirement change, or anything else that affects bank reserves, matters as much as monetization. Failing to make explicit this distinction between monetization and adjusted bank reserves is a serious shortcoming of Blinder's paper. It is important to recognize that not only Federal Reserve monetization matters, all actions taken by the Federal Reserve are meaningful.[3]

Does Monetization Matter Empirically?

How important have other Fed actions been over the sample period in comparison to monetization as actually defined by Blinder? If the Fed has not changed any other factors affecting bank reserves in an appreciable way, then monetization has a singular importance for the period considered. It would then be appropriate to conclude that only monetization has mattered empirically. On the other hand, if the Fed has changed other factors as well, monetization, per se, is not singularly important. Thus, we are left with the empirical question: Has the Fed relied primarily on open market operations to alter adjusted bank reserves or has it used other channels as well?

The Federal Reserve has significantly altered adjusted bank reserves through many channels other than changing its holdings of federal debt since 1952. Probably the most empirically meaningful alteration over the period investigated by Blinder was produced by reserve requirement changes.

Considering the period as a whole, effective reserve requirements have been reduced substantially from 1952 to 1981.[4]

Of the $32.7 billion increase in adjusted bank reserves from 1952 to 1981, $11.8 billion (36 percent of the increase) arose from reductions in reserve requirement ratios. Thus, if reserve requirement ratios had been kept at their 1952 level, the Federal Reserve would have had to buy $11.8 billion more federal debt to achieve the same $32.7 billion increase in adjusted bank reserves. Clearly, reserve requirement ratio changes have played an significant role in altering adjusted bank reserves.

Moreover, the change in reserve requirements over the period considered has not followed a smooth pattern, so we are ignoring a factor which has little trend when we solely consider monetization. In order to observe graphically the historical importance of reserve requirement changes, merely look at figure 2–4 which shows the growth rates of two separate $M1$ multipliers. The first money multiplier is the ratio of $M1$ to adjusted bank reserves. The difference between the two is simply RAM—an adjustment for past reserve requirement changes. The first multiplier contains an adjustment for changes in reserve requirement ratios, the second does not.

The lesson to be learned from figure 2–4 is that the relationship between money and adjusted bank reserves is much more stable than the relationship between money and unadjusted bank reserves. In fact the variance in the growth rate of the unadjusted bank reserve multiplier is over three times that of the adjusted bank reserve multiplier. This indicates that over this period, the Fed often changes the level of bank reserves—monetizing or demonetizing the Federal debt—simply to offset reserve requirement changes.

To those who believe that money is an important determinant of economic activity, the poor relationship between money and unadjusted bank reserves suggests a rather weak connection between monetization and economic activity. In fact, if Federal Reserve holdings of government debt are used instead of adjusted bank reserves as an explanatory variable in a reduced-form GNP relationship, no significant statistical relationship is observed. The top panel of table 2–5 reports estimation results for such an equation for fiscal years 1952–81. None of the individual coefficients on the change in Federal Reserve holdings of government debt (FRDH) are significantly different from zero. Thus, had Blinder actually sought to ascertain the individual importance of monetization as he has defined it, he would have found no systematic relationship. This is not because monetization does not matter. Rather, it simply indicates that looking at what the Fed is doing with one hand is not enough.

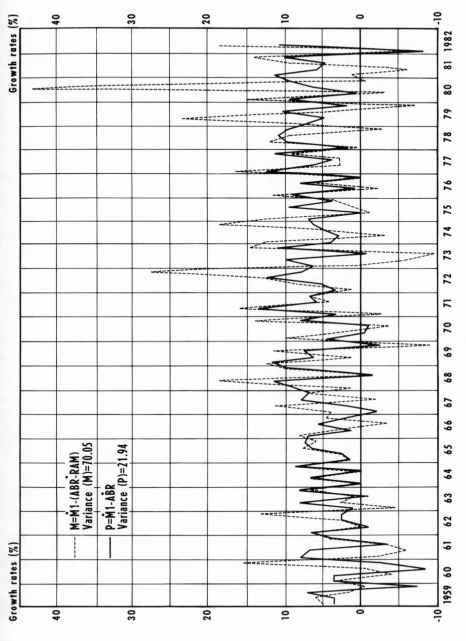

Figure 2–4   Alternative Money Multiplier Growth Rates

Table 2-5. Regression Results (absolute value t-statistics in parenthesis)

(A) Monetization and Economic Activity (1952–81)

$$(\Delta Y/Y)_t = 3.29 + 0.08\ (\Delta Y/Y)_{t-1} + 0.17\ (\Delta Y/Y)_{t-2}$$
$$\ (1.73)\quad (0.39)\qquad\qquad (0.83)$$

$$+\ 0.01\ (\Delta Y/Y)_{t-3} + 0.10\ (\Delta FRDH/FRDH)_t$$
$$\ (0.02)\qquad\qquad (0.55)$$

$$+\ 0.14\ (\Delta FRDH/FRDH)_{t-1} + 0.08\ (\Delta FRDH/FRDH)_{t-2}$$
$$\ (0.82)\qquad\qquad\qquad (0.63)$$

$$+\ 0.02\ (\Delta FRDH/FRDH)_{t-3}$$

$$R^2 = 0.24 \qquad DW = 1.84 \qquad F(8,22) = 0.98$$

(B) Determinants of Monetization (1949–81)

$$(\Delta FRDH/Y)_t = 0.09 + 0.03\ (DEF/Y)_t + 1.08\ (\Delta C/Y)_t$$
$$\ (1.20)\quad (0.80)\qquad (3.29)$$

$$-\ 0.60\ (\Delta RAM/Y)_t$$
$$\ (3.55)$$

$$R^2 = 0.55 \qquad DW = 1.90 \qquad F(4,29) = 11.76$$

Y = nominal GNP
$FRDH$ = federal Reserve holdings of government securities
DEF = federal government deficit (N/A measure)
C = currency holdings of nonbank public
RAM = reserve adjustment magnitude

The Determinants of Federal Reserve Policy and Monetization

Blinder's confusion between monetization per se and the sum of all Fed actions carries over to Blinder's discussion of "the determinants of monetization." We cannot conclude from Blinder's empirical work, relating adjusted bank reserve growth behavior inversely to past inflation and the rate of growth of real Federal purchases, that these two variables determine the rate of growth in the Fed's holding of government securities. Blinder's findings simply suggest that the Fed takes actions to restrain money stock growth in the face of greater inflation or real government spending. We do not know by considering the growth of the adjusted bank reserves alone, whether the Fed necessarily responds by slowing the rate of increase in its holdings of Federal debt, or whether it achieves its desired result by any of the other channels previously discussed.

The previous section does suggest, however, that changes in the Fed's holdings of government securities are likely to be related to reserve requirement ratio changes. It appears, historically, that many changes in reserve requirement ratios were not designed solely with the intent of altering money growth. In this regard, the Fed usually has changed its portfolio holdings of government securities to offset, at least partially, the effects of reserve requirement changes on money growth.

Empirical evidence supports this view. Consider the relationship between the Federal Reserve's holdings of Federal debt (FRDH) and three variables: (1) the federal government deficit (DEF); (2) currency holdings of the nonbank public (C); and (3) the change in the reserve adjustment magnitude (ΔRAM). The results obtained by estimating this relationship using fiscal year observations from 1949–81 are reported in the second panel of table 2–5.

The coefficient on the ΔRAM variable is negative and different from zero at conventional significance levels. The point estimate suggests that, on average over this period, when $1 billion in bank reserves were freed by a reserve requirement ratio reduction, approximately $0.6 billion in the Fed's holdings of government securities would be sold to offset the expansionary effects of the reserve requirement ratio reduction. This means that what the Fed did with one hand, was undone with the other. Again, in such a setting, only looking at one hand is quite misleading.

The estimation results further suggest that the Federal reserve accommodates any demand for currency on the part of the public. The near unity coefficient estimate on the currency varible indicates that the Federal Reserve buys $1 billion in government securities for each $1 billion

Table 2-6.　Simplified Federal Reserve Balance Sheet
(in millions of dollars)

Assets	Level Sept. 29, 1982	Liabilities	Level Sept. 29, 1982
Gold certificates	$ 11,148	Monetary base:	
Foreign currencies	5,041	Deposits of financial	$ 18,734
Federal Reserve credit:		institutions	
Security holdings	139,254	Federal Reserve notes	135,259
Loans to financial		Treasury deposits	8,320
institutions	1,154	Foreign central	
Float	1,937	bank deposits	295
Other assets	9,128	Other liabilities	
		and capital	5,054

increased demand for currency. Finally, the equation indicates that the level of the federal government deficit (NIA measure) has no significant bearing on the Federal Reserve's purchase of government securities.

Conclusion

I have very little to quarrel with regarding Blinder's empirical findings. Blinder finds much empirical support for the general propositions that I strongly believe in: (1) monetary actions as measured by adjusted bank reserves are a significant determinant of nominal GNP growth and inflation; and (2) federal deficits have little direct effect on inflation. He also finds support for the proposition that the Federal Reserve seeks to restrain money growth in the face of rising inflation—a proposition that I do not find all that implausible.

I have much to quarrel with regarding Blinder's interpretation of his findings, however. Although he claims to have shown that monetization matters, and claims to have provided new insights into the determinants of monetization, his analysis is inconsistent with his definition of monetization as the change in the central bank's holdings of Federal debt. Rather than examining the determinants of monetization and showing that monetization matters, Blinder has examined the determinants of monetary policy and has shown that monetary policy matters. In this regard, all actions taken by the Federal Reserve are shown to be important. Although I certainly would not deny the validity of this proposition it has nothing to do with the issue of monetization per se.

Notes

1. See for example, Blinder and Solow (1974).

2. Those familiar with the original Andersen-Jordan equation will not be too perplexed by the fact that the long-run adjusted bank reserve multiplier for nominal GNP growth is found to be somewhat less than unity over the sample period considered by Blinder. This simply reflects a general decline in the ratio of $M1$ to adjusted bank reserves over the period, as a result of a general increase in the currency to checkable deposit ratio. Estimating the relationship with $M1$ still yields a steady-state effect of unity. Using the adjusted bank reserve series yields a slightly smaller effect due to the general negative trend in the adjusted bank reserve multiplier.

3. I stress this point fearing that someone reading Blinder's paper should erroneously conclude that only monetization matters and thus only follow developments with regard to the Fed's holdings of government debt. Equation 2.4 shows explicitly that any change in the Fed's holdings of government debt can be either attenuated or offset by many alternative channels. In this regard, looking only the change in the Fed's holdings of government securities can be very misleading.

4. In calendar year 1952 the average level of RAM was -8.73. By the end of Blinder's sample period, 1981, the average level of RAM was $+3.08$.

References

Anderson, L.C. and J.L. Jordan. "Monetary and Fiscal Actions: A Test of Their Relative Importance in Economic Stabilization." *Federal Reserve Bank of St. Louis Review* (November 1968), 11–24.

Balback, A.B. and A.W. Burger. "Derivation of the Monetary Base." *Federal Reserve Bank of St. Louis Review* (November 1976), 2–8.

Balbach, A.B. "How Controllable is Money Growth?" *Federal Reserve Bank of St. Louis Review* (April 1981), 3–12.

Blinder, A.S. and R.M. Solow "Analytical Foundations of Fiscal Policy." In: *The Economics of Public Finance.* Washington DC: The Brookings Institution, 1974, pp. 3–118.

Gilbert, R.A. "Revision of the St. Louis Federal Reserve's Adjusted Monetary Base," *Federal Reserve Bank of St. Louis Review* (December 1980), 3–10.

Tatom, J.A. "Issues in Measuring an Adjusted Monetary Base." *Federal Reserve Bank of St. Louis Review* (December 1980), 11–29.

Thornton, D.L. "The Budget Constraint, Endogenous Money and the Relative Importance of Fiscal Policy Under Alternative Financing Schemes." Federal Reserve Bank of St. Louis Working Paper No. 82-007, 1982.

APPENDIX

Adjusted Bank Reserve Growth and Debt Monetization

The source base is defined to be the sum of the two largest liabilities of the Federal Reserve System: (1) Reserve balances of financial institutions; and (2) currency outstanding.[1] To more directly relate the source base to central bank holding of federal debt—which is of direct concern here—we can employ the balance sheet identity. This identity says that the source base must equal the value of all assets of the Federal Reserve system less all of its liabilities other than deposits of financial institutions and outstanding Federal Reserve notes. If we use the balance sheet in table 2–6 we see that: $SB_t \equiv$ Gold certificates$_t$ + Foreign currencies$_t$ + Security holdings$_t$ + Loans to financial institutions$_t$ + Float$_t$ + Other assets$_t$ − Treasury deposits$_t$ − Foreign central bank deposits$_t$ − Other liabilities and capital$_t$.

Two definitional steps separate adjusted bank reserves from the source base. Because a given amount of source base can support very different money stock levels—depending on current reserve equipment ratios in place—an adjustment for reserve requirement ratio changes is made. This adjustment is made by determining how much of the monetary base would be freed (or absorbed) if some base period reserve requirements had constantly prevailed through time.[2] This magnitude, known as RAM, is simply added to the source base to obtain the adjusted monetary base (AMB): $AMB_t = SB_t + RAM_t$.

The second step required to determine adjusted bank reserves (ABR) is to subtract currency held by the nonbank public (C) from the adjusted monetary base: $ABR_t \equiv AMB_t - C_t$. Using the first two balance sheet identities we can write: $ABR_t =$ Gold Certificates$_t$ + Foreign currencies$_t$ + *Security holdings$_t$* + Loans to financial institutions$_t$ + Float$_t$ + Other assets$_t$ − Treasury deposits$_t$ − Foreign central bank deposits$_t$ − Other liabilities and capital$_t$ + $RAM_t - C_t$. This identity shows quite clearly the relationship between the Federal Reserve's ability to influence bank deposits and its holdings of government debt (italicized for emphasis).

Notes

1. For a more detailed discussion of the source base see Balbach, A.B. and A.E. Burger. "Derivation of the Monetary Base," *Federal Reserve Bank of St. Louis Review* (November 1976), 2–8, and Balbach, A.B. "How Controllable is Money Growth?" *Federal Reserve Bank of St. Louis Review* (April 1981), 3–12.

2. For a discussion of the present measurement of the reserve adjustment magnitude (RAM) and other issues involved see, Gilbert, R.A. "Revision of the St. Louis Federal Reserve's Adjusted Monetary Base," *Federal Reserve Bank of St. Louis Review* (December 1980), 3–10, and Tatom, J.A. "Issues in Measuring An Adjusted Monetary Base," *Federal Reserve Bank of St. Louis Review* (December 1980), 11–29.

For a theoretical discussion which recognizes the difference between monetization and reserve requirement changes see, Thornton, D.L. "The Budget Constraint, Endogeneous Money and the Relative Importance of Fiscal Policy Under Alternative Financing Schemes," Federal Reserve Bank of St. Louis Working Paper No. 82-007, 1982.

II THE IMPACT OF DEFICITS ON INTEREST RATES AND CAPITAL FORMATION

3 ASSET SUBSTITUTABILITY AND THE IMPACT OF FEDERAL DEFICITS

V. Vance Roley

The large federal deficits since 1975, and the prospect of their further rapid expansion through the mid-1980s, have caused greater attention to be focused on the economic consequences of federal deficits. Much of the discussion has centered on the issue of whether a rise in the deficit crowds out interest-sensitive private spending. This discussion is properly directed, as a vast majority of deficits since the late 1960s have been debt financed. In particular, while marketable Treasury securities net of Federal Reserve holdings actually declined during the 1964–69 period, private investors have purchased about 85 percent of the cumulative rise in federal debt since 1969. Moreover, during 1980 and 1981, private investors purchased over 90 percent of the rise in outstanding federal debt.[1].

Any of several conditions have been shown to imply situations in which a debt-financed increase in the federal deficit due to a rise in government expenditures crowds out an equal amount of private expenditures, even in the

I am grateful to David Johnson and Rick Troll for research assistance, to Benjamin Friedman for the use of his expanded MPS model, and to Benjamin Friedman, Alan Hess, Karlyn Mitchell, Carl Walsh, and Charles Webster for helpful comments. The views expressed here are solely my own and do not necessarily represent the views of the Federal Reserve Bank of Kansas City or the Federal Reserve System short run.[2] One unambiguous case emerges when all factors of production are already fully employed (M. Friedman, 1970). However, even in the presence of unemployed resources, if households view the tax liability associated with an increase in federal debt as being equal to the value of the debt, then debt-financed increases in government spending would again crowd out private spending. (Bailey, 1971, Barro, 1974, and Kochin, 1974) That is, if the Ricardian equivalence theorem holds, systematic fiscal policy cannot affect aggregate demand.[3]

In the absence of full employment and Ricardian equivalence, Tobin (1961, 1963) and subsequent writers have noted that the extent of short-run crowding out depends on the substitutability among assets. If federal debt and private capital are perfect substitutes, for example, complete crowding out is again possible if the demand for money depends on wealth. (Silber, 1970 and Meyer, 1975) However, if money and federal debt are perfect substitutes, a debt-financed increase in the deficit causes total spending to rise. Allowing imperfect substitutability among money, federal debt, and capital, the possible outcomes span these extremes and therefore range from crowding out to crowding in. (B. Friedman, 1978) Moreover, even if federal debt and capital are perfect substitutes, Blinder and Solow (1973) have demonstrated that bond-financed deficits may be more stimulative than those that are money-financed in the long run.[4]

The purpose of this paper is to examine empirically the role asset substitutability plays in determining the impact of federal deficits on interest rates and capital formation. In the first section, the issues are examined in a simple analytical model including three assets: money, federal debt, and corporate bonds. Following B. Friedman (1978), the impact of federal deficits is shown to depend primarily on the relative magnitudes of the interest-rate coefficients in the aggregate demands for these three assets. The empirical model used to evaluate asset substitutability is presented in the second section. The model consists of estimated demands for corporate bonds, equities, and four different maturity classes of Treasury securities by eleven disaggregated investor categories. In the third section, the short-run impact of deficits on interest rates is estimated using simulations in which the supply of each of the four maturity classes of Treasury securities is separately increased in each period. The dynamic effects of deficit shocks are then calculated in this partial equilibrium framework. The general equilibrium effects of deficits on both interest rates and capital formation are considered in the fourth section. These general equilibrium effects are obtained from the model developed by B. Friedman (1981, 1982), which in turn is comprised of the disaggregated asset demands estimated by Roley (1980, 1982) combined with the MIT-PENN-SSRC (MPS) model. The main conclusions of this paper are summarized in the final section.

Issues in a Simple Analytical Model

In this section, a basic analytical model is presented to consider the role of asset substitutability in determining the impact of a change in the federal deficit on interest rates.[5] Two permutations of this simple model are also considered. First, the corporate financing decision is endogenized to examine whether substitutability between financing alternatives moderates the impact of deficits on interest rates. Second, similar effects are investigated in the context of financial intermediation. Although the empirical results reported in later sections are obtained from a disaggregated structural model comprised of 51 behavioral equations, the empirical model in its aggregated form is similar to the illustrative models analyzed here.

In each of the models presented below, only the financial effects of an increase in the federal deficit are considered. Thus, income is exogenous and the financial effects examined are analogous to shifts in the LM curve in traditional IS-LM analysis. Using B. Friedman's (1978) terminology, such shifts in the LM curve determine the amount of "portfolio crowding out," which is separate from the amount of "transactions crowding out." This latter effect corresponds to the movement along a given LM curve associated with shifts in the IS curve. As long as the LM curve has a positive slope, some transactions crowding out—and a subsequent rise in interest rates—will occur in response to stimulative fiscal actions. However, if the LM curve is not vertical, transactions crowding out cannot be of sufficient magnitude to inhibit altogether a rise in total spending. Thus, the question of whether crowding out is complete depends also on the sign and magnitude of the portfolio crowding out effect considered below. Moreover, depending on the substitutability among assets, some portion of transactions crowding out could actually be offset resulting in an unambiguous rise in total spending with perhaps only a trivial rise in interest rates.

To investigate these questions, the first model considered is comprised of the aggregate demands for money (M^d), federal debt (T^d), and corporate bonds (B^d):

$$M^d = \beta_{mt}r_t + \beta_{mb}r_b + \gamma_m W + \delta_m Y$$
$$T^d = \beta_{tt}r_t + \beta_{tb}r_b + \gamma_t W + \delta_t Y$$
$$B^d = \beta_{bt}r_t + \beta_{bb}r_b + \gamma_b W + \delta_b Y \qquad (3.1)$$

where r_t, r_b = yields on Treasury securities and corporate bonds, respectively, W = financial wealth, Y = income, and β_{ij}, γ_i, δ_i ($i, j = m, b, t$) = coefficients. Throughout this section, it is assumed that own-yield and wealth elasticities of demand are nonnegative such that $\beta_{ii} > 0$, $0 \leqq \gamma_i \leqq 1$, ($i = t, b$), and that assets are not gross complements $[\beta_{ij} \leqq 0, i \neq j, (i, j = m, t, b)]$.[6] The Brainard-Tobin (1968) portfolio balance conditions place further restrictions on the coefficients, and they may be represented as $\beta_{mt} + \beta_{tt} + \beta_{bt} = 0$; $\beta_{mb} + \beta_{tb} + \beta_{bb} = 0$; $\gamma_m + \gamma_t + \gamma_b = 1$; $\delta_m + \delta_t + \delta_b = 0$. In this model, the interest-bearing securities are assumed to have variable coupons and fixed market values, and businesses are assumed to finance all capital accumulation with bonds. It is also assumed that the cumulative supply of bonds (B^s) equals the value of the capital stock, K. Thus, total wealth has the usual representation

$$W = M + T + K \tag{3.2}$$

Combining the aggregate demands (3.1) with fixed supplies of money (M^0), Treasury securities (T^0), and capital ($K^0 = B^s$), the model determines two endogenous yields, r_t and r_b. Because of its presumed effect on business investment decisions and hence total spending, the impact of bond-financed deficits on the corporate bond rate is examined here. That is, the corporate bond rate is taken as the relevant rate for the *IS* curve.

Following Christ (1968), Silber (1970), and Meyer (1975), any increases in government expenditures (G) or decreases in taxes (R) are related to increases in federal debt and outside money through the government budget constraint

$$dG - dR = dT + dM \tag{3.3}$$

In the case of a bond-financed increase in the deficit, $dM = 0$ and $dT = dW > 0$; the impact on the corporate bond rate may be expressed as

$$\frac{\partial r_b}{\partial T} = \frac{-(1 - \gamma_t)\beta_{bt} - \gamma_b\beta_{tt}}{\beta_{tt}\beta_{bb} - \beta_{tb}\beta_{bt}} \tag{3.4}$$

where the denominator is positive if all assets are gross substitutes. Thus, the presence of portfolio crowding out or crowding in depends on the numerator. In turn, the sign and magnitude of the numerator depend on the degree of asset substitutability and the effect of wealth on the individual demands.

With the above assumptions, it can be shown that if wealth does not affect money demand ($\gamma_m = 0$), then a rise in the deficit unambiguously reduces the corporate bond rate and therefore leads to crowding in. In this case, the wealth effects on the demands for interest-bearing securities more than offset the impact of the rise in the supply of Treasury securities. Alternatively, if the demands for Treasury securities and corporate bonds are not functions of wealth ($\gamma_m = 1$), a bond-financed increase in the deficit unambiguously leads to crowding out. Interest rates must rise in this case to offset the increased demand for money due to the rise in wealth.

The interest rate coefficients in the demand equations—which relate directly to asset substitutability—are equally important in determining the impact of larger deficits on the corporate bond rate. As others have previously noted, if money and Treasury securities are close substitutes, implying that β_{bt} is near zero, then bond-financed increases in the deficit cause the corporate bond yield to fall. Alternatively, if Treasury securities and corporate bonds are close substitutes, leading to a value of $-\beta_{bt}$ near β_{tt}, crowding out is the result.[7] For asset substitutability between these extremes, the outcome could be either crowding out or crowding in.

Corporate Financing Decision

In the model examined above, businesses are assumed to finance capital accumulation solely by selling bonds. This assumption is now relaxed in perhaps the simplest manner by allowing corporations to either sell bonds or reduce their money holdings to finance investment spending. As is shown below, the extent of crowding out or crowding in is reduced if corporations view alternative funding sources as substitutes.

In this extended model, corporations are assumed to demand money and supply bonds according to

$$M^c = b_{mb}r_b + b_m K + b_{my}Y$$
$$B^s = b_{bb}r_b + b_b K + b_{by}Y \qquad (3.5)$$

where the coefficients b_{ij}, b_i, b_{iy} ($i, j = m, b$) satisfy $b_{bb} \leq 0$, $0 \leq b_b$, $b_m \leq 1$, $0 \leq b_{by}$, $b_{bm} \leq 1$ as well as the portfolio-balance constraints

$$b_{bb} - b_{mb} = 0, \ b_b - b_m = 1, \ b_{by} - b_{my} = 0 \qquad (3.6)$$

Implicit in equation 3.6 is the constraint $K = B^s - M^c$. The aggregate demands for assets by households equation 3.1 are assumed to remain unchanged, but equilibrium in the money market is now described by the market clearing identity $M^d + M^c = M^0$.

Combining equations 3.1 and 3.5, the impact of a bond-financed increase in the deficit on the corporate bond rate may be determined as before. In this case, it may be shown that the impact is

$$\frac{\partial r_b}{\partial T} = \frac{-(1 - \gamma_t)\beta_{bt} - \gamma_b\beta_{tt}}{\beta_{tt}(\beta_{bb} - b_{bb}) - \beta_{tb}\beta_{bt}} \qquad (3.7)$$

Under the reasonable assumption that the supply of bonds is negatively related to the corporate bond rate ($b_{bb} < 0$), the impact on this rate (equation 3.7) is unambiguously less in absolute value than that in the previous case (equation 3.4). Not surprisingly, then, allowing some substitutability among corporate financing decisions moderates the effect of increased deficits on the corporate bond rate. The importance of substitutability in the corporate financing decision is empirically examined in the third section.

Financial Intermediation

If the portfolio behavior of financial intermediaries such as banks, insurance companies, and pension funds is different from that of households due to regulation or other institutional features, and if households do not view intermediaries simply as mutual funds and adjust their own portfolio behavior accordingly, then financial intermediation may modify the impact of increased deficits on interest rates. Indeed, Hansen (1973) and Meyer and Hart (1975) have examined such effects in a model similar to that employed here, and found that the addition of financial intermediaries alters the crowding out effect in a nontrivial way. Because financial intermediaries are explicitly represented in the empirical model discussed in subsequent sections, it may be useful to examine their impact in the context of the illustrative framework presented above.

In the model, banks are taken as the representative intermediaries and they are assumed to hold required reserves (RR), excess reserves (ER), and corporate bonds (B^b). The sum of their asset holdings equals total money liabilities (M) and net worth (NW). The behavior of these intermediaries is described by the following set of equations

$$H = RR + ER$$

$$RR = \alpha M$$

$$EE = c_{eb}r_b + c_e(NW + M - RR)$$

$$B^b = c_{bb}r_b + c_b(NW + M - RR) \tag{3.8}$$

where H represents outside money and the coefficients satisfy $0 \leq \alpha \leq 1$. $0 \leq c_{bb} \leq 1$, $0 \leq c_e, c_b \leq 1$ as well as the portfolio adding-up restrictions

$$c_{eb} + c_{bb} = 0, \quad c_e + c_b = 1 \tag{3.9}$$

Thus, for a given required reserve ratio (α), banks determine their allocation of assets between excess reserves and bonds. In addition, the market clearing condition for bonds now becomes $B^d + B^b = B^s$ and household wealth may be expressed as[8] $W = H + T + K$.

Combining equation 3.8 with equations 3.1 and 3.5, the impact of a bond-financed increase in the deficit on the corporate bond rate may be shown to equal

$$\frac{\partial r_b}{\partial T} =$$

$$\frac{[-(1-\gamma_t)\beta_{bt}-\gamma_b\beta_{tt}]-(1-\gamma_t)c_b(1-\alpha)\beta_{mt}-\gamma_m c_b(1-\alpha)\beta_{tt}}{[\beta_{tt}(\beta_{bb}-b_{bb})-\beta_{bt}\beta_{tb}]+\beta_{tt}[c_{bb}+c_b(1-\alpha)(\beta_{mb}+b_{mb})]-c_b(1-\alpha)\beta_{mt}\beta_{tb}}$$

$$(3.10)$$

The effects of financial intermediation may be illustrated by several special cases. First, if the required reserve ratio equals one ($\alpha = 1$), then the impact of an increased deficit (equation 3.10) is unambiguously smaller in absolute value than before if banks exhibit some interest elasticity in their allocation of net worth between excess reserves and bond holdings. Second, this same result follows if banks' demand for bonds has zero elasticity with respect to the value of total discretionary asset holdings ($c_b = 0$). Finally, in comparison to equation 3.7, changes in the interest sensitivity in banks' portfolio allocation (c_{bb}) have ambiguous effects. As a whole, the presence of financial intermediation may accentuate or diminish any crowding out or crowding in effect.

To summarize, simple extensions to the illustrative model considered at the outset can significantly alter the portfolio crowding out effect. Before turning to the empirical investigation of the crowding out effect, the empirical analogue of the analytical model dicussed in this section is presented.

Specification and Estimation of the Model

Various aspects of the empirical model used to estimate the impact of bond-financed deficits on interest rates are discussed in this section.[9] The model consists of disaggregated demands for Treasury securities, corporate bonds, and equities by eleven categories of investors. The yields on these securities are determined from market clearing identities which equate aggregate demands with supplies for each type of security. As such, the reduced-form expressions for security yields implicit in the model are restricted by the underlying portfolio behavior of the different categories of investors.[10] Thus, as was the case in the illustrative model considered in the previous section, the substitutability among assets in the individual asset demands is a primary determinant of the impact of bond-financed deficits on interest rates.

Specification

The approach used to specify the financial asset demands attempts to capture the basic determinants of investor's short-run portfolio allocation. One such determinant is surely the risk return trade-off associated with different attainable portfolios. This trade-off may be modeled formally using the mean-variance portfolio selection model, which serves to identify investors' desired portfolios in terms of their risk aversion and the risk and return characteristics of individual securities. Following Friedman and Roley (1979b), the mean-variance model may be shown to be consistent with the following linear homogenous demands:

$$\alpha_{it}^* = A_{it}^*/W_t = a_{i0} + \sum_j b_{ij} r_{jt}^e + \sum_k c_{ik} \sigma_{kt}, \quad i = 1, \ldots, N \quad (3.11)$$

where the α_{it}^* are desired portfolio shares, the A_{it}^* are desired asset holdings in dollars, $W(= \Sigma_i A_{it}^*)$ is total portfolio wealth, the r_{jt}^e are expected asset yields, and the σ_{kt} are variances associated with these yields. These latter terms are added to the asset demands obtained from utility maximization to represent the possible nonstationarity of yield variances—i.e., changes in the riskiness of different types of securities over time. The a_{i0}, b_{ij}, and c_{ik} are fixed coefficients that satisfy the usual adding-up constraints $\Sigma_i b_{ij} = \Sigma_i c_{ik} = 0$, for all j and k, and $\Sigma_i a_{i0} = 1$.

Although, investors desire to hold the portfolio shares described in equation 3.11, actual short run portfolios are often thought to be different from those desired due to transactions costs. Because of this important role of transactions costs, their effects should be represented with some care. In this respect, the general portfolio adjustment model used here distinguishes among the costs associated with reallocating the securities currently held by the investor, the smaller costs associated with purchasing securities from new investable wealth flows, and the possible asymmetric costs in buying and selling securities.[11] Analytically, all of these features are represented in the model

$$\Delta A_{it} = \sum_{k}^{N} \pi_{ikt}(\alpha_{kt}^{*}W_{t-1} - A_{k,t-1}) + \delta_{it} \cdot \Delta W_{t}, \quad i = 1, \ldots, N \quad (3.12)$$

where ΔA_{it} represents net purchases of asset i; the indices i and k ($i, k = 1, \ldots, N$) are associated with endogenous assets; δ_{it} describes the marginal allocation of new investable wealth flows ΔW_{t}; and the π_{ikt} are flexible portfolio adjustment parameters.

One way this model (equation 3.12) differs from the standard stock adjustment model is that it allows wealth flows to affect the reallocation of assets already held in investors' portfolios. In particular, the parameter describing the adjustment of last period's assets $A_{k,t-1}$ to those desired $\alpha_{kt}^{*}W_{t-1}$ is not constant. Instead, this parameter is defined as

$$\pi_{ikt} = \theta_{ik} + \psi_{ik}'(\Delta W_{t}'/W_{t-1}) + \psi_{ik}''(\Delta W_{t}''/W_{t-1}) \quad (3.13)$$

where θ_{ik}, ψ_{ik}', and ψ_{ik}'' are fixed coefficients satisfying the constraints $\Sigma_{i}^{N}\psi_{ik} = \overline{\theta}$, $\Sigma_{i}^{N}\psi_{ik}' = \overline{\psi}'$, and $\Sigma_{i}^{N}\psi_{ik}'' = \overline{\psi}''$, for all k; and $\Delta W_{t}'$ and $\Delta W_{t}''$ are positive and negative wealth flows, respectively. For positive wealth flows, for example, $\Delta W_{t}''$ equals zero, and the larger the magnitude of the flow, the less an investor will reallocate currently held assets. In this case movement toward desired portfolio composition may be achieved with less cost by simply investing the wealth flow according to desired portfolio composition.

The final term in the model (equation 3.12) reflects this less costly investment strategy. This term describes the marginal allocation of new investable wealth flows. For positive wealth flows, it is defined to equal α_{it}^{*}, investors' desired long-run portfolio composition. For negative wealth flows, investors may not sell assets according to desired portfolio composition for a variety of reasons—including differential transactions costs and a possible aversion to realizing capital losses—implying that a separate term may be needed to represent portfolio behavior in this case. Thus, the coefficient determining marginal purchases or sales is defined as

$$\delta_{it} = \begin{cases} \alpha_{it}^{*}, & \text{for } \Delta W_{t} > 0 \\ \gamma_{it}^{*}, & \text{for } \Delta W_{t} < 0 \end{cases} \quad (3.14)$$

where γ_{it}^{*} depends on the same factors as α_{it}^{*} in equation (3.11), but it is not constrained to imply identical responses by investors to positive and negative wealth flows.

All of the terms that are additional to the standard stock adjustment model are tested to judge their relevance. As might be expected because of the diverse institutional and behavioral characteristics of the categories of investors included in the structural model, several subcases of the general portfolio adjustment model (3.12) are actually applied. Statistical tests involving zero constraints on the ψ'_{ik} and ψ''_{ik} parameters and equality constraints on the α^*_{it} and γ^*_{it} terms are used to determine which sub-model is appropriate for each investor category.

Data and Estimation Techniques

The investor categories included in the disaggregated structural model are indicated in table 3–1. As of year-end 1981, the investor categories with endogenous demands held 96 percent of the total amount of outstanding Treasury securities net of the Federal Reserve System and foreign holdings, 98 percent of the total supply of corporate bonds, and 96 percent of the total supply of equities. The primary data source of the disaggregated structural model is the Federal Reserve System's flow-of-funds accounts (1975). Quarterly observations are used, with the sample period beginning in 1960:Q1 and ending in 1975:Q4.

The data for Treasury securities consist of four weighted maturity classes of federal debt that are consistent with the flow-of-funds accounts. The data are defined in terms of four "definite" areas and three "borderline" areas. The definite areas include the following maturities: (1) within one year (short-term); (2) two to four years (short-intermediate-term); (3) six to eight years (long-intermediate-term); and (4) over twelve years (long-term). Treasury securities with maturities in the borderline areas are allocated to the definite classifications according to a weighting scheme. The principal advantage of this procedure is that it avoids the otherwise perverse effects that occur when large debt issues cross fixed maturity boundaries.

Financial flow variables corresponding to the individual assets of the 11 investor categories are defined in terms of seasonally adjusted net changes during the quarter. The wealth flow variables are generally defined as quarterly net acquisitions of financial assets, seasonally adjusted. Financial stock variables, including individual asset stocks and total portfolio wealth, are formed by decrementing seasonally adjusted quarterly flows from the value of year-end outstandings in 1975:Q4. This procedure serves to guarantee the mutual consistency of the asset stock and flow data throughout the sample period. When asset stock data contain market valuation changes, these components are included without seasonal adjustment. The endogenous yields correspond to the published series for the three month

Table 3-1. Treasury Securities, Corporate Bonds, and Equities Outstanding as of Year-end 1981

Securities Held By:	Treasury Securities[a]		Corporate Bonds		Equities	
	Amount	Percent	Amount	Percent	Amount	Percent
Households*	$162.0b	22.0%	76.5	14.5	1,084.2	72.5
Foreign	141.4	19.2	22.0	4.2	64.1	4.3
Federal Reserve System	131.0	17.8	—	—	—	—
Commercial Banks†	113.1	15.4	7.6	1.4	0.1	0.0
State-Local General Funds†	60.7	8.3	—	—	—	—
Private Pension Funds*	30.6	4.2	61.7	11.7	167.1	11.2
State-Local Retirement Funds*	27.3	3.7	102.8	19.4	47.8	3.2
Other Insurance Companies*	18.2	2.5	30.8	5.8	31.0	2.1
Credit Unions	14.1	1.9	—	—	—	—
Life Insurance Companies*	8.6	1.2	187.9	35.5	49.7	3.3
Nonfinancial Corporate Businesses†	8.0	1.1	—	—	—	—
Savings and Loan Associations†	8.0	1.1	—	—	—	—
Mutual Savings Banks*	5.4	0.7	20.2	3.8	3.2	0.2
Sponsored Credit Agencies	2.9	0.4	—	—	—	—
Investment Companies‡	2.8	0.4	10.1	1.9	37.4	2.5
Security Brokers and Dealers	1.0	0.1	9.1	1.7	11.7	0.8
Total	735.1	100.0	528.7	100.0	1,496.4	100.0

Source: Board of Governors of the Federal Reserve System (1975) and subsequent issues.
Amounts are in billions of dollars.
Detail may not add to total because of rounding.
[a] Agency issues and non-negotiable savings bonds are excluded.
*Endogenous demands for all three types of securities.
†Endogenous demands only for Treasury securities.
‡Endogenous demands only for equities.

Treasury bill yield, the three to five year Treasury security yield, the long-term (ten year and over) Treasury security yield, the yield on new issues of corporate bonds (Aa utilities), Standard and Poor's dividend-price ratio, and a weighted average of yields on Treasury securities maturing in six, seven, and eight years for the long-intermediate-term yield. When statistically significant, distributed lags on the percentage change of the Standard and Poor's composite common stock price index are also included to represent expected capital gains or losses on equities.[12] Variances of holding period yields are represented by lagged four or eight quarter moving average variances of the sum of the coupon return and the capital gain (or loss) on the respective securities.

The estimated demand equations correspond to various submodels embodied in equation 3.12. For the simplest case—involving the constraints $\psi'_{ik} = \psi''_{ik} = 0$ and $\gamma^*_{it} = \alpha^*_{it}$—expansion of equation 3.12 implies that net purchase of a security depend on lagged stocks of assets, products of expected yields with wealth flows and stocks, and products of variances with wealth flows and stocks. The set of lagged asset stocks consists not only of the six securities modeled here, but also such assets as commercial paper, state and local bonds, mortgages, and components of the monetary aggregates. Similarly, yields and variances of yields are included for all of these categories of assets.

The structure of the supply-demand model necessitates the use of a simultaneous equations estimation technique. This is the case because yields on securities are jointly dependent variables along with investors' demands. Thus, ordinary least squares estimation results in inconsistent estimates. Because the direct application of $2SLS$ is not possible due to the undersized sample problem—i.e., more predetermined variables than sample observations—the application of an instrumental variables technique described by Brundy and Jorgenson (1971) is used to gain consistent estimates for the structural equations.

The particular instrumental variables procedure used involves replacing current values of dependent variables appearing in the righthand side of the structural equations with fitted values obtained from a first stage regression. The first stage regression for an individual structural equation has righthand side variables consisting of a subset of the principal components of the entire set of predetermined variables in the system of equations, augmented by the set of predetermined variables appearing in the structural equation. In addition, since the dependent variables being instrumented appear as products with either wealth flows or stocks, the proper procedure of forming an instrument for the entire multiplicative term is followed here.

Empirical Results

In total, 51 behavioral equations representing the net purchases of four maturity classes of Treasury securities, corporate bonds, and equities are estimated over 64 quarterly observations beginning in 1960:Q1 and ending in 1975:Q4. Summary statistics for the estimated equations are presented in table 3–2. As indicated by the multiple correlations ($\bar{R}^2$), these equations explain much of the variation of the net purchases of the six types of securities. The multiple correlations range from 0.53 to 0.91 for equities, 0.64 to 0.87 for corporate bonds, and 0.35 to 0.93 for the much more volatile net purchases of Treasury securities. Comparing the individual categories of investors using this criterion, the short-run demands of life insurance companies are explained the most successfully with multiple correlations ranging from 0.83 to 0.96. Within individual investor categories, the statistics reported in table 3–2 also indicate that the net purchases of each type of security are modeled with approximately equal success. The standard errors of the estimated equations are additionally reported to indicate the accuracy of the estimated equations in dollar amounts.

Individual parameter estimates also support the short-run portfolio selection model. As reported by Roley (1980, 1982), all coefficients on own yields and own asset stocks have the anticipated sign, and virtually all are statistically significant. Moreover, in the set of 51 estimated demands, there is evidence that at least some asset substitutability exists as 45 statistically significant cross yield terms are included.

By combining the 51 estimated equations with six market clearing identities that place aggregate demands equal to exogenous supplies (net of exogenous demands) of the four maturity classes of Treasury securities, corporate bonds, and equities, the yields on these six types of securities along with the 51 endogenous security demands may be simultaneously determined. The endogenous variables are determined in this framework using both one period and dynamic simulations beginning in 1960:Q1 and ending in 1975:Q4. The dynamic simulation differs from the one period (or static) simulation in that the former uses simulated values for all lagged endogenous variables.

The results from these simulations are summarized for the six endogenous yields in the lower half of table 3–2. In both simulations, the root-mean-square errors (RMSE) monotonically decrease for Treasury security yields as the maturity becomes longer, reflecting the greater volatility of shorter term yields. Moreover, for long-term yields, the root-mean-square errors range from only nineteen basis points for the long-term Treasury yield in the

Table 3-2. Summary of Estimation and Simulation Results (Sample Period: 1960:Q1–1975:Q4)

	Net Purchases of:											
	US1		US2		US3		US4		CB		EQ	
Investor Category	$\bar{R}^2$	SE	$\bar{R}^2$	SE	$\bar{R}^2$	SE	$\bar{R}^2$	SE	$\bar{R}^2$	SE	$\bar{R}^2$	SE
Commercial Banks	.75	1,190	.57	841	.87	366	.64	136	–	–	–	–
Households	.76	978	.76	426	.66	318	.71	154	.69	660	.61	637
Investment Companies	–	–	–	–	–	–	–	–	–	–	.53	325
Life Insurance Companies	.85	45	.83	21	.96	30	.93	39	.87	238	.88	120
Mutual Savings Banks	.55	74	.67	50	.72	57	.71	52	.82	187	.84	21
Nonfinancial Corporate Businesses	.65	665	.77	169	–	–	–	–	–	–	–	–
Other Insurance Companies	.44	71	.53	57	.81	35	.64	24	.77	108	.78	110
Private Pension Funds	.55	90	.77	45	.85	35	.80	38	.64	262	.85	217
Savings and Loan Associations	.52	172	.59	158	.61	103	.66	53	–	–	–	–
State-Local General Funds	.62	515	.43	186	.35	122	.52	108	–	–	–	–
State-Local Retirement Funds	.60	98	.37	26	.58	32	.57	117	.80	197	.91	104

Simulation Results (in percent)

	One Period		Dynamic	
Yield	ME	RMSE	ME	RMSE
Short-Term Treasury (r_T)	.02	.66	.06	.69
Short-Intermediate-Term Treasury (r_2)	.03	.40	.06	.47
Long-Intermediate-Term Treasury (r_3)	.01	.32	–.11	.43
Long-Term Treasury (r_4)	.00	.19	.02	.21
Corporate Bond (r_C)	–.01	.31	.04	.37
Equity (r_E)	.00	.34	.01	.37

Notes: US1 = short-term Treasury securities
US2 = short-intermediate-term Treasury securities
US3 = long-intermediate-term Treasury securities
US4 = long-term Treasury securities
CB = corporate bonds

EQ = equities
$\bar{R}^2$ = adjusted multiple correlation coefficient
SE = standard error in millions of dollars
ME = mean error
RMSE = root-mean-square error

one period simulation to 37 basis points for the corporate bond and equity yields in the dynamic simulation. Thus, the disaggregated structural model explains yields remarkably well with only small biases evident in the reported results.

Financial Effects of an Increase in the Federal Deficit

In this section, the disaggregated structural model of the Treasury security, corporate bond, and equity markets is used to examine empirically the effect of an increase in the federal deficit on interest rates. In particular, two sets of simulation experiments are performed. First, the initial impacts of increases in each of the four maturities of Treasury securities on the six endogenous yields are considered. Second, the longer run effects of deficit shocks— financed according to the historical maturity distribution of the outstanding federal debt—are investigated. Since these experiments involve only the financial sector, the results correspond to the portfolio crowding out effects reviewed in the first section.

Initial Effects of an Increase in the Deficit

To examine the short-run impact of debt-financed increases in the deficit on interest rates, simulations involving one percent increases in the stocks of the four different maturity classes of Treasury securities are performed, with all other predetermined variables taking historical values in each period. These experiments are not only suggestive in indicating the initial financial effects of increased debt-financed deficits, but they may also be used to examine whether alternative financing schemes involving the four maturities of Treasury securities have different consequences. Indeed, in a previous study (Roley, 1982), this model was shown to imply that debt management operations involving changes in the maturity composition of the federal debt significantly affect corporate bond and equity yields. In the expanded model employed in the next section, B. Friedman (1981) found similar effects.

As is discussed in more detail in the next subsection, the one percent changes in the different maturity classes of Treasury securities are quite small in comparison to the historical innovations in the respective net supplies. Thus, in the context of actual deficit financing policy which occurred during the sample period, the changes in asset stocks used in the simulation experiments may be thought of as innovations in the time-series

significantly affect relative yields if different investors have different "preferred habitats."

One period simulations utilizing the model exactly as outlined in the previous section are reported on the top half of table 3–3. For short-term Treasury securities (US1), for example, the results indicate that a one percent rise in the amount outstanding causes the bill yield (r_T) to rise 32 basis points above its value in the control simulation in 1966:Q1, 19 basis points in 1971:Q1, and an average of 32 basis points in one period

(Corporate Bond Supply Exogenous):[a]

	US3			US4	
1966:Q1	*1971:Q1*	*Average*	*1966:Q1*	*1971:Q1*	*Average*
−.01%	.00%	−.01%	.05%	.03%	.01%
−.01	.00	−.00	.01	.02	.01
.21	.07	.12	.18	.09	.12
.00	.00	.01	.18	.09	.14
−.00	−.00	.01	.16	.07	.12
.04	.00	.01	.05	.01	.01
Supply Endogenous)					
−.01	.00	−.01	.05	.02	.01
−.01	.00	−.00	.01	.02	.01
.22	.07	.12	.18	.09	.11
.00	.00	.01	.18	.09	.14
−.00	−.00	.00	.14	.06	.09
.05	.00	.01	.05	.01	.01
$0m	$1m	−$1m	−$41m	−$55m	−$53m

r_3 = 6- to 8-year Treasury security yield
r_4 = long-term (10-year and over) Treasury security yield
r_C = yield on new issues of corporate bonds (Aa utilities)
r_E = Standard and Poor's dividend-price ratio
Average = average impact over the entire sample period (1960:Q1–1975:Q4)
[a]Difference from control simulation values.

simulations over the entire sample period. Similarly, one percent increases in outstanding short-term Treasury securities results in an average rise in the corporate bond rate of four basis points, and a decline in the equity yield of three basis points.

As a whole, the results from these simulations are somewhat mixed. However, in comparing short- and long-term debt financing, the model suggests that the former is less likely to result in crowding out. In particular, under long-term debt financing, the average impacts on the corporate bond and equity yields are twelve and one basis points, respectively, or about eight and four basis points higher than those calculated under short-term debt financing. This difference occurs despite the fact that the average increase in short-term Treasury securities is over three times larger than the rise in long-term Treasury securities.

In the next set of simulations, the supply of corporate bonds is made endogenous by adding B. Friedman's (1979) corporate bond supply equation to the model.[13] This specification is particularly well suited for the experiments conducted here as it emphasizes the substitutability between long- and short-term debt financing. In this expanded model, the same simulations as before are performed, and the impacts of increased Treasury security supplies on both yields and the supply of corporate bonds are reported in the bottom half of table 3–3.

In terms of the impacts on yields, the simulation results are virtually the same as those reported in the top half of the table. The average impact on the corporate bond yield is, however, reduced slightly in the experiments concerning increases in long-term Treasury securities. With respect to quantity effects, the substitution away from corporate bond financing is quite small in three of the four sets of experiments. The average reductions in net issues of corporate bonds are $17m, $10m, $1m, and $53m for 1 percent increases in US1, US2, US3, and US4, respectively, where average increases in these four maturities of Treasury securities are $118m, $52m, $66m, and $31m. The results therefore indicate a high degree of substitutability between long-term federal debt and corporate bonds, as a $31 million average increase in long-term Treasury securities results in an average reduction of $53 million in corporate bonds.

Dynamic Effects of an Increase in the Deficit

The longer run financial effects of an increase in the deficit are considered in two sets of dynamic simulations. In these experiments, the innovation technique suggested by Mishkin (1979) is employed. This approach is implemented by first estimating an equation representing the time-series process of the cumulative debt-financed deficit over the 1960:Q1 to 1975:Q4 sample period.[14] Using the Box-Jenkins (1970) identification procedures, the time-series model ultimately obtained is[15]

$$\Delta Debt_t = .5734 \; \Delta Debt_{t-1} + .3850 \; \Delta Debt_{t-2} + \varepsilon_t \qquad (3.15)$$
$$\quad\;\; (4.6) \qquad\qquad\quad (2.6)$$

$$R^2 = .90 \qquad SE = \$3479m \qquad Q(26) = 10.48$$

where $Debt_t$ = cumulative debt-financed federal deficit at time t and ε_t = serially uncontrolled random error. This estimated equation 3.15 is then shocked by \$3.5 billion, or about one standard error, and the dynamic cumulative changes in the federal debt are computed. The increases in the cumulative deficit which result are financed according to the historical proportions of the amount outstanding in each of the maturity classes of Treasury securities to the total privately held federal debt in each quarter. It may be verified from (3.15) that the \$3.5 billion shock cumulates to \$26.1 billion after twelve quarters, and averages \$15.3 billion over the same period.

As before, simulations are performed both with and without an endogenously determined supply of corporate bonds. In the case of an exogenously determined supply, dynamic simulations beginning in 1966:Q1 and 1971:Q1 are reported in the top half of table 3–4. In each case, the dynamic simulations span twelve quarters. In comparison to the results in table 3–3, each of the simulations exhibit much larger impacts in the initial quarter reflecting the significantly larger magnitude of the federal debt shock. In the experiment initiated in 1966:Q1, the corporate bond yield rises throughout the twelve quarters, while the equity yield reaches a peak and then declines to 21 basis points above its value in the control simulation. In contrast, in the dynamic simulation initiated in 1971:Q1, both private security yields actually fall below their control simulation values after twelve quarters.

With an endogenously determined supply of corporate bonds, the yields exhibit similar patterns, as is apparent in the bottom half of table 3–4. In this case, however, several of the initial impacts of the deficit shocks are somewhat smaller. Moreover, after twelve quarters, the corporate bond yield is significantly lower in comparison to the exogenous supply case. The declines in net issues of corporate bonds are also fairly small relative to the increase in the cumulative deficit. After twelve quarters, outstanding corporate bonds fall by about \$7.7 and \$4.9 billion in the experiments initiated in 1966:Q1 and 1971:Q1, respectively, while the cumulative change in federal debt equals \$26.1 billion in each simulation. However, to

Table 3–4. Dynamic Simulation Results

Yields	*(Corporate Bond Supply Exogenous)* Deficit Shock of $3.5b in 1966:Q1[a]			Deficit Shock of $3.5b in 1971:Q1[a]		
	1966:Q1	1968:Q4	Average	1971:Q1	1973:Q4	Average
r_T	.92%	.17%	.17%	.47%	−.19%	.09%
r_2	.67	−.06	.31	.65	.00	.13
r_3	1.27	−.04	.98	.81	−.13	.22
r_4	.52	.66	.63	.28	.02	.18
r_C	.46	.80	.74	.32	−.08	.17
r_E	.22	.21	.34	.12	−.14	−.05
(Corporate Bond Supply Endogenous)						
r_T	.93	−.09	.01	.47	−.41	−.04
r_2	.67	−.43	.14	.63	−.15	.04
r_3	1.27	.03	1.01	.79	−.10	.21
r_4	.52	.71	.66	.28	.00	.16
r_C	.40	.12	.43	.24	−.19	.03
r_E	.22	.29	.36	.11	−.04	−.02
Supply: CB	−$117m	−$7,671m	−$2,784m	−$234m	−$4,854m	−$2,212m

Notes: For variable definitions, see Table 3–3.

Average = average change over the first 12 quarters after the experiment is initiated (1966:Q1 or 1971:Q1)

[a]Differences from control simulation values.

the extent that the quantity of as well as the yield on corporate bonds influences business investment decisions, these results could be consistent with some crowding out of investment expenditures. These general equilibrium effects are examined in the next section.

Deficits, Capital Formation, and Economic Activity

In this section, both the nonfinancial and financial effects of an increase in the federal deficit are examined in a model developed by B. Friedman (1981, 1982). The model consists of B. Friedman's (1977, 1979) structural model of the corporate bond market, the structural model of the Treasury securities market discussed in preceding sections, and the MPS model. The principal differences between this model (hereafter MPS-CGB) and the MPS model are that yields are determined in an explicit supply-demand market clearing framework, and that the government budget constraint is explicitly imposed.

Deficits are increased in the simulation experiments by adding $10 billion to government expenditures in each quarter.[16] The money stock is held at its control simulation path, thereby allowing virtually all of the rise in the deficit to be reflected in net sales of federal debt to the public. In implementing the simulation experiments, the Treasury bill yield is determined in the money market as in the unaltered MPS model, and the quantity of Treasury bills (US1) is then proximately determined in the short-term Treasury securities market. The remainder of the deficit that must be financed is allocated to the other three maturities of Treasury securities according to their historical proportions to total privately held federal debt.

The results of two dynamic simulations are reported in table 3–5. As before, the simulations begin in 1966:Q1 and 1971:Q1. The experiments consist of increasing real government expenditures by $10 billion in each of four quarters. In terms of interest rates, the pattern is similar to that found in the partial equilibrium financial model, although the long-intermediate-term yield appears to be somewhat unstable. Nevertheless, all yields initially rise above control simulation levels in response to the increase in debt-financed government expenditures, while the longer run effects on the long-term yields are ambiguous.[17] The impact on the supply of outstanding corporate bonds is on average smaller than before, reflecting a larger amount of total corporate external financing resulting from the cumulative rise in investment spending.

The effect of this debt-financed fiscal policy action on economic activity is much smaller in the MPS-CGB model than would be expected in the unaltered MPS model. In the MPS-CGB model, real GNP rises by slightly more than the increase in government expenditures in the initial quarter, but by the end of four quarters real spending equals about one third of the rise. Real business fixed investment exhibits a small initial rise due to accelerator effects, but in the 1966:Q4 experiment, some real investment is crowded out after four quarters. Moreover, the nominal federal deficit rises over the four quarters, and since prices remain virtually unchanged from their control simulation levels, the rise mainly reflects gains in real deficits.

As a whole, the results suggest that while a debt-financed increase in government spending provides stimulus over four quarters, the multiplier is less than one after a year. Moreover, the results suggest that capital formation could be adversely affected, although it rises on average in the simulations. One source of these rather pessimistic results is the deficit-financing scheme adopted in the experiments. In particular, as a consequence of the bill yield being determined in the money market, the supply of bills held by the public actually falls by over $1 billion after four quarters in each of the simulations.[18] Thus, the rise in the deficit in addition to this $1 billion must be financed by issuing longer term debt instruments. In particular,

Table 3–5. Simulation Results in the MPS-CGB Model

Yields	Increase in G of $10b in 1966:Q1[a]			Increase in G of $10b in 1971:Q1[a]		
	1966:Q1	1966:Q4	Average	1971:Q1	1971:Q4	Average
r_T	.36%	.46%	.43%	.21%	.25%	.28%
r_2	.59	.37	.89	.79	.46	.75
r_3	1.83	1.44	3.62	1.23	1.74	1.81
r_4	.77	−.08	1.31	.54	.78	.84
r_C	.48	−.02	.79	.36	.56	.60
r_E	.03	.28	.27	.03	.27	.18
Bond Supply						
CB	−$320m	$111m	−$67m	−$373m	−$276m	−$379m
Real Expenditures						
G	$10b	$10b	$10b	$10b	$10b	$10b
Y	12.6	3.8	6.5	10.7	2.7	6.9
IPE	0.6	−0.4	0.4	0.4	0.3	0.6
Deficit						
DEF	5.3	8.2	7.4	6.4	8.8	7.5

Notes: For variable definitions, see table 3–3.
G   = real federal government purchases ($1972 billion)
Y   = real gross national product ($1972 billion)
IPE   = real investment in plant and equipment ($1972 billion)
DEF = federal government deficit ($billion)
Average = average change over the first four quarters after the experiment is initiated (1966:Q1 or 1971:Q1)
[a]Differences from control simulation values.

slightly less than one half of the cumulative rise in the deficit is financed with long-intermediate and long-term Treasury securities. On the basis of debt-managements experiments using this model (B. Friedman, 1981), a greater emphasis on short-term debt financing would lead to a more expansionary fiscal policy impact on both total spending and capital formation.

Summary of Conclusions

Asset substitutability played an explicit role in determining the effects of federal deficits on interest rates and economic activity in this paper. The role of asset substitutability was made explicit by considering the impact of deficits in a disaggregated structural model of the US Treasury securities, corporate bond, and equity markets. In this model, the relationships among yields depend on the substitutability of assets in the portfolios of different categories of investors. As indicated in the sample illustrative model considered at the outset of this paper, the presence of imperfect asset substitutability implies that the possible impact of an increase in the federal deficit may range from crowding out to crowding in.

In simulations which examined both portfolio and total crowding out, the results suggest that the manner in which the deficit is financed affects interest rates. When the increased deficit is financed with short-term Treasury securities, the partial equilibrium experiments indicated that corporate bond and equity yields change only slightly. In contrast, when long-term debt-financing is employed, both yields rise, particularly the corporate bond yield. Simulations in a general equilibrium setting tended to coincide with these results, as an increase in government expenditures financed by new issues of Treasury securities exclusive of Treasury bills was found to be offset significantly, but not completely, by a reduction in private expenditures.

Notes

1.   The source of these data are Board of Governors of the Federal Reserve System (1975) and subsequent issues. For purposes of this introductory section, total marketable US Treasury securities are disaggregated into Federal Reserve and non-Federal Reserve holdings.

2.   For a reduction in taxes, private spending remains at its initial level implying an unchanged level of total spending in both of the cases considered below.

3.   This theory also hinges on operative intergenerational transfers in which the size of bequests varies with the presumed tax liability of future generations. For evidence on the importance of intergenerational transfers as a determinant of private saving, see Kotlikoff and Summers (1981). For arguments and evidence against the Ricardian equivalence view, see Feldstein (1982).

4.   For other dynamic long-run analyses of the two-asset model, see, for example, Burmeister and Phelps (1971), Infante and Stein (1976), Tobin and Buiter (1976), and Turnovsky (1978).

5.   In this model it is assumed that investors regard federal debt as wealth, that resources are not fully employed, and that the price level is constant.

6.   A system of asset demands similar to the set of equations (3.1) may be derived from expected utility maximization. In the expected utility maximization models presented by Blanchard and Plantes (1977) and Roley (1979), positive covariances between asset yields are a necessary but not a sufficient condition for gross substitutability. Moreover, Roley (1983) has shown that symmetry in the yield coefficient matrix implies constant absolute risk aversion, and

hence is not a general property of asset demands. Symmetry is not, therefore, imposed in the asset demands equations 3.1).

7.   For previous studies which examine the consequences of asset substitutability in the three-asset model, see, for example, Tobin (1961, 1963), Brunner and Meltzer (1972), B. Friedman (1978), Cohen and McMenamin (1978), and Walsh (1983). In contrast to the other studies listed above and to the illustrative model discussed here, Cohen and McMenamin (1978) consider the dynamic and long-run consequences of asset substitutability in determining the effect of deficits. Also, Walsh (1983) is unique in considering the impact of deficits in models based on explicit utility maximizing behavior and rational expectations.

8.   Households are also assumed to regard the net worth of banks (NW) as exogenous and to allocate $W-NW$ among money, federal debt, and corporate bonds. Thus, $W-NW$ replaces W in equations 3.1, where $W = M^d + T^d + B^d + NW = H + T + K$.

9.   For a more complete description of this model, see Roley (1980).

10.   For a discussion of alternative models of interest rate determination, see Friedman and Roley (1980). For a comparison of a version of this disaggregated structural model to the "efficient markets" model as advanced, for example, by Pesando (1978) and Mishkin (1978), see Roley (1981).

11.   The portfolio adjustment models specified by Brainard and Tobin (1968), Modigliani (1972), Bosworth and Duesenberry (1973), and B. Friedman (1977) exhibit some, but not all, of these properties.

12.   In a test of rational, unitary, and autoregressive models of expectations in the context of a disaggregated structural model of the corporate bond market, the autoregressive model used here to represent expected capital gains on equities dominates the other expectations models. See Friedman and Roley (1979a).

13.   This corporate bond supply equation was re-estimated through 1975:Q4. The estimated coefficients remained basically unchanged from those reported by B. Friedman (1979).

14.   To conform with the simulation experiments in the next section, the aggregated debt variable—as opposed to the stocks of the individual maturity classes of Treasury securities—is used to evaluate the impact of deficit shocks. These deficit data should correspond to those used by Barro (1980). However, in calculating deficit shocks, Barro does not use an ARIMA model.

15.   This model was estimated using Chase Econometrics' automated Box-Jenkins program. The Q(26) statistic is distributed as $\chi^2(24)$, and is not significantly different from zero at the five percent significance level, indicating that the null hypothesis of white noise residuals cannot be rejected.

16.   While this procedure departs from the innovation technique implemented in the previous section, the numerical values are not drastically different. In particular, an ARIMA model was estimated for the five exogenous categories of government expenditures in the MPS-CGB model, and the combined standard error was about $6 billion. Over the next three quarters, a one standard error shock yielded values of $7.5, $7.3, and $8.1 billion. In the current version of the program used to simulate the MPS-CGB model, only constant changes in government expenditures may be used.

17.   In a reduced-form model, Makin (1982) estimates the impact of deficit shocks to be less than one third of the magnitude reported here for the Treasury bill yield. In representing deficit shocks, Makin employs a demand shock involving exports instead of the government expenditures variable used in table 3–5.

18.   In the simulations, the increase in the demand for Treasury bills resulting from the rise in the Treasury bill yield is more than offset as a result of rises in other yields, particularly r_2 and r_3.

References

Bailey, M. J. *National Income and the Price Level.* New York: McGraw Hill, 1971.

Barro, R. J. "Are Government Bonds Net Wealth?" *Journal of Political Economy* (November/December 1974), 1095–1117.

Barro, R. J. "Federal Deficit Policy and the Effects of Public Debt Shocks." *Journal of Money, Credit, and Banking* (November 1980), 747–62.

Blanchrad, O. J. and M. K. Plantes. "A Note on Gross Substitutability of Financial Assets." *Econometrica* (April 1977), 769–71.

Blinder, A. S., and R. M. Solow. "Does Fiscal Policy Matter?" *Journal of Public Economics* (November 1973), 319–37.

Board of Governors of the Federal Reserve System. *Flow of Funds Accounts 1946–1975.* Washington: 1975.

Bosworth, B. and J. S. Duesenberry. "A Flow of Funds Model and Its Implications." In *Issues in Federal Debt Management.* Boston: Federal Reserve Bank of Boston, 1973.

Box, G. and G. M. Jenkins. *Time Series Analysis: Forecasting and Control.* San Francisco: Holden Day, 1970.

Brainard, W. C. and J. Tobin. "Pitfalls in Financial Model-Building." *American Economic Review* (May 1968), 99–122.

Brundy, J. M. and D. W. Jorgenson. "Efficient Estimation of Simultaneous Equations by Instrumental Variables." *Review of Economics and Statistics* (August 1971), 207–24.

Brunner, K. and A. H. Meltzer. "Money, Debt, and Economic Activity." *Journal of Political Economy* (September/October 1972), 951–77.

Burmeister, E. and E. S. Phelps. "Money, Public Debt, Inflation and Real Interest." *Journal of Money, Credit, and Banking* (May 1971), 151–82.

Christ, C. F. "A Simple Macroeconomic Model With a Government Budget Constraint." *Journal of Political Economy* (January/February 1968), 53–67.

Cohen, D. and J. S. McMenamin. "The Role of Fiscal Policy in a Financially Disaggregated Macroeconomic Model." *Journal of Money, Credit, and Banking* (August 1978), 322–36.

Feldstein, M. "Government Deficits and Aggregate Demand." *Journal of Monetary Economics* (January 1982), 1–20.

Friedman, B. M. "Financial Flow Variables and the Short-Run Determination of Long-Term Interest Rates." *Journal of Political Economy* (August 1977), 661–89.

Friedman, B. M. "Crowding Out or Crowding In? Economic Consequences of Financing Government Deficits." *Brookings Papers on Economic Activity* (No. 3 1978), 593–641.

Friedman, B. M. "Substitution and Expectation Effects on Long-Term Borrowing Behavior and Long-Term Interest Rates." *Journal of Money, Credit, and Banking* (May 1979), 131–50.

Friedman, B. M. "The Effect of Shifting Wealth Ownership on the Term Structure of Interest Rates: The Case of Pensions." *Quarterly Journal of Economics* (May 1980), 567–90.

Friedman, B. M. "Debt Management Policy, Interest Rates, and Economic Activity." National Bureau of Economic Research, Working Paper No. 830, 1981.

Friedman, B. M. "Interest Rate Implications for Fiscal and Monetary Policies: A Postscript on the Government Budget Constraint." *Journal of Money, Credit, and Banking* (August 1982), 407–12.

Friedman, B. M. and V. V. Roley. "Investors' Portfolio Behavior Under Alternative Models of Long-Term Interest Rate Expectations: Unitary, Rational, or Autoregressive." *Econometrica* (November 1979a), 1475–97.

Friedman, B.M. "A Note on the Derivation of Linear Homogenous Asset Demand Functions." National Bureau of Economic Research, Working Paper No. 345, 1979b.

Friedman, B.M. "Models of Long-Term Interest Rate Determination." *Journal of Portfolio Management* (Spring 1980), 34–45.

Friedman, M. "A Theoretical Framework for Monetary Analysis." *Journal of Political Economy* (March/April 1970), 193–238.

Hansen, B. "On the Effects of Fiscal and Monetary Policy: A Taxonomic Discussion." *American Economic Review* (September 1973), 546–71.

Infante, E. F. and J. L. Stein. "Does Fiscal Policy Matter?" *Journal of Monetary Economics* (November 1976), 473–500.

Kochin, L.A. "Are Future Taxes Anticipated by Consumers?" *Journal of Money, Credit, and Banking* (August 1974), 385–94.

Kotlikoff, L. J. and L. H. Summers. "The Role of Intergenerational Transfers in Aggregate Capital Accumulation." *Journal of Political Economy* (August 1981), 706–32.

Makin, J. H. "Real Interest, Money Surprises, Anticipated Inflation and Fiscal Deficits." University of Washington; Mimeo, 1982.

Meyer, L. H. "The Balance Sheet Identity, the Government Financing Constraint, and the Crowding-Out Effect." *Journal of Monetary Economics* (January 1975), 65–78.

Meyer, L. H. and W. R. Hart. "On the Effects of Fiscal and Monetary Policy: Completing the Taxonomy." *American Economic Review* (September 1975), 762–67.

Mishkin, F. S. "Efficient Markets Theory: Implications for Monetary Policy." *Brookings Papers on Economic Activity* (No. 3 1978), 707–52.

Mishkin, F. S. "Simulation Methodology in Macroeconomics: An Innovation Technique." *Journal of Political Economy* (August 1979), 816–36.

Modigliani, F. "The Dynamics of Portfolio Adjustment and the Flow of Savings Through Financial Intermediaries." In *Savings Deposits, Mortgages and Housing.* E. Gramlich and D. Jaffe, (Eds.) Lexington: D.C. Heath & Company, 1972.

Pesando, J. E. "On the Efficiency of the Bond Market: Some Canadian Evidence." *Journal of Political Economy* (December 1978), 1057–76.

Roley, V. V. "A Theory of Federal Debt Management." *American Economic Review* (December 1979), 915–26.

Roley, V. V. "A Disaggregated Structural Model of the Treasury Securities, Corporate Bond, and Equity Markets: Estimation and Simulation Results." National Bureau of Economic Research, Technical Paper No. 7, 1980.

Roley, V. V. "The Determinants of the Treasury Security Yield Curve." *Journal of Finance* (December 1981), 1103–26.

Roley, V. V. "The Effect of Federal Debt Management Policy on Corporate Bond and Equity Yields." *Quarterly Journal of Economics,* (November, 1982), 645–668.

Roley, V. V. "Symmetry Restrictions in a System of Financial Asset Demands: Theoretical and Empirical Results." *Review of Economics and Statistics,* forthcoming, 1983.

Silber, W. L. "Fiscal Policy in IS-LM Analysis: A Correction." *Journal of Money, Credit, and Banking* (November 1970), 461–72.

Sims, C. A. "Policy Analysis With Econometric Models." *Brookings Papers on Economic Activity* (No. 1 1982), 107–52.

Tobin, J. "Money, Capital, and Other Stores of Value." *American Economic Review* (May 1961), 26–37.

Tobin, J. "An Essay on the Principles of Debt Management." In *Fiscal and Debt Management Policies.* Commission on Money and Credit. Englewood Cliffs: Prentice-Hall, 1963.

Tobin, J. and W. Buiter. "Long-Run Effects of Fiscal and Monetary Policy on Aggregate Demand." In *Monetarism.* Ed. J. Stein. Amsterdam: North-Holland, 1976.

Turnovsky, S.J. "Macroeconomic Dynamics and Growth in a Monetary Economy: A Synthesis." *Journal of Money, Credit, and Banking* (February 1978), 1–26.

Walsh, C.E. "Asset Prices, Asset Stocks, and Rational Expectations." *Journal of Monetary Economics,* forthcoming, 1983.

DISCUSSION
FREDERIC S. MISHKIN

This paper uses a structural econometric model of the demand and supply for financial securities to analyze the impacts of federal deficits. Structural econometric models are rich in detail and are the most desirable models for analyzing policy questions if the structure is well specified. Unfortunately, the model that Roley uses for his simulation experiments has such severe deficiencies that it cannot be used to provide information on the policy questions he asks. It is important to emphasize that the sins in the model that Roley uses are not brand new. Indeed the most severe sins—that is, those that can be classified as mortal rather than venal—are ones that are frequently a standard feature of financial markets models in the macro-economics literature. Thus, Vance can at least take comfort that he is far from being alone in taking the brunt of my criticisms.

To focus my discussion, I will concentrate on Roley's asset demand equation 3.11, which is repeated below

$$\frac{A_{it}^*}{W_t} = a_{io} + \sum_j b_{ij}\, r_{jt}^e + \sum_k c_{ik}\, \sigma_{kt}, \qquad i = 1, \ldots, N \qquad (3.11)$$

where $A_{it}^* =$ desired asset holdings, $r_{jt}^e =$ expected asset yields, $\sigma_{kt} =$ variance

117

associated with those yields, and $W_t =$ total non-human wealth. Roley claims that the mean-variance model is consistent with the above linear homogeneous demand equation, but this claim is not quite correct. As Tobin's (1958) seminal work and the later treatments of mean-variance models in the finance literature indicate, in order for equation 3.11 to be valid the r_{jt}^e must be the expected holding period returns and not expected yields to maturity as appear in the econometric model Roley uses.

Clearly if expected capital gains on securities were always expected to be zero then the yield to maturity would equal the expected holding period return, but there is no reason to expect this to be the case. Indeed, casual empirical evidence obtained by looking at the correlation of actual quarterly holding period returns on long-term bonds with their yields to maturity indicates that the correlation of expected returns and yields not only might not be high in the postwar period, but it might even be negative.

One response to the criticism above is to say that a yield on a twenty year bond might belong in the asset demand equations because the decision period, and hence holding period, for the bond purchaser is twenty years long. The most serious objection to this view is that the decision period in financial markets is almost certainly much shorter, especially since this is a market with low transaction costs and homogeneous commodities. But even if the decision period were really twenty years long, then although a twenty year bond yield would belong in the asset demand equations, the yield on a three month Treasury bill would not. Instead, the expected twenty year return from rolling over the three month T-bill would be appropriate.

Why is this criticism of the econometric model used by Roley so important? The argument above demonstrates that the r_{jt}^e variables in the asset demand functions are seriously misspecified and the estimates of the b_{ij} coefficients will suffer severe errors-in-variables bias. This might explain an important empirical result in the econometric model in this paper: assets are not found to be very substitutable even though reduced-form work on preferred habitats, such as Modigliani and Sutch (1969), gives some indication that bonds of different maturity are close substitutes. My suspicion is that the errors-in-variable problem which usually leads to coefficients being biased towards zero causes the estimates of asset substitutability to be strongly underestimated.

What does the above criticism say about the validity of the main conclusion in Roley's paper? He finds that the way a government deficit is financed—that is whether by long-term rather than short-term government securities—is crucial to the macroeconomic effects of the deficit. In other words, an Operation Twist debt management operation where the mix of long-term versus short-term bonds is changed will be a valuable government policy tool. The criticism raised above indicates that this may be a misleading conclusion because of potential underestimation of the degree of asset substitutability. My own priors tend to side with Modigliani and Sutch (1969) who do not see a major impact from Operation Twist.

Before I go onto another topic, I want to point out that the crime of using yields to maturity rather than expected holding period returns is usually the norm rather than the exception. A prominent example where this occurs is empirical work on the demand for money. A common practice in this literature is to use long-term bond yields as explanatory variables for money demand. [See the survey in Laidler (1977) and the more recent literature on the term structure of interest rates and money demand, Heller and Khan (1979) and Friedman and Schwartz (1982)]. As discussed above, if the decision period is short, as is most sensible, then the expected return on the long bond belongs in the money demand function and not its yield to maturity. It should be pointed out that the above argument does not rule out using yields on short-term securities such as three month Treasury bills in money demand equations. For a short holding period, let's say three months, the expected return of a three month Treasury bill equals the actual return and is just equal to the three month Treasury bill yield. Thus in this case, the bill yield is a valid description of the expected holding period return. This reasoning suggests that money demand functions which only include short-term interest rates as explanatory variables are on much firmer theoretical ground than specifications making use of long-term yields.

One final comment about the econometric modeling of the asset demand function in 3.11 is worth making. The r_{jt}^e are usually measured by estimating them as an unrestricted distributed lag on past r_{jt}. One problem with this procedure is that it allows the researcher to conduct a specification search on the distributed lag that will yield results which confirm his or her prior. This is obviously a dangerous situation, as Leamer (1978) has pointed out. One attractive aspect of the rational expectations, or equivalently market efficiency, hypothesis is that it provides structure on what form distributed lags in expectations equations should take. Furthermore, it is well supported as a first approximation in financial markets. The advantage of using rational expectations to impose more structure on our models of financial market behavior is that it will restrict specification searches and so give us more confidence in a researcher's results, and it will lead to restrictions that will increase the statistical power of the empirical analysis. An important direction for future research is to attempt the structural modeling of financial market behavior using the rational expectations hypothesis as a basic building block. This would help us get better answers to the interesting questions that Roley addresses in his paper.

References

Friedman, M. and A. Schwartz. "The Effect of the Term Structure of Interest Rates on the Demand for Money in the United States." *Journal of Political Economy* 90 (February 1982), 201–212.

Heller, H. R. and M. S. Khan. "The Demand for Money and the Term Structure of Interest Rates." *Journal of Political Economy* 87 (February 1979), 109–29.

Laidler, D. *The Demand for Money: Theories and Evidence.* New York: Dun–Donnelley, 1977.

Leamer, E. *Specification Searches: Ad Hoc Inference With Nonexperimental Data.* New York: John Wiley and Sons, 1978.

Modigliani, F. and R. Sutch. "Debt Management and the Term Structure of Interest Rates: An Empirical Analysis of Recent Experience." *Journal of Political Economy,* Supplement (August 1967).

Tobin, J. "Liquidity Preference as Behavior Towards Risk." *Review of Economic Studies* 25 (February 1958), 65–86.

4 INVESTMENT VERSUS SAVINGS INCENTIVES: THE SIZE OF THE BANG FOR THE BUCK AND THE POTENTIAL FOR SELF-FINANCING BUSINESS TAX CUTS

Alan J. Auerbach
and Laurence J. Kotlikoff

Introduction

In closed economies, saving and investment represent, respectively, the supply of and demand for new domestic capital. Saving incentives shift the supply curve for new domestic capital, while investment incentives shift the demand curve. The basic public finance equivalence theorem—the real effects of a tax (subsidy) are independent of who nominally pays the tax (receives the subsidy)—applies equally well to the market for new capital.

We are grateful to the National Bureau of Economic Research and the National Science Foundation for financial support. Andrew Myers provided excellent research assistance. The views expressed are solely those of the authors.

121

Hence, in closed economies, saving and investment incentives do not represent conceptually distinct policies, and the real effects of taxes or subsidies applied to the supply of new capital, saving, can be replicated by taxes or subsidies applied to the demand for new capital, investment.

While economically meaningful distinctions between saving and investment incentives do not arise, there are meaningful distinctions between policies that affect savings, the sum of past and current saving, and those that directly affect only current saving, or, in equilibrium, current investment.

This chapter examines the closed economy effects of government policies that vary with respect to whether they treat newly produced capital differently from old capital. Policies that distinguish new capital from old are denoted investment policies, while those that do not are labelled savings policies. While both types of policies alter marginal incentives to accumulate new capital, investment incentives can generate significant inframarginal redistribution from current holders of wealth to those with small or zero claims on the existing stock of capital. In the context of a neoclassical growth model, this redistribution runs, in large part, from the elderly to young and future generations. The direction of this intergenerational transfer is opposite to that associated with the "burden of government debt;" in the case of debt, the government passes the tax bill for current expenditures on to future generations.

Intergenerational transfers can have important effects on national saving and capital formation in the life cycle model that posits zero or limited intergenerational altruism. The process by which these transfers affect capital formation is often referred to as the crowding out of investment. A natural question to pose in a life cycle model is whether the crowding in of new capital formation arising from investment incentives exceeds the crowding out produced by deficits potentially associated with these incentives. This question has particular relevance to present economic affairs since current and projected US deficits reflect, in large part, business tax cuts.

In addition to analyzing the net impact on capital formation of deficit-financed business tax cuts, this chapter considers the potential for self-financing business tax cuts. A self-financing business tax cut is defined here as a deficit-financed investment incentive that produces an increase in the economy's long-run tax base sufficient to permit the government to reach long-run budget balance without ever raising tax rates.

A third issue of considerable relevance to current economic policy is whether gradual increases in investment incentives delay investment until the incentives have been fully phased in. The 1981 Economic Recovery Tax Act (ERTA) provided for even greater investment incentives after 1984 than between 1981 and 1984. The 1982 Economic Report of the President indicated a potential decline in the effective tax rate on equity financed new investment in general industrial equipment from 21 percent in 1982 to negative 54 percent in 1986. In part, these figures reflect steadily declining projected inflation rates interacting with historic cost depreciation provisions. In addition, ERTA authorized more favorable depreciation schedules starting in 1985. While the 1982 tax act reduced future increases in the acceleration of depreciation, the 1981 act may, in part, be responsible for the historically low investment rate in 1982.

The principal findings of this paper with respect to these three issues are:

(1) Investment incentives, even those financed by short-run increases in the stock of debt, significantly increase capital formation in life cycle economies.

(2) Deficit-financed savings incentives, in contrast, typically reduce the economy's rate of capital formation in the long run.

(3) Deficit-financed investment incentives can be self-financing for particular, but not unreasonable, parameterizations of neoclassical life-cycle growth models.

(4) Gradual phasing in of investment incentives can actually reduce rather than stimulate short-term investment.

(5) The underlying explanation for the relative efficacy of investment as opposed to savings incentives in stimulating capital formation in life cycle models is that investment incentives redistribute from the old to the young. Since the old in life cycle models have higher marginal propensities to consume out of lifetime resources than the young, this transfer reduces current consumption, permitting the crowding in of current investment.

The analysis of investment incentives is based on the Auerbach-Kotlikoff (1983) life cycle computer simulation model. The model describes the perfect foresight growth path of life cycle economies in response to a wide variety of fiscal policies. For purposes of this study the model has been expanded to include full or partial expensing of new capital as a policy option. Expensing is only one of several types of currently legislated investment incentives; its use is limited to a small subset of total US investment. However, expensing is a convenient devise for analyzing a variety of other investment incentives including the investment tax credit (ITC) and the acceleration of depreciation; rates of fractional expensing can be chosen that produce effective tax rates on new investment equal to those arising from these other policies. In addition, if deficit policy is chosen appropriately, expensing policies can produce a time path of cash flows to the government similar to those that would arise from changes in the ITC or depreciation schedules.

The second substantitive addition to the model is the inclusion of cost of quickly adjusting the economy's capital stock. As described by many authors (including Abel, 1979; Hayashi, 1981; and Summers, 1981), such increasing marginal costs of investment generate inframarginal rents to existing capital. As a consequence, the market valuation of the economy's existing capital stock can differ from its replacement cost. The assumption of quadratic adjustment costs leads to a theory of investment in which the rate of investment is a linear function of Tobin's q (Tobin, 1969), the ratio of the stock market value of capital to its replacement cost. Tobin's q is also an important variable in determining household consumption and labor supply decisions. These decisions are based on the current and future wages and rates of return households foresee, but also on the household's initial wealth, including the market value of its claims to existing capital.

Since the elderly are the primary owners of capital in a life cycle model, consideration of adjustment costs, with their associated implications for changes in the wealth of the elderly, can be quite important in assessing the redistributive impact of numerous fiscal policies. One example is a switch from an income to an equal revenue consumption tax. Such a policy suggests a significant loss in welfare to the elderly, whose wealth holdings must now be spent, in part, to meet taxes on the purchase of consumption goods. With capital adjustment costs, however, there is a countervailing effect serving to increase the wealth and welfare of the elderly. The stimulus to capital formation associated with the consumption tax produces an immediate increase in stock market values, reflecting increased inframarginal rents to the existing capital stock. The higher initial stock market values obviously redound to the advantage of the elderly.

In addition to mitigating the intergenerational redistribution from the old to the young in the case of a switch to a consumption tax, the inclusion of adjustment costs in the model cushions the fall in stock market values associated with investment incentives that discriminate against old capital. Permitting expensing of new capital at higher rates than were previously allowed and restricting this expensing solely to new capital is an example of a policy injurious to the elderly, since it places existing capital at a financial disadvantage relative to new capital. But the welfare loss to the elderly is mitigated to the extent that the economy's desire for an ultimately greater level of capital per worker raises inframarginal rents on previously installed, i.e. existing, capital.

The next section of this paper ignores the issue of adjustment costs in order to clarify, in a simple framework, differences between investment and savings incentives. The discussion points out equivalence relationships between investment incentives and other fiscal policies. In particular, permitting 100 percent expensing of new capital in the presence of a capital income tax (levied either on individuals or on businesses, in the form of a profits tax) is equivalent to imposing a one time wealth tax at a rate equal to that of the capital income tax. If the economy also taxes labor income at this same rate, introducing 100 percent expensing taxes wages and initial wealth at the same rate. This tax structure, in turn, is equivalent to a proportional consumption tax.

With the exception of the investment tax credit, new US business investment incentives are available to old as well as new capital; the old capital must, however, be sold to qualify for the new incentives. The sale of old capital requires payment of recapture taxes calculated on the difference between the asset's new sale price and its adjusted basis. If the taxes incurred in turning over old assets exceed the present value gain in investment incentives from such a transaction, turnover will not be stimulated; in this case the economic outcome of new investment provisions that do not explicitly exclude old capital will be identical to that which would have occurred had the new incentives been restricted solely to new capital.

The third section considers the potential for turning over old capital under the 1981 Tax Act; for much of US capital produced prior to 1981 the costs of turnover exceed the benefits. For the remaining assets, however, turnover, in the absence of transaction costs, is profitable, but turnover taxes still recapture most of the gains from these transactions. Hence, with respect to recent tax legislation, the effective, if not the nominal, tax treatment of new and old capital is quite different, and the new law primarily provides investment as opposed to savings incentives.

The fourth describes the version of the Auerbach-Kotlikoff simulation model used to compare savings and investment incentives in both the presence and absence of capital adjustment costs. The following section presents simulations of these policies and examines the extent of short-run and long-run crowding out.

The sixth section considers three alternatives to the deficit-financing of investment incentives. One involves a delay in the introduction of expensing. A second involves actually increasing the tax on capital income in conjunction with full expensing, while a third involves a reduction in the extent to which expensing is permitted.

The first simulation shows that a time path of increasingly generous investment incentives can be associated with simultaneous declines in stock market values, quite low and, possibly, negative short-term interest rates and fairly large, positive long-term interest rates. Such a policy actually suppresses short-run investment. The second simulation demonstrates the somewhat paradoxical result that, given a structure of investment incentives, increases in capital income tax rates (e.g., corporate or dividend tax rates) will generally stimulate, rather than retard, capital formation, while requiring an immediate decline in wage taxes to avoid running surpluses. Finally, our third simulation shows that the government, through a policy of partial expensing, can raise investment and generate a surplus without ever raising either the capital income tax or the labor income tax.

The last section of the paper summarizes major findings and relates these results to recent economic events.

Investment Incentives—Structural Relationship to Other Fiscal Policies

A simple two period life cycle model of economic growth provides a convenient framework for examining the underlying nature of investment incentives. Consider such an economy with a tax $\tau_{w,t}$ on labor income, a tax $\tau_{r,t}$ on business profits, and an expensing rate for new capital of e_t. The subscript t denotes the period in which the three instruments are applied. To simplify the analysis further, assume individuals work only when young and that the depreciation rate, the rate of population growth, and the rate of technological change are zero.

Equations 4.1 and 4.2 characterize the economy's process of capital formation:

$$K_t = (W_{y,t-1} (1 - \tau_{w,t-1}) - C_{y,t-1}/q_{t-1} \tag{4.1}$$

$$C_{0,t} = q_{t-1} K_t (1 + r_t) \tag{4.2}$$

In equation 4.1, $W_{y,t-1} (1 - \tau_{w,t-1}) - C_{y,t-1}$ is the saving of the young in period $t - 1$, their after tax wages in period $t - 1$ less their consumption in period in $t - 1$. The net price of a unit of capital in period $t - 1$ is given by q_{t-1}. Dividing the financial saving of the young by q_{t-1} determines their purchase of physical capital. The physical capital acquired by the young at the end of period $t - 1$ equals the economy's capital stock at the beginning of period t, K_t; the old generation in period t (those young in $t - 1$) hold claims to all the economy's capital, since the young in period t have no beginning of period assets.

For the old in period t, consumption, $C_{0,t}$, equals the return of principal, $q_{t-1}K_t$, plus the after tax return on the investment, $q_{t-1} K_t r_t$. The after tax return, r_t, includes capital gains and losses:

$$r_t = \frac{F_{K,t}\,(1 - \tau_{r,t}) + q_t - q_{t-1}}{q_{t-1}} \tag{4.3}$$

In equation 4.3 $F_{K,t}\,(1 - \tau_{r,t})$ equals marginal after tax profits per unit of capital. In combination, (4.2) and (4.3) imply:

$$C_{0,t} = q_t K_t + K_t\,F_{K,t}\,(1 - \tau_{r,t}) \tag{4.4}$$

This new expression is also intuitive: the consumption of the old in period t (the young of period $t - 1$) equals after tax business profits plus the value of the sale of their capital at the prevailing asset price q_t.

Equation 4.5 expresses q_t, the net price of purchasing a unit of capital, in terms of $\tau_{r,t}\,e_t$:

$$q_t = 1 - \tau_{r,t}\,e_t \tag{4.5}$$

For new capital the net acquisition cost is 1, the price of new capital, less the tax rebate from expensing, $\tau_{r,t}\,e_t$. Equation 4.5 also determines the price of old capital. Since old capital and new capital are perfect substitutes in production, their net acquisition costs must be identical in equilibrium; hence, old capital sells for $\tau_{r,t}\,e_t$ less than new capital because the purchaser of new capital receives $\tau_{r,t}\,e_t$ from the government, while the purchaser of old capital receives no tax rebate. Since the value of old capital depends on the product of $\tau_{r,t}\,e_t$, the price of old capital falls not only when expensing is increased (and $\tau_{r,t}$ is positive), but also when the rate of business profits taxation rises, given an expensing policy.

Equations 4.1, 4.4, and 4.5 may now be combined to indicate the lifetime budget constraint of the young in period $t - 1$,

$$C_{y,t-1} + C_{0,t}\,\frac{(1 - \tau_{r,t-1}\,e_{t-1})}{(1 - \tau_{r,t}\,e_t) + F_{K,t}\,(1 - \tau_{r,t})} = W_{y,t-1}\,(1 - \tau_{w,t-1}) \tag{4.6}$$

and the old in period $t - 1$:

$$C_{0,t} = K_{t-1}\,(1 - \tau_{r,t-1}\,e_{t-1}) + K_{t-1}\,F_{K_{t-1}}\,(1 - \tau_{r,t-1}) \tag{4.7}$$

These equations suffice to describe the relationship of savings and investment incentives to other tax structures. First, consider the case of zero expensing $(e_{t-1} = e_t = 0)$. This assumption produces an economy with period t capital income and wage tax rates of $\tau_{r,t}$ and $\tau_{w,t}$ respectively. In such an economy, the return to new capital, capital produced in period $t - 1$ and old capital, capital produced prior to period $t - 1$, are taxed at the same effective rates in period t and beyond. With zero expensing, there is no discrimination in favor of newly produced capital; the relative price of new and old capital is always unity. Changes in the time path of $\tau_{r,t}$ and $\tau_{w,t}$ that satisfy the government's long-term budget constraint (see Auerbach and Kotlikoff, 1983) are classified, in our taxonomy, as savings incentives. The fifth section indicates that lowering capital income tax rates will typically depress rather than stimulate long-term capital formation if such savings incentives are deficit-financed.

The essential feature of investment incentives can be illustrated most simply by assuming zero wage taxation, permanent capital income taxation at rate τ_r, zero expensing prior to period $t - 1$, and a permanent move to 100 percent expensing starting at time $t - 1$. Under these assumptions, all tax terms drop out of equation 4.6; the young of period $t - 1$ and all future generations face zero effective taxation over their lifetimes. While the young and future generations nominally pay business profits taxes in their old age, the reduced cost of purchasing capital when they are young exactly offsets the present value cost of this taxation. Stated differently, new generations starting in year $t - 1$ are subsidized when young to purchase capital and taxed when old on its return. The subsidy and tax cancel in present value and the young face no net taxation on their capital investments.

While this new tax structure effectively exempts the young of period $t - 1$ and all future generations from paying any taxes over their lifetime, elderly individuals at time $t - 1$ suffer a capital loss on their assets equal to $K_{t-1}\, \tau_r$. According to equation 4.7, the consumption of the elderly falls by this amount; the $K_{t-1}\, \tau_r$ capital loss constitutes a one time wealth tax on the old of period $t - 1$. Considering the tax treatment of the young and old together, this new tax system is equivalent to the government's collecting K_{t-1} $(1 + F_{k_{t-1}})\, \tau_r$ in taxes from the old period in $t - 1$ and abolishing taxation thereafter.[1]

This example highlights the special feature of investment incentives, namely that they tax initial holdings of wealth. A second important feature is that they lower the effective tax on the return to saving of young and future generations. With 100 percent expensing the effective capital income tax rate is reduced to zero.

The presence of wage taxation alters the analysis somewhat. Let us now assume positive and permanently fixed values of τ_r and τ_w. In this case moving to full expensing leaves young individuals facing a lifetime wage tax, or equivalently a lifetime consumption tax, since equation 4.6 can now be rewritten as:

$$C_{y,t-1} (1 + \tau_C) + C_{0,t} \left(\frac{1 + \tau_C}{1 + F_{K,t}} \right) = w_y \qquad (4.6')$$

where

$$1 + \tau_C \equiv \frac{1}{1 - \tau_w}$$

The elderly in period $t - 1$ again face an additional wealth tax of $K_{t-1} \, \tau_r$ in addition to business profits taxes of $K_{t-1} \, F_{K_{t-1}} \, \tau_r$. If τ_r equals τ_w, the case of a proportional income tax, equation 4.7 becomes:

$$C_{0,t-1} (1 + \tau_C) = K_{t-1} (1 + F_{K_{t-1}}) \qquad (4.7')$$

Equations 4.6' and 4.7' demonstrate that the movement to full expensing in the presence of a proportional income tax produces a consumption tax, or equivalently, a wage tax plus a one time wealth tax on the elderly where the wage and one time wealth tax rates are identical. Other proposals, which are billed as "providing consumption tax treatment" of income flows, such as unlimited use of IRAs and abolition of the corporate income tax, produce wage tax rather than consumption tax structures. In the case of unlimited IRAs, the initial owners of capital can place all their holdings of capital into IRAs, receiving tax deductions that equal in present value the taxes on withdrawals of principal plus interest from the IRA. Thus the owners of existing capital face no effective taxation on the conversion of their capital into consumption expenditures; a policy of unlimited IRAs effectively eliminates the capital income tax component of the income tax with no effective wealth tax on existing assets. For those with no initial assets, wage taxation and consumption taxation are structurally equivalent. Hence, a policy of unlimited IRAs and a zero corporate income tax replicates a wage tax. It does not replicate a consumption tax.

Another complication of the foregoing analysis is that the actual US tax law permits existing assets to qualify for new tax incentives, if they are sold by the existing owner. For example, the 1981 Accelerated Cost Recovery System (ACRS) does not explicitly exclude old capital, though application of ACRS to old capital requires a change in the capital's ownership. It is important to distinguish here between direct capital ownership and indirect ownership through firms. One normally thinks of life cycle transfers of assets as being accomplished by the sale of shares in firms owning capital goods. This is not considered to be a change in the ownership of the capital goods themselves, which would require the sale of the actual goods by one firm to another. Thus, we may imagine that in selling off their assets the elderly can choose whether to transfer ownership of assets or ownership of firms, with the only resulting difference being whether sale of the capital goods themselves is recognized for tax purposes. We refer to the former case as turnover of assets.

If old capital is eligible for new investment incentives (expensing) subject to recapture taxation, the budget constraint facing the elderly is no longer equation 4.7, but rather:

$$C_{0,t-1} = K_{t-1}(1 - R_{t-1}) + K_{t-1} F_{K_{t-1}} (1 + T_{r,t-1}) \qquad (4.7'')$$

where R_{t-1} is the recapture tax per unit capital.

A comparison of equations 4.7 and 4.7″ implies that the sale of old capital to acquire eligibility for current investment incentives available to new capital will only occur if $\tau_{r,t-1} e_{t-1}$ exceeds R_{t-1}. If these two terms are equal, the elderly are indifferent between selling their capital as old capital, e.g., selling equity title to previously expensed capital, or selling the actual capital at its replacement cost of unity and paying recapture taxes.

If turnover is advantageous, equation 4.7″ indicates that recapture taxes are equivalent to lump sum taxes of equal size on the initial generation of elderly. For the young in period $t - 1$, the lifetime budget constraint is no longer equation 4.6 but:

$$C_{y,t-1} + \frac{C_{0,t} (1 - \tau_{t-1} e_{t-1})}{1 - R_t + F_K (1 - \tau_{r,t})} = W_y (1 - \tau_{w,t-1}) \qquad (4.6'')$$

For given values of F_K, $\tau_{r,t-1}$, $\tau_{r,t}$ and e_{t-1}, values of R_t that make turnover profitable imply a larger effective after tax return on the saving of the young. In the case of a zero recapture tax, expensing implies no additional taxation of the elderly, and an effective subsidy on capital income to the young.

Recapture Taxes and the Exclusion of Old Capital From the Accelerated Cost Recovery System

The extent to which recapture taxation inhibits turnover is an empirical question that depends on the size of changes in investment incentives. The set of new incentives considered here are those provided by the Accelerated Cost Recovery System. Though the business tax provisions have again been altered by the Tax Equity and Fiscal Responsibility Act of 1982, the more recent legislation represents a small change from previous law, and introduces no additional incentives to turn over old assets to obtain the tax treatment accorded new assets. This is because the 1982 Act maintains current depreciation allowances indefinitely.

The 1981 Act introduced a sharp increase in the present value of depreciation allowances for a new asset purchased under pre-1981 law, we increase in the expensing fraction restricted to newly produced capital, accelerated depreciation can lower the value of existing assets. While the new ACRS provisions are available to owners of old assets provided they sell (turn over) their old assets, the sale of these assets generates recapture taxes that may exceed the net increase in depreciation allowances. To the extent that such a sale is attractive, the fraction of the loss in value that the seller recoups represents a leakage to old capital of the investment incentive embodied in ACRS.

The recapture treatment of structures and equipment differs and they must be considered separately. For structures, the seller must pay a tax on the difference between the sale price and the depreciated basis, with the difference between sale price and hypothetical straight line basis taxed as a capital gain, and the additional difference between straight line basis and actual basis (positive if a more accelerated depreciation method has been used), taxed as ordinary income. Thus, the total tax due on an asset with a one dollar sale price is:

$$R = c(1 - B_{SL}) + \tau(B_{SL} - B) \qquad (4.8)$$

where c is the capital gains tax rate (equal to .28 for corporations) and τ is the income tax rate (.46 for corporations). The basis B and hypothetical straight line basis B_{SL} depend on the age of the asset, which determines the extent to which depreciation allowances have been taken, and the asset's initial purchase price. If a t year old asset physically depreciates at a constant exponential rate δ, and the inflation rate is π, then its initial purchase price was $e^{(\delta - \pi)t}$. Thus, letting b_{SL}^t and b^t be the straight line basis and actual basis for an asset aged t per initial cost, we have from equation 4.8

$$R_t = c(1 - b_{SL}^t \, e^{(\delta - \pi)t}) + \tau e^{(\delta - \pi)t} (b_{SL}^t - b^t) \qquad (4.9)$$

In return for this recapture tax, the potential seller receives one dollar times the number of units of capital (at replacement cost) for his asset rather than the value it would command with its old depreciation allowances. Since investors must be indifferent between old and new capital, the price of an asset not turned over must reflect the differences in depreciation allowances afforded new capital and those available to old capital.

$$q^t = 1 - \tau(Z_{ACRS} - Z_0^t\, e^{(\delta - \pi)t}) \qquad (4.10)$$

where Z_0^t is the present value of remaining depreciation allowances for an asset of age t initially purchased for a dollar and Z_{ACRS} is the present value of allowance per dollar of new capital under $ACRS$. Equation 4.10 corresponds to the earlier equation 4.5 derived for the case of expensing. Here, the expensing fraction e is replaced by the more general expression of the difference between the values of prospective depreciation allowances on new and old assets.

Using equations 4.9 and 4.10, we may now ask whether the turnover tax R_t exceeds the increase in sale price $(1 - q^t)$ that the seller can obtain by opting for recapture. In addition, letting Z_0 be the present value of depreciation allowances for a new asset purchased under pre-1981 law, we may calculate what fraction of the capital loss generated by ACRS is avoided when turnover is profitable. Since the price of an asset of age t would have been

$$q_0^t = 1 - \tau(Z_0 - Z_0^t\, e^{(\delta - \pi)t}) \qquad (4.11)$$

had there been no change in tax regime, the capital loss caused by ACRS for existing assets not turned over is

$$q_0^t - q^t = \tau(Z_{ACRS} - Z_0) \qquad (4.12)$$

per dollar of age t capital.

Our calculations require parameter values for δ and π, the depreciation and inflation rates, and prior depreciation provisions. For purposes of illustration, we set $\delta = .03$ and $\pi = .08$. We assume an after tax nominal discount rate of .10 and that prior tax depreciation followed the 150 percent declining balance formula with optimal straight line switchover, based on a tax lifeline of 35 years. These estimates of both actual and tax depreciation are meant to correspond roughly to a typical structures investment (see Jorgenson and Sullivan, 1982). We assume assets are purchased six months into the tax year and that tax payments are made annually, midway through the tax year as well. Post-1981 tax depreciation follows the 175 percent declining balance formula with optimal straight line switchover, based on a tax lifetime of 15 years, as dictated by ACRS.

Table 4–1 shows the results of calculations of q^t and R^t for structures purchased t years before the enactment of ACRS. The last column shows the fraction of the capital loss caused by ACRS (equal to 12.1 cents per dollar of capital) that could be recouped by turnover. Though turnover would not be useful for structures already completely written off, it appears advantageous for the bulk of structures. Because of growth and depreciation, a large fraction of the structure's capital stock is represented by assets purchased in recent years. For those assets, recoupment is substantial. For structures purchased within four years of the 1981 tax change, turnover allows a recoupment of over half the capital loss caused by ACRS. This figure is 85 percent for assets only one year old. Overall, if we assume a constant real rate of annual investment growth of three percent, this recoupment from turnover amounts to about one third of the capital loss on structures, given our parameterization. This result also suggests that, absent transaction costs,

Table 4–1.   The Incentive to Resell Assets (Structures)

Age (t)	Recapture Tax — R^t	Per Dollar of Age t Capital Value without Resale — q^t	Gain from Resale $(1 - q^t - R^t)$	Fraction of Capital Loss Recovered
1	.021	.876	.103	.85
2	.046	.864	.090	.74
3	.069	.853	.078	.64
4	.090	.843	.067	.55
5	.107	.834	.059	.49
6	.124	.825	.051	.42
7	.139	.818	.043	.36
8	.153	.811	.036	.30
9*	.164	.805	.031	.26
10*	.174	.800	.026	.21
.	.	.	.	
.	.	.	.	
.	.	.	.	
> 35	.280	.727	−.007	—

*Once an asset is 100 months old, the fraction of $(B_{SL}-B)$ subject to ordinary income taxation declines by one percent per month until it reaches zero at 200 months. This is accounted for in these calculations.

a large fraction of the structures capital stock ought to have been turned over upon the enactment of ACRS. However, such costs are clearly substantial for certain assets, such as factories and buildings, complementary to other productive factors in a company's production process. However, one would expect to see a greater turnover activity in commercial structures, such as apartment buildings and office buildings.

We turn next to the recapture treatment of equipment. Here, the analysis is complicated by the fact that most equipment qualifies for the investment tax credit, but only if the asset is new. The law greatly restricts the ability of an investor in used property to obtain the ITC. Moreover, the credit obtained by the original purchaser is also subject to recapture if the number of years the asset has been held is less than the minimum number of years required to qualify for such a credit. For example, equipment purchased before 1981 needed a tax lifetime of at least seven years to qualify for the full ten percent credit. Assets with lifetimes of between five and seven years received only a 6⅔ percent credit, and those with lifetimes between three and five years received a 3⅓ percent credit. If an asset with a lifetime exceeding seven years were sold after, say, six years, the seller would have to repay one third of the original credit received; if the sale were after four years, two thirds of the original credit would be repaid, and so on.

A second difference in recapture treatment of equipment is that the entire differential between sale price and basis is taxed as ordinary income, unless sale price exceeds initial purchase price, in which case the gain on purchase price is taxed as a capital gain. These two differences in the recapture treatment of equipment make turnover less attractive than in the case of structures.

As long as the sale price of the asset is less than original purchase price, the total recapture tax on one dollar of equipment aged t is

$$R_t = \tau(P - b^t\, e^{(\delta - \pi)t}) + (k - k^t)\, e^{(\delta - \pi)t} \qquad (4.13)$$

where b^t, δ, π and T are defined as before, k is the investment tax credit claimed originally, and k^t the credit that, *ex post,* the asset lifetime t would have dictated for the asset. P, less than unity, is the sale price. It accounts for the fact that, unlike a dollar of new capital, this asset will only receive the ACRS depreciation deductions and not the investment tax credit. Thus:[2]

$$P = 1 - (k + \tau Z_{ACRS} - \tau P\, Z_{ACRS}) \qquad (4.14)$$

or

Table 4-2. The Incentive to Resell Assets (Equipment)

Age (t)	Recapture Tax — R^t	Per Dollar of Age t Capital Value without Resale — q^t	Gain from Resale $(P - q^t - R^t)$
1	.054	.847	−.062
2	.135	.796	−.092
3	.167	.753	−.081
4	.215	.718	−.103
5	.220	.690	−.071
6	.255	.667	−.083
7	.246	.645	−.052
.	.	.	.
.	.	.	.
.	.	.	.
>10	.386	.521	−.068

$$P = \frac{1 - k - \tau Z_{ACRS}}{1 - \tau Z_{ACRS}}$$

If the asset is not sold, then the value of the t year old capital per dollar of replacement cost is:

$$q^t = 1 - (k + \tau Z_{ACRS} - \tau Z_0^t e^{(\delta - \pi)t}) \qquad (4.15)$$

which differs from the equation for structures 4.10 only in the inclusion of the investment tax credit.

The seller of an asset will gain from turning the asset over if $P - q^t$ exceeds R^t. However, for representative parameters for equipment, this will not occur. Table 4–2 shows the values of R^t and q^t for an asset that depreciates at a rate of .12 and under old law was written off over a tax lifetime of ten years using the double declining balance method with a switchover to straight line. The value of P is .839, and the inflation rate and discount rates are, as above, set at .08 and .10. As the results show, the prospective seller would always lose by turning assets over on resale. Thus, owners of equipment can escape none of the capital loss induced by the liberalization of depreciation allowances for new capital goods. This loss is described by equation 4.12 and equals 10.5 cents of capital (measured at replacement cost).

Thus no equipment, but a substantial fraction of structures, could gain by being brought under ACRS. In the case of structures, a large fraction of the capital loss induced by ACRS could be avoided in this way. However, the presence of transaction costs of unknown magnitude makes it difficult to know how much of this turnover would take place. We may place upper and lower bounds on the size of the capital loss induced by the introduction of ACRS. With no turnover, the loss equals approximately 10.5 cents per dollar of existing equipment and 12.1 cents per dollar of existing structures. With the maximum gain from turnover, about one third of the loss on structures is recouped. Using estimates of the equipment/structures break-down of 44.4 percent and 55.6 percent, respectively, obtained from data for 1975,[3] and with an estimate of 2.56 trillion dollars for the value in 1980 of the replacement cost of the business capital[4] stock, we obtain a range of 233 to 292 billion dollars as the effective wealth tax induced by the introduction of ACRS.

This result is only a rough calculation, and ignores the actual heterogeneity of the capital stock. Moreover, in the presence of adjustment costs (see below), the prices of all capital goods, including old ones, may rise with a surge in demand induced by an investment incentive such as ACRS. This would act to offset part of the capital loss induced by the more generous tax treatment of new capital versus old. However, the losses just calculated still are meaningful in that they represent the drop in value of existing capital relative to the value such capital would have had, had the additional tax benefits of ACRS applied to all capital.

The Simulation Model and Its Parameters

The Auerbach-Kotlikoff simulation model calculates the equilibrium growth path of an economy consisting of government, household, and production sectors. The life cycle version of the model used in this study incorporates expensing of new capital and costs of adjusting the level of the capital stock. In addition to expensing, the government's policy instruments include capital income, consumption, and wage taxes, the level of government consumption, and the choice of a deficit policy.

The household sector consists of fifty-five overlapping generations, with the total population growing at a constant rate. The fifty-five period life span corresponds roughly to the life span of an adult. In each generation there is a single, representative individual, and generations differ only with respect to their opportunity sets. The production sector is characterized by firms maximizing the present value of their profits by choosing both annual levels of labor input and annual rates of investment.

Each household chooses life cycle labor supply and consumption by maximizing an intertemporally separable CES utility function (Auerbach, Kotlikoff, and Skinner, 1983) with a constant static elasticity of substitution between consumption and leisure at a point in time and a constant intertemporal elasticity of substitution between consumption at different points in time, leisure at different points in time, and consumption and leisure at different points in time. The simulation presented below incorporates a one percent population growth rate, a static elasticity of substitution of .8, and an intertemporal elasticity of substitution of .25. These elasticities are suggested by recent empirical studies of saving and labor supply.[5]

The production function used here is Cobb-Douglas, with capital's income share equal to twenty-five percent. The costs associated with investment are quadratic as in the simulation model of Kotlikoff, Leamer, and Sachs (1981); that is, the marginal cost of a new dollar of capital, including installation costs, is:

$$\phi(I) = 1 + b \left(\frac{I}{K}\right) \tag{4.16}$$

where I is investment and K is existing capital. The term b is the adjustment cost coefficient. Larger values of b imply greater marginal costs of new capital goods for a given rate of investment.

The government choice of policy instruments is constrained by an intertemporal budget that holds over infinite time. This budget constraint requires that the present value of government capital income, wage, and consumption tax receipts be sufficient to pay for the present value of government consumption, the present value of expensing deductions, and the value of existing government net debt. The assumption that government debt (surplus) per capita cannot grow infinitely large is sufficient to generate this constraint on the time path of government policies.

The constraint implies that government policies are necessarily interdependent. A corollary is that certain deficit policies are not feasible. For example, the government cannot permanently change its expensing policy and permanently meet the consequent change in its receipts by simply altering its issue of debt. Such a policy would lead, over the long term, to either an infinite debt or an infinite surplus per capita. The probability that the change in the present value of tax receipts exactly equals the present value loss in revenues from changes in expensing is zero. Hence, to meet its budget constraints, the government must eventually raise or lower a tax instrument or its level of consumption in response to changes in its expensing policy. The next section indicates that, for certain expensing policies, the government need never raise any tax rate and, indeed, must lower tax rates at some point in the future to bring government finances into long-term balance. Investment incentives that require no increases in current or future tax rates or reductions in current or future government consumption are described here as self-financing.

Investment versus Savings Incentives— Illustrative Simulations

No single comparison of policies that do and do not discriminate against old capital can meaningfully summarize all differences in economic growth paths associated with investment versus savings incentives; the government's intertemporal budget constraint requires adjusting other government policies in response to these incentives in order to maintain a present value equality between its receipts and expenditures (including interest and principal repayments on debt). The differences in capital formation arising from the implementation of investment rather than savings incentives depends on the choice and timing of these other necessary policy adjustments.

Contrast, for example, two policies that begin with a proportional income tax, one introducing permanent, 100 percent expensing, and the other permanently removing the tax on capital income. The reduction or possible increase in revenues from either of these policies could be financed by immediate or future changes in the tax rate on labor income, current or future changes in government consumption, or some combination of changes in these and/or other available instruments. Given the range of possible concommitant adjustments in other policies, statements such as "investment incentives stimulate more capital formation than savings incentives" are meaningless. Comparisons of investment and savings incentives for explicitly specified policies of adjusting to the associated revenue changes do, however, permit meaningful conditional comparisons of investment and savings incentives.

The first simulation we present involves a permanent removal of capital income taxes, with debt policy used to maintain the wage tax rate at thirty percent for five years, and wage taxes adjusted thereafter to maintain a constant level of debt per capita. This simulation also assumes that there are no adjustment costs involved in changing the capital stock.

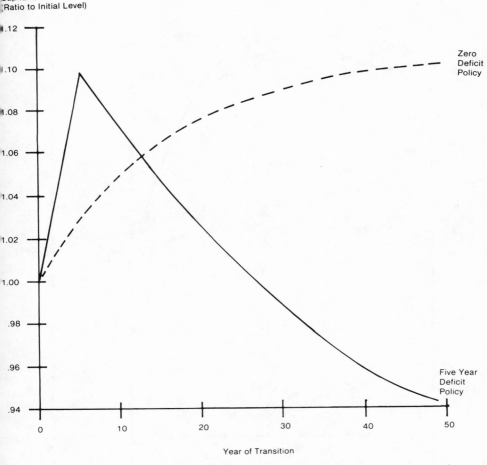

Figure 4–1   Capital Paths (Per Capita), Capital Income Tax Removal

The initial steady state is characterized by a capital output ratio of 3.04 and a gross interest rate of 8.22 percent. The specified policy leads to a 7.35 percent reduction in capital per capita, and a greater reduction in labor supply, with the resulting drop of 8.90 percent in output per capita. The wage tax rises to 47.8 percent in the long run. The path of per capita capital stocks over the transition period is shown by the solid line in figure 4–1.

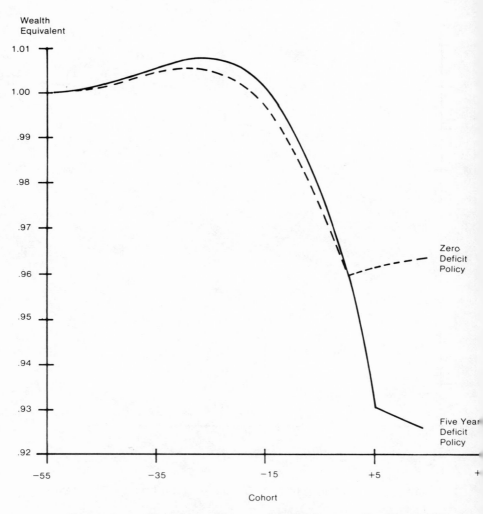

Figure 4-2   Wealth Equivalents, Capital Income Tax Removal

The solid line in figure 4-2 shows the welfare effects on transition cohorts of this deficit financed elimination of capital income taxation; the horizontal axis indexes the cohort's year of birth (relative to the first transition year, 1), and the vertical axis measures the amount by which the cohort's labor endowment vector would need to be increased (or decreased) under the old regime to allow the achievement of the same utility level as that attained under the new regime. The long-run welfare loss is 8.7 percent, but, in the short run, older generations gain relative to their *ex ante* prospects. This pattern of gains and losses is similar to that occurring under a policy (examined in Auerbach *et al.*, 1983) of switching immediately to wage taxation without running deficits, represented by the dotted line in figure 4–2. However, both the short-run gains and the long-run losses are larger when debt policy is used, because of the further shifting of tax liabilities onto future generations. The impact on capital formation is another difference associated with the use of deficits to finance savings incentives; the dotted line in Figure 4–1 shows the path of capital per capita arising from a balanced budget switch from income to wage taxation. Rather than falling, the capital stock rises in the long run.

The next policy we consider is a move to immediate expensing of all investment, with the income tax held at thirty percent for five years and deficits used to finance the loss in revenue. After five years, income taxes rise to maintain a constant level of debt per capita. The capital stock and welfare transitions are shown by the solid lines in figures 4–3 and 4–4, with corresponding paths under immediate balanced budget expensing (as discussed in Auerbach *et al.*, 1983), shown by the dotted lines. The effects of the implicit wealth tax on the original owners of capital is evident in both diagrams. The utility of older transition cohorts is decreased, and capital accumulation enhanced by the reduction in their consumption.

The five year delay in allowing tax rates to rise again leads to a lower long run capital stock, but to a much smaller degree. The reason for this is that the deficits created by the policy during its first five years are much smaller. The long-run level of debt to capital is just 2.13 percent, compared to 13.8 percent in the case of the first simulation. In fact, the long-run rate of income taxation is 28.9 percent—lower than the value that obtained before the creation of the debt.

Thus far in our simulations, we have ignored the possibility that the short-run supply curve for capital goods may slope upward. That is, attempts to increase quickly the amount of capital in response to an increased investment or savings incentive may result in a higher price of capital goods relative to consumption goods. If this is true, then our results may overstate the capital loss borne by holders of existing capital arising from an investment incentive such as expensing.

Setting the adjustment parameter b (see equation 4.16) equal to the empirically plausible value of five for the simulation of a transition to expensing with a five year deficit policy yields the following results. First, the drop in capital stock values by the full value of expensing is not immediate, because of the offsetting effect of the increasing supply price of new capital

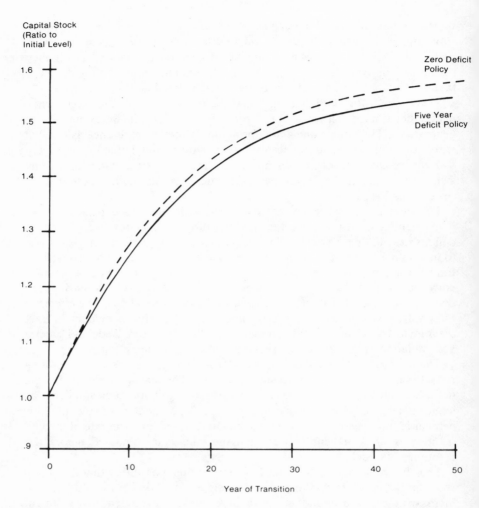

Figure 4–3   Capital Paths (Per Capita), Full Investment Expensing

goods. The price drops by 22.5 percent in the first year of the transition rather than thirty percent. Second, the welfare loss of older transition cohorts is smaller and the long-run gain also smaller (5.92 percent) than in the simulation without adjustment costs (6.29 percent). The welfare paths are compared in figure 4–5. Finally, the capital stock grows by a smaller amount, because not all of the demand induced by the investment incentives translates into increased output of capital.

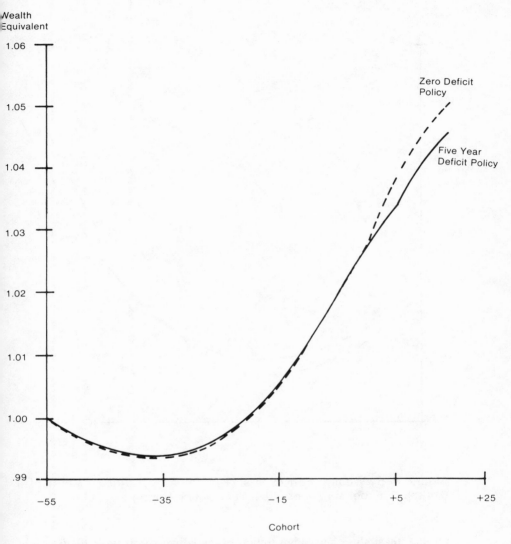

Figure 4–4   Wealth Equivalents, Full Investment Expensing

Dealing with Deficits

Various strategies have been offered to reduce short-run deficits associated with tax cut policies. In this section, we present three simulations that bear

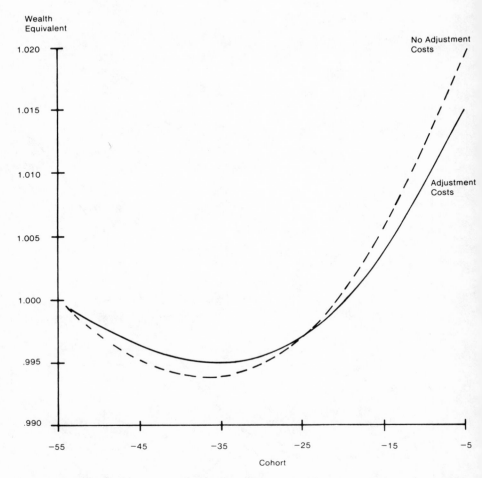

Figure 4–5 Wealth Equivalents. The Impact of Adjustment Costs (Switch to Expensing under Five Year Deficit Policy)

on the feasibility and advisability of avoiding short-run deficits while increasing the incentive to invest.

A typical solution to short-run revenue losses is a phase-in of investment incentives. This characterized the Economic Recovery Tax Act of 1981, which called for the acceleration of depreciation allowances to increase in 1981 and again in 1985 and 1986.[6] The problem with policies of this kind is that they induce capital losses gradually over the phase-in period. The awareness of potential investors of such future losses discourages investment in the short run, defeating the entire purpose of the legislation. This can be seen in the next simulation, which measures the effects of a five year phase-in of expensing without deficits, with the expensing fraction rising linearly from .2 in the first transition year to 1 in the fifth. Deficits are avoided by the adjustment of the income tax.

Though investment eventually expands under this policy, the short-run impact is to discourage investment. Figure 4–6 compares per capita capital stocks for the first twenty years of this policy with those arising from an immediate balanced budget switch to full expensing. The short-run disincentive to invest is also reflected by the drop in interest rates. The initial steady state interest rate is 8.22 percent. Under the investment phase-in policy, the gross interest rate (the yield that bonds would have to offer to provide the same after tax return as capital, inclusive of capital gains and losses) is negative until the phase-in is completed, and then jumps to over twelve percent. Thus, such a policy would sharply increase the slope of the yield curve.

A more successful way of avoiding deficits recognizes that investment incentives can often be achieved by raising rather than lowering capital income taxes. Recall that under a policy of full expensing that is effectively restricted to new capital the effective tax rate on capital income is zero. While the return on savings is not taxed at the margin, the increase in the statutory capital income tax rate increases the implicit wealth tax on existing capital. This reduces the consumption of wealth holders, permitting an expansion of national saving and investment. In addition, the extra revenue from the capital income tax allows the government to lower other taxes. Starting from an initial steady state with full expensing and a thirty percent income tax, raising the capital income tax rate to fifty percent allows an immediate drop in the wage tax rate to 26.5 percent (falling eventually to 21.6 percent) and an eventual increase in capital per person of 34.6 percent.

Finally, investment incentives may be self-financing in the long run, requiring no current or future increase in statutory tax rates to achieve a more capital intensive long-run steady state with no debt. As an example, from an initial steady state with no expensing consider a policy of moving directly to fifty percent fractional expensing, with the income tax held constant at thirty percent for twenty years; while there are short-run deficits, the expansion of the income tax base over time raises revenue sufficient to retire this debt. Indeed, in the twentieth year the debt-capital ratio is −.36 percent. This surplus permits a slight decrease in the income tax thereafter (to avoid an expanding surplus), to 29.2 percent in the twenty first year and 29.0

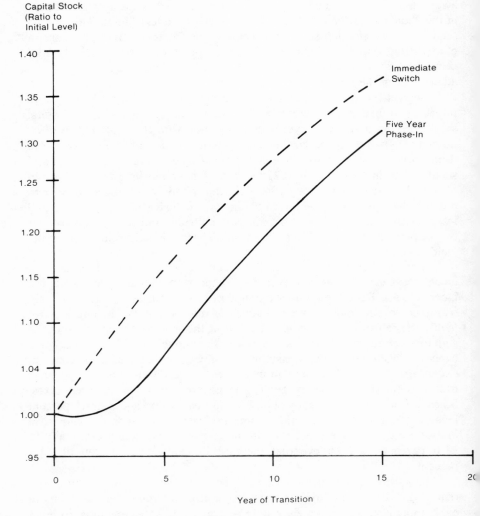

Figure 4-6   Capital Paths, Expensing Without Deficits

percent in the long run. The per capita capital stock increases by 25.9 percent in the long run.

Part of the explanation of this result is that, while taxes on capital income and, eventually, labor income decline, existing capital owners face increased implicit wealth taxation under this same policy. Their welfare declines, thus distinguishing this policy from those offered by the "free lunch" theorists. A second aspect of this policy is that the economy has shifted to a more efficient tax structure, substituting lump sum taxes on initial wealth holders for distortionary income taxes on current and future generations. These efficiency gains also provide economic resources to "cut taxes and raise revenues."

While this policy of fractional expensing eventually leads to surpluses and tax rate reductions, a policy of full expensing (discussed at the beginning of the previous section) does not have this feature, indicating the presence of nonlinearities in the functions determining the economy's behavior. One such nonlinearity is associated with the well known result that the excess burden of a tax rises at a rate proportional to the square of the tax rate itself. Thus, the initial reduction in the effective tax rate on saving induced by a policy of fifty percent expensing does proportionally more to reduce the distortion of savings behavior than does a policy of moving from fifty percent to full expensing.

Summary

The key difference between savings and investment incentives in closed economies is the applicability of these incentives to old as well as new capital. Investment incentives discriminate against old capital; savings incentives do not. This discrimination reduces the market value of old capital and, therefore, the economic resources of owners of the existing capital stock. The reductions in the resources and welfare of initial wealth holders under investment policies are essentially identical to those arising from a one time wealth tax.

In life cycle economies, the remaining resources of the elderly are held primarily in form of nonhuman as opposed to human wealth. The effective wealth tax generated by investment incentives falls, therefore, most heavily on the elderly. For a given time path of government consumption and given characteristics of tastes and technology, extra taxes on the currently elderly imply offsetting receipts of resources of young and future generations. In life cycle economies, the elderly have a greater marginal propensity to consume than the young because of their shorter life expectancies; future generations obviously have zero current marginal propensities to consume. Hence, the intergenerational redistribution of resources away from the elderly, arising from investment incentives, leads to a major reduction in the economy's current consumption. The reduction in the consumption of the elderly effectively finances the crowding in of investment.

For certain ranges of investment policy instruments, the long-term tax revenues arising from the increase in capital intensity are sufficient to finance the short-run loss in revenue from these incentives. Hence, there is a range of investment incentives that are self-financing. In general, deficits associated with investment incentives are less injurious to capital formation than those associated with savings incentives.

In contrast to investment incentives, savings incentives such as permanent reductions in the taxation of profits at the corporate level typically redistribute towards rather than away from the elderly. The impetus to current consumption arising from this redistribution—the income effect—is offset to some extent by the greater marginal incentive to save—the substitution effect of a higher after tax rate of return. The net impact of savings incentives on capital formation depends on the use of deficits to finance these incentives. As demonstrated here, deficit-financed reductions in capital income tax rates can sharply lower national capital formation.

The policy most conducive to capital accumulation involves simultaneously increasing investment incentives and capital income tax rates. Such a policy could eliminate deficits, raise the after tax return to marginal saving, and produce income and substitution effects that both operate in the direction of stimulating capital formation.

Notes

1.   For the government to maintain long-term budget balance, it needs to choose a path of government consumption that equals $K_{t-1} (1 + F_{K_{t-1}}) \tau_r$ in present value.

2.   After the effective date of the 1982 Act, this result would be altered by the application of a fifty percent basis adjustment for new credits taken.

3.   US Department of Commerce, Bureau of Economic Analysis, "Fixed Non-Residential Business and Residential Capital in the US, 1925–1975," PB 253 725, 1976.

4.   *Flow of Funds*, "Balance Sheets for the U.S. Economy, 1945–1980," Board of Governors of the Federal Reserve System, Washington, D.C., 1981.

5.   Auerbach, Kotlikoff and Skinner (1983) survey this literature.

6.   The 1985 and 1986 changes have been repealed by the Tax Equity and Fiscal Responsibility Act of 1982.

References

Abel, A. B. *Investment and the Value of Capital.* New York: Garland Publishing, 1979.

Auerbach, A. J. and L. J. Kotlikoff. "National Savings, Economic Welfare and the Structure of Taxation." In: *Behavioral Simulation Methods in Tax Policy*

Analysis M. Feldstein (Ed.). Chicago: University of Chicago Press, 1983 forthcoming.

Auerbach, A. J., L. J. Kotlikoff, and J. Skinner. "The Efficiency Gains from Dynamic Tax Reform." *International Economic Review* (February 1983, forthcoming).

Hayashi, F. "Tobin's Marginal and Average q: A Neoclassical Interpretation." *Econometrica* 50 (January 1982), 213–224.

Jorgenson, D. and M. Sullivan, "Inflation and Corporate Capital Recovery." In: *Depreciation, Inflation and the Taxation of Income from Capital* C. Hulton (Ed.). Washington: Urban Institute, 1981.

Kotlikoff, L. J. E. Leamer and J. Sachs. "The International Economics of Transitional Growth—the Case of the United States," NBER Working Paper No. 773 September 1981.

Summers, L. "Taxation and Corporate Investment: A q Theory Approach." *Brookings Papers on Economic Activity* II (1:1981), 67–127.

Tobin, J. "A General Equilibrium Approach to Monetary Theory." *Journal of Money Credit Banking* 1 (February 1969), 15–29.

DISCUSSION
FRANCO MODIGLIANI

It is a pleasure to comment on the Auerbach and Kotlikoff (AK) paper. I have found it fascinating, full of surprises and rich in paradoxes, though, admittedly, my enthusiasm may not be wholly unbiased. It turns out that their most unexpected and paradoxical results rely heavily on an unadulterated life cycle model, a model to which I am, understandably, attached and partial. In fact, their use of this model is even more extreme than some of my own applications in that they have "posited zero intergenerational altruism," or, in other words, they totally disregard the possibility and implications of an estate motive. I will come back to this issue. I am sure that the reader will hardly ever find a dull moment in their paper, although the presentation is frequently difficult and a bit too compact. I suspect that they have lived and become accustomed to those unusual results and paradoxes and thus overestimate the ability of the average reader to catch on.

I am happy to find that their paper largely confirms my long held conviction that common garden variety investment incentives, such as reductions in the taxation of profits and other property income, if financed by deficit, can be expected on balance to reduce rather than lift capital formation and the long-run stock of capital through its negative effect on net national saving. Their novel contribution consists in showing that different

151

types of incentives can produce widely different results and that there is in particular a class of incentives that may succeed in increasing saving and investment without requiring any significant increase in some taxes in order to finance them. These incentives belong to a type that they label investment incentives. They are characterized by the feature that, like the investment tax credit, they apply only to newly produced capital goods. What makes these incentives work differently is the simple fact that they can be expected to reduce the market value of all preexisting capital. This can be seen quite clearly in the most elementary case where the government offers, for example, a fifty percent subsidy on new investment. Since the impact effect of this is to double the rate of return on new investments, the rate at which returns from capital are capitalized must double, halving the value of any infinite lived assets and reducing the value of all other, depending on their remaining life.

Now suppose that, for some reason, the community wishes, in long-run equilibrium, to maintain a stable ratio of wealth at market value to income. Then, in response to the initial decline in the market value of its wealth, the community will increase its saving rate, and accumulate capital, until the market value of wealth goes back to the initial level. But this same market value will now represent a larger physical quantity. (More generally, the value of capital will rise back to the initial multiple of incomes which, presumably, will also have risen because of the additional real capital).

The additional accumulation of capital and consequent increase in productivity is clearly a desirable outcome. But it should be noted that it is achieved at the expense of those who owned the capital that lost value; they are made poorer and need to save to reconstruct the capital lost. In other words, as the authors point out, the investment incentive acts like a capital levy. The authors rightly refer to this rise in the capital stock as a crowding in effect since it is the mirror image of the crowding out effect that occurs when the government finances a deficit on current account by tapping the current flow of saving and reducing thereby capital formation and the future stock of capital. But just like crowding out is basically beneficial to the current generation at the expense of future generations that will have less capital, so, investment incentives and the resulting crowding in benefit future generations at the expense of the current one. As the authors well put it, this distinguishes "this policy from those offered by 'free lunch' theorists."

The effects of investment incentives just described should hold, in particular, under life cycle saving, since such a model has precisely the property that the wealth income ratio tends to a constant (which depends on the rate of growth of income). In addition, by relying on a life cycle model, one can make inferences as to who is likely to lose and how the additional savings comes about. As to the first question, the loss should fall prevailingly on the old, and notably on the retired, who finance their consumption from the past accumulation of capital; and the additional aggregate saving basically comes about because the old can command less consumption goods as they sell their unexpectedly less valuable assets to the young. On the other hand, the young have no reason to consume more. If anything, they might be more likely to consume less, if the higher return on capital produces a substitution effect larger than the income effect. The reduction of consumption or rise in saving which occurs while the older generation leaves the scene, produces a one time increase in the stock of real capital.

Given these characteristics, I am not sure I am prepared to share the authors' enthusiasm for their newly discovered gadget. At any rate, as a representative of those oldsters who presumably stand to lose most from investment incentives, I would like to suggest that one can make a strong case that a redistribution of wealth from the old to the young is the most cruel type of redistribution. The old, in contrast to the young, have no opportunity to recoup. Indeed, it is precisely on this ground that in a number of my writings I have suggested that unexpected inflation is particularly bad because, like investment incentives, it redistributes wealth to future generations at the expense of the old. And, there are, of course, other devices that would work in the same general way: e.g., a Henry George type of tax on pure rent.

In the light of these equity considerations, I would suggest that, if there is a clear case for a higher capital intensity—which the authors implicitly assume by considering a stationary economy with a positive rate of return—then it should be achieved at the expense of the young who will benefit from it, rather than at the expense of the old. Thus, I would favor a policy of reducing capital income tax financed by higher wage taxes, which is illustrated in figures 4–1 and 4–2 by the dotted lines. I hope I am not unfairly swayed by that rising section of the curve in figure 4–2 between ages -55 and -30.

Another valuable aspect of the paper consists in pointing out that the incentives can take many forms—an outright subsidy or capital contribution is only one, but there are others, like investment credit and expensing; it is the latter device that the authors consider explicitly. This specific incentive has, among other things, the nice feature of giving rise to what is clearly the prized paradox in their analysis: namely, under appropriate conditions, investment and the capital stock can be increased by raising rather than lowering the tax on capital income. The condition is the existence or introduction of a full or high rate of expensing, since the reduction in the value of existing capital is larger the larger the benefit of expensing, and that benefit in turn clearly rises with the tax rate.

In closing I would like to speculate briefly on the extent to which their results would be affected by allowing for a bequest motive. Clearly the answer must depend on the determinant of bequests. Presumably in a pure Barro-type world, the investment incentive would leave the consumption path entirely unchanged, and just permanently reduce the market value of wealth carried by the community (on the assumption of course that the old have enough wealth to enable them to maintain their consumption at the expense of bequests, or can count on the help of their living children—the potential gainers). I personally assign zero belief to Barro's hypothesis as a model of prevailing behavior, in part because I have shown that, at least for the US, the evidence is strikingly inconsistent with the prediction of that model (see Modigliani, "The Life Cycle Hypothesis of Saving, the Demand for Wealth and the Supply of Capital," *Social Research,* Vol. 33, 1966, 160–217, and some forthcoming updating). I assign, instead, high credence to a model in which the share of life wealth bequeathed by a given household is a rising function of its position in the distribution of life wealth. With some further assumptions about the stability in time of the distribution of life wealth, that model again implies a constant ratio of income to the market value of wealth. But this means that, by and large, AK's conclusions should continue to hold in the long run, though a difference could still arise from the fact that it would take longer to reach long-run equilibrium.

III THE POLITICAL SOURCES AND CONSEQUENCES OF DEFICITS

5 PUBLIC DEFICITS IN NORMATIVE ECONOMICS AND POSITIVE POLITICAL THEORY

Peter H. Aranson

The scholar who comes fresh to the study of macroeconomic theory, policy, and history, no less than the layman who undertakes the same task but at a popularized level, confronts a bewildering array of complicated relationships among several variables. Measures of employment and unemployment, public sector deficits, rates of inflation, gross national product, and the money supply appear very much like balls attached by springs, each to the other. Perturbing one will obviously perturb all of the others, but experts disagree over both the direction and magnitude of the resulting trajectories.

A closer inspection of the economic theories underlying various macroeconomic predictions reveals less a rigorously deductive framework and more a set of quasi-theories based on competing but sometimes weak behavioral assumptions. For example, concerning money illusion one finds an inherent conflict between the positive decision models underlying a rational expectations approach to money creation and a myopic Keynesian approach. The same kind of conflict prevails between the rational expectations view and so-called "supply-side" economics. Supply side views rest on assumptions about entrepreneurship and innovation, neither of which we can anticipate theoretically and therefore model sensibly in terms of their causes and consequences. Even the predictions emanating from individual macroeconomic theories may be contradictory. For example, supply siders bought the three stage Reagan administration tax cut but then explained its failure to stimulate economic activity on the grounds that (1) it was not a tax cut at all, because it just kept taxpayers even, and planned increases in Social Security taxes made taxpayers worse off (that is, a reduction of expected increased costs has no expectational effect); and (2) people were withholding increments of production until the full force of the tax cut became manifest in its third year (that is, there are expectational effects on production). Thus, in the supply side view, margins of productivity simultaneously are and are not occupied. Nor are supply siders alone in uttering inherently contradictory sentences when it comes to applying their theories to real public policies.

One thus comes away from a brief sojourn in the territory of macroeconomics with the impression that there is no coherent theory, and certainly not one that commands a consensus. Moreover, one gains the impression that an explanation for the absence of such a theory may rest on a fundamental indeterminateness and incoherence in aggregate economic behavior, a view that Frydman, O'Driscoll, and Schotter (1982) have recently argued. That is, even if scholars could agree upon a clear and consistent economic theory of macroeconomic behavior, such a theory might not yield consistent predictions, or any predictions at all, about the movement of aggregate measures as a function of decisions taken in the public sector.

But this much we know already from positive political theory. Government decisionmakers can vary the level of government spending, the deficit or surplus, the division of the deficit between borrowing and money creation, the targeting of increased or diminished public sector spending, and the targeting of tax increases or tax cuts. While the relationships among these policies seem partially constrained by accounting identities, at least in the short run, nevertheless sufficient policy dimensions remain to create a situation in which there is no apparent pure strategy equilibrium in a political contest over those dimensions, even if a single elected politician controlled all of these variables following a two candidate race (Plott, 1967; McKelvey, 1979). Because these policies are controlled by a large number of elected and nonelected officeholders in different and often competing governmental institutions, and because they are reacted to differentially and expectationally by economic agents in the private sector, the problem of prediction becomes all the more complex. In sum, the behavior of macroeconomic aggregate measures and the underlying states that they seek to reflect depend crucially upon political as well as economic decisions, and we do not now have anything approaching a rudimentary positive political theory of macroeconomic policy, nor can we agree on an appropriate and consistent economic theory of macroeconomic policy.

This essay does not provide a positive political theory of macroeconomic policy in general, or of deficits in particular. Indeed, it may be impossible to do so until a coherent economic theory of macroeconomic aggregates is first worked out.[1] Instead, I focus here on the consequences (and by implication, the causes) of public sector deficits, and try to apply to that subject some recently gained knowledge about the political nature of public policy decisionmaking in representative democracies. My intent is to show that decisions about public sector deficits, if indeed we can ever say that decisions are made about such deficits, have little to do with any of the sometimes conflicting normative reasons given for accumulating those deficits. And, even when we can trace a relationship between a normative purpose for deficit spending and an actual policy or event, the shape of the resulting spending decisions so distorts the normative intent that the deficit becomes larger than it otherwise need be.

The outline of the essay is thus. First, I briefly review commonly acknowledged (although sometimes disputed or severely qualified) normative justifications for public sector action in general and public sector spending in particular. Then I apply some of these justifications to the problem of deficits as a special case, paying attention to public investment, capital expenditures, passive counter-cyclical policies, and active counter-cyclical policies. Second, I report on some recent research in the theory of representative democracy, which argues that a successful pursuit of the policies recommended under the previously stated normative justifications is difficult if not impossible in such political systems. Third, I apply that research to the problem of deficit spending and also sketch the very preliminary outlines of a positive political theory of macroeconomic policy. Finally, I reflect on our present discontent with public sector deficits and examine some proposed correctives.

Public Sector Deficits and
the Normative Theory of the State

To evaluate deficits in the abstract, with no regard for the reasons that they are accumulated, seems pointless. Presumably, we would distinguish between a person who borrows $100,000 to buy a home and one who borrows the same amount to support his local bookie. We need not claim that the homesteader is morally superior to the gambler (especially if the gambler doubles his money and buys a home that costs twice as much). But public deficits ought to be accumulated for public purposes that command majoritarian consent. Here, we tersely review these purposes and then apply them to the deficit spending problem.

Welfare Theory

The theoretical justifications for public sector action seem well established, although their boundaries and implications for public policy are hotly disputed (Baumol, 1965; Buchanan, 1971; Steiner, 1974). Very generally, a necessary condition for government action is the presence of a divergence (or potential divergence) between private and social cost.[2] We can partition in several ways the universe of situations in which such a divergence occurs. I have chosen to do so here and elsewhere by dividing these situations into the not mutually exclusive categories of public goods, public bads, property rights, monopoly, and redistribution.

Public goods include those goods, services, and states of the world that are either theoretically jointly supplied or jointly consumed, such as national defense, or are made so by law, such as elementary and secondary education (Samuelson, 1954). Because we cannot or do not withhold these goods from those who fail to contribute to their supply, nonsupply or suboptimal supply may occur. Because government enforces contribution, it is sometimes called upon to overcome the inherent free rider problem.

Public bads are negatively valued goods, such as air and water pollution. If transactions costs are high, if property rights are undefined, or if people otherwise have no restrictions on their activities, then a greater than optimal production of public bads may occur. The theoretical purpose of much health, environmental, and safety regulation relies on a public bads justification for its enactment. Public goods and public bads represent the same phenomenon, because we may view an unproduced public good (whose production would be publicly efficient) as a public bad and an unproduced public bad (whose nonproduction would be privately efficient) as a public good.

The property rights problem is a species of the public goods public bads problem. For instance, if we could secure to a producer (for example, a lighthouse owner (Coase, 1974)) the right to a return for his production in all cases, then the public goods problem would disappear, and if we could impose on producers the social cost of their activities (securing rights for those otherwise damaged), then the public bads problem would also be resolved. However, we ordinarily reserve the term property rights to refer to specific institutional arrangements for entitlement, ownership, and control, such as broadcast frequency allocations (Coase, 1959), job tenure (Martin,

1977), and fishing rights (Smith, 1969). If correctly designed, property rights efficiently internalize external costs and secure returns to productive activity. activity.

The monopoly problem, following the old learning, occurs if a buyer or seller is large enough to affect output and price.[3] If the monopolist or monopsonist grows large as a result of the global decline in its long-run average total cost curve, then it is a natural monopoly; otherwise, not. Natural monopolies usually are either regulated or incorporated into the public sector. Other monopolies may be sued, regulated, or influenced by legislation. Monopolies are said to produce less output at a higher price than is optimal, and thus the alleged goal of public policy with regard to monopolies is to increase output and reduce price. The monopoly problem has been interpreted as a public goods problem, because "subsequent" consumers of a monopolist's output affect the prices paid by "prior" consumers (Lerner, 1964). But this view probably deprives the concepts of both public goods and monopoly of their analytical power (Buchanan, 1971).

Finally, resource or wealth redistribution has been posited as a proper public sector goal. In a sense, redistribution may be a public goods problem, because one philanthropist may benefit from another's giving, if the object of the giving is made better off (Hochman and Rogers, 1969). Redistribution may also resolve a public bads problem, because it might avoid civil strife (Brennan, 1973).

Welfare Theory and Public-Sector Deficits

This exercise in recapitulating welfare theory, though pedestrian and truncated, reflects an agreement with Buchanan (1958, pp. 151–152) that, "The question as to when the government should borrow cannot be answered apart from the fundamental normative question in fiscal theory: When should government spend? Or, differently phrased: How much should government spend? What proportion of the community's resources should be devoted to collective or public ends as opposed to private employments?" Thus, in a normative view of the state, a decision to create or to add to a public-sector deficit resembles a private decisionmaker's choice to create or to add to his own level of debt: the public-sector deficit, like its private sector counterpart, must be justified by the nature of the activities that it supports. But what is the substance of such activities and of the resulting deficits?

First, suppose that a plant producing a public good, such as a national defense installation, has a useful life of several decades.[4] Presumably, its cost should be allocated over time to taxpayers in all positively affected generations. Otherwise, the benefit of the installation in year $t + 1$ comes to rest as a cost on the taxpayer in year t. Simply stated, capital expenditures for production of public goods ought to be paid for over a period of years. The consequence of not doing so is an underinvestment in such goods, on the one hand, or an unfair burden placed on a single year's taxpayers, on the other.[5]

An application of the same principle concerns deficit financing to wage war. We no longer live in an age when it is respectable to argue that expenditures for a war are identical to expenditures for a capital good, although such an argument doubtless must have prevailed in Disraeli's Parliament and in other imperial minded councils of state. Nevertheless, we can interpret the costs of (defensive) wars as payments to preserve preexisting capital goods, including the political system and culture. Thus, we can reasonably incur a debt, imposing an obligation on future generations, to pay for the war. The necessary assumption to adopt this deficit spending policy on welfare grounds is that our children and grandchildren will find the present enemy, say the Nazis, as distasteful as we do.

Second, more generally, at any time the fisc may be at a sufficiently low level that it cannot pay currently for public sector projects that are quite reasonable on cost-benefits grounds. The reason for the current depletion of the treasury is immaterial. What matters is that there is a potential program that, properly discounted, will return more to the treasury or to the "catchment" than its cost. Such an opportunity is a proper reason for the public sector to engage in deficit spending: the present embarrassment is merely a cash-flow problem.

Third, public sector deficits may arise for passive reasons. These are unanticipated deficits that result from economic conditions, such as a swing in the business cycle, that were not foreseen. Since such deficits are unanticipated, there is really nothing that we can do about them, and therefore there is no way that we can plan for them. In this sense, we may interpret them as proper only because they are not improper.

It is important to add two qualifications to this characterization of passive deficits, however. (1) Just as deficits may be unanticipated, so, too, surpluses may be unanticipated. In the absence of conscious manipulation, there is no reason to suppose that deficit-surplus situations would not be symmetric. Therefore, in this view, the surplus must be used to offset the accumulated deficits or must be saved to offset future ones. (2) Even before the age of Keynes, the countercyclical nature of passive deficits had been fully recognized.

Fourth, there is the highly disputed purpose of public sector deficits involved in active deficit spending: creating fully anticipated deficits to stimulate the economy through fiscal policy. I need not settle here, nor indeed take a position on, the question of whether such a policy has been and is always appropriate, whether it once was appropriate but no longer remains so (Feldstein, 1982), or whether it is and was never appropriate. If we postulate that the active deficit policy is correct, *ad arguendum,* and if that policy improves everyone's economic position, then it would be equivalent to a public good; if it improves some people's positions to the detriment of others, then it would be equivalent to redistribution.[6] None of the subsequent argument here depends on this theory being valid or invalid. I merely note that it is a postulated normative purpose of public sector deficits that rests comfortably within the traditional categories of welfare theory.

Two implications emerge effortlessly from this review of the normative functions of deficits. First, we cannot judge whether a deficit is appropriate or inappropriate merely by its absolute size or by changes in its size, for that matter. We would also have to know why the deficit was accumulated in each specific instance. Presumably, the deficit actually might be too small, and we would have to judge it as such. For example, it would have been foolish not to conclude the Louisiana Purchase or not to buy Alaska, because of a temporary lack of funds. Nor, perhaps, would we have the right to argue about this matter today (nor might many of us be here today) had not annual federal deficits as a percentage of GNP exceeded 100 percent for two years during the Second World War. Although these examples reflect deficits of forty years ago and more, it would be foolish to suppose that such opportunities for appropriate public sector activity requiring deficit spending do not or cannot exist today.

Second, it is also apparent that the "correct" or "optimal" level of the deficit, in the sense that we have just described, will probably maximize the public sector's ability to bear additional present and future deficits. That is, "good" deficit spending today should increase correctly measured GNP in the future, and therefore, *ceteris paribus,* should increase tax receipts, while diminishing the level of the presently anticipated deficit as a percentage of GNP. This possibility enrages, befuddles, and otherwise infuriates many scholars, who reject Laffer-like policy prescriptions based on the notion that lower tax rates will result (desirably) in greater tax revenues.[7] The position of such scholars has often been painted in caricature to suggest that they oppose any and all forms of public sector activity. But such is not the case. Rather, they have a comprehensive view of the public sector that the term "leviathan" best describes, and they are convinced that the behemoth grows unconstrained.[8]

A Reconstructed Theory of Representative Democracy

It was, and in some quarters remains, a commonplace among economists and others that the private sector is riddled with imperfections and untoward constraints, which the public sector effortlessly and costlessly corrects; that the marketplace fails but that the public sector does not; that monitoring costs, transactions costs, and free-rider problems abound in the private sector but are nowhere to be found in the public sector; that human beings, motivated by narrow self-interest in the private sector, suddenly become self-effacing saints when they occupy positions in the public sector. Stated differently, this view of the politics of representative democracies comprehends a universe in which public policies would be appropriately fashioned and carried on at optimal levels, thus leading to a correct level of spending and, therefore, deficits.

Elections in the Virtuous State

It proves useful to describe briefly the manner in which the unassembled preferences of the members of the electorate would be converted into appropriate and optimal public policies, and therefore an optimal public sector deficit, in such a universe (Downs, 1957). Very generally, citizens would have preferences over various levels of the production of public goods, say, depending upon their respective tax and benefit shares. It would be possible to hypothesize a distribution of bliss points (most preferred positions) over the resulting n-dimensional policy space, one dimension of which (assuming payment fungibility among programs) would measure the amount of the tax share paid now and the amount paid in future years. Two candidates would compete over this n-dimensional policy space, converging at the median voter's most preferred position. The winner would then go into government and get that policy enacted and implemented.

Several theoretical and empirical studies of actual institutions—legislatures, administrations, bureaus, and courts—make this very simple model look much simpler than it actually is, and we shall consider some of these momentarily. Here, though, we consider three separate challenges to this model, which accept the model on its own terms. The first of these challenges, as I have suggested in the introduction to this essay, points out that elections over multidimensional issue spaces more commonly than not possess no pure strategy equilibria to which candidates might converge. Rather, each strategy can be defeated by some other strategy, and therefore electoral competition may cycle endlessly, coming to rest only at the artificial stopping point imposed by the first Tuesday in November. By this view, the resulting public policies seem random at best, and possibly subject to manipulation, and therefore are entirely uncompelling on normative grounds (McKelvey, 1979; Plott, 1967; Riker, 1980). Of course, this judgment would extend immediately to any resulting deficit.

A second criticism of the simple election model rests on the notion of a "fiscal illusion" (Goetz, 1977; Wagner, 1976). By this view, citizens more readily perceive the benefits of public sector activity than they do its costs. The illusion occurs, *inter alia,* because by the nature of the tax structure and public sector programs, benefits tend to be concentrated while costs tend to be dispersed. Furthermore, politicians, whose welfare may be positively related to a larger public sector (Niskanen, 1971), fashion programs that induce the illusion, merely as a response to competitive political pressures. Relatedly, but more important for our purposes, the possibility of deficit financing allows the costs of public spending to be dispersed intergenerationally. The fiscal illusion hypothesis would thus predict a larger than optimal budget size and a larger than optimal shift to deficit spending over immediate taxation. However, if we assume that political competition leads to an equilibrium in the presence of such an illusion, then we have an explanation for why the public sector is larger than desirable, but not for why it grows larger still; an explanation for why the public debt is larger than optimal, but not for why it grows larger still.

A third criticism of the simple election model is the direct opposite of the fiscal illusion hypothesis. This view hypothesizes that citizens do not fully discern the benefits of public sector programs, because these programs create public goods, such as highway systems and national defense, which are commonly taken for granted; but citizens more completely perceive the costs of such programs (Galbraith, 1969; Downs, 1960). Furthermore, the public sector, for various reasons, fails to advertise sufficiently. The advertisement argument has been subject to severe criticism (Clarkson and Tollison, 1979). But the differential perception argument concerning public goods may hold merit. If so, then the public sector may be too small and therefore, assuming that the debt would increase with an increase in the size of the public sector, the public debt itself may be too small.

The principal difficulty with both the fiscal illusion model and the opposite view of inadequate public spending is that each fails to explain why some politician does not simply build a campaign on repairing the obvious defect. If this strategy is impossible or politically unproductive, then the underlying model itself may be fundamentally defective. A reasonable model of public sector activity must address this problem. Nevertheless, each of these criticisms of the simple election model has inherent merit, and we shall draw on elements of each criticism to create a more realistic view of public sector processes in general, and of those that apply to deficit financing in particular.

Groups in the Electoral Process

We begin this reconstruction by considering the position of organized groups in the electorate, as an interpretation of that position has developed in a recent line of research (Aranson and Ordeshook, 1977a, 1977b, 1978, 1981a, 1981b). Suppose that in an electorate of 500,000 persons, about the size of an average congressional district, there are two groups of people composed of 1000 voters each, and suppose that each group holds a policy preference opposed to the interests of the other group but about which the general electorate, for the moment, remains entirely disinterested. Group A, say, is organized, with a set of officers, a communications network (such as a newsletter), a dues structure, and the ability to include or exclude and reward or sanction members at will, depending on their contribution to the group. Group B remains entirely unorganized. Plainly, the average election candidate or incumbent would detect, respond to, and try to enact and implement the public policy preferences of the members of group A as compared with those of group B, of whom he may be only dimly aware, if at all.

Now let us suppose that group B has 2000 members, not 1000. We still would expect that group A will continue to be heard while group B would go ignored. Indeed, *a priori* it is difficult to say at what size a politician will begin to discern the preferences of the members of group B and to act on them, contrary to the interests of group A. (Of course, we have not explained the fact of organization of group A, nor the nonorganization of group B.) However, at the limit group A might be made up of the original group, while group B might embrace the entire electorate, which is damaged by the public sector program that the legislator creates for the members of group A. It is not unusual to find such programs and to have group A continue to be heeded, while the members of group B, the general electorate, go ignored.

Nor is it difficult to explain the advantages of organization over the disadvantages of its absence. The mere problem of efficiently communicating a candidate's position to a large number of people gives any organized group a presumptive political advantage. But the fact of organization also gives evidence of an ability to form complex transactions among officeholders and the members of a group when such transactions require complicated bargaining and monitoring of compliance. Whatever other form the coin of payment might assume between the members of an organized group and an elected officeholder, a limitation of payment to a secretly cast ballot, the only currency available to the unorganized, places the unorganized at a distinct disadvantage, if not a fatal one.

That organized groups enjoy a clear political advantage over disorganized, unaggregated voters may be apparent. But that observation alone does not tell us anything about the resulting public policy. Perhaps, as political pluralists believe, group action is the means by which optimal public policies, fulfilling a normative purpose, and therefore by implication, optimal public deficits, occur (Dahl, 1961).

However, that is not the case, because the incentives at work in representative democracies remain inconsistent with the welfare economist's civics book model (Aranson and Ordeshook, 1977b, 1978). In particular, under reasonably general conditions, and in the presence of a political budget constraint, when an interest group's leader must decide to lobby for a public good, as welfare theory would contemplate, or for a private good for the members of his group, to be supplied at collective cost, he will lobby for the private good.[9] Furthermore, when he must choose between lobbying for his own group's private benefit or opposing the private benefit to be supplied to another group, he will lobby for his own benefit and ignore the other group's benefit, unless his group must bear a disproportionate share of the burden of that other benefit. In sum, organized groups in the political process prevail over the interests of the unorganized, and such goups demand private benefits, private goods, not public goods.[10]

Finally, though general sentences seem hard to come by, it appears that this kind of political action may be an inferior good, because expenditures on it represent a larger and larger percentage of each group's budget as that budget grows smaller (Aranson and Ordeshook, 1981b). Furthermore, there is an inherent logic to the kinds of benefits that such groups would demand for their members. If these goods, or programs, were efficient in a cost-benefit sense, then a group could purchase them in the private sector. But if they are inefficient, then there is a presumption that the group would seek to have the cost spread over all taxpayers.

The resulting prediction about the group based demand for public sector activity is that it is for the public-sector supply of inappropriate and inherently inefficient programs that create private benefits at collective cost. Were this force to go unabated, the fisc would come to resemble a putatively overused common resource (one without divisible property rights). The result for public debt would be increases to the point at which the (hypothesized) rate of inflation, or interest, or both would be so great and differentially experienced by particular groups (as we shall see momentarily) that those increases in these aggregate measures, and the misery that they reflect, would begin to lose more votes than the flow of associated private benefits would gain.

But we are ahead of our story, and the political response to this possibility is not so obvious. For the moment, we hasten to point out that we really cannot say whether the debt under the reconstructed view that we have reported is larger or smaller than it would be under a regime that was entirely public-regarding. However, we would nevertheless prefer the debt accumulated under the public-regarding regime to that accumulated under the regime that the reconstructed view describes, just as we might approve of the homesteader's debt but not the gambler's.

We can now begin partially to understand the central inadequacy of both the fiscal illusion model and the Downs-Galbraith hypothesis. We criticized both views, because they fail to explain why a candidate for office would not adopt the platform that maximized welfare as we have understood it. Part of the answer is that it is difficult to assemble payment for such a politician to act righteously. It is far simpler to assemble payment for him to be a delegate for a special, limited interest, and a special pleader. While there may be virtue in representing the public interest, there is seldom lucre in it, nor does it often secure reelection.

Representative Legislatures

In a sense, the legislator's interests overlay perfectly those of interest groups and their leaders. It is far easier for a legislator to form transactions with a single leader of an organized group than with all of the members of an unorganized group. With the unorganized, his transactions costs would be enormous, he could not monitor their compliance with any bargains struck, nor could he easily and efficiently convey information about his activities to them (possibly to the strategic exclusion of all others). Hence, the legislator has a positive incentive to listen to the organized, and therefore there is every presumption that he will heed their demands and none others.

We can say more, however, much, much more. Recent writing about legislative decisionmaking has sought to tease out various conflicting demands placed on legislators and expose the nature of their decisions, so conditioned (Fiorina, 1977; Mayhew, 1974). Much of this research distinguishes between "universalistic" and "particularized" benefits, "programatic" and "private" legislation, "position taking" on large issues of national concern and "casework" and "credit claiming" for bringing home the "pork." In each of these juxtapositions, the first term referred to is very much like a public good, while the second term (or terms) resembles a private benefit. The overriding conclusion from this literature is that the stuff of legislative action concerns the exchange of private benefits, collectively supplied, for votes, endorsements, and campaign contributions, rather than the principled creation or pursuit of the public interest.

Indeed, such a result is not merely reasonable, but its opposite seems most unreasonable. Were a legislator to produce through his activity a purely public—completely nondivisible—good, he could not insure payment in return of the sort that would compete successfully against an opponent who could secure such payment. Thus, even if the boast were true, claiming credit for singlehandedly reducing the rate of inflation or unemployment or for increasing the GNP is simply not believable (Mayhew, 1974). Claiming credit for securing a new public works project for one's district or a subsidy or tariff for a local industry, or performing case work for individual constituents, by contrast, remain not merely credible but perfectly reasonable in the sense that no legislator from another district would commit resources to secure such results.

There remains the problem of ascertaining whether or not legislators would understand the nature of the effects that their activities have on the population and band together to oppose the resulting public policy. But when this possibility is embedded in the context of three-person cooperative and noncooperative games as well as of more general n-person noncooperative games, the results indicate that the antiprivate benefit coalition may form in transitory situations but that it is subject to constant defection, making it an irrational strategy for legislators to follow (Aranson and Ordeshook, 1978).[11]

Table 5-1 illustrates the nature of the problem facing those who would construct a coalition to oppose this variety of federal spending and public policy. It reports 1982 voting in the House of Representatives on two issues: the recently proposed balanced budget amendment to the Constitution and the override of President Reagan's veto of an appropriations bill, whose terms satisfied several private groups in various constituencies across the nation. The balanced budget amendment failed, and the veto override succeeded. Both required two thirds votes. The table reports percentages of the 408 House members who cast ballots, paired, or announced their positions on both of these two votes (nearly all actually voted). The table labels as "conservative" those who voted for the amendment and against overturning the veto; as "liberal," those who shared the opposite voting pattern; and as "hypocritical," those who voted for the amendment but against overturning the veto.[12] The highest degree of ideological consistency appears among Northern Democrats, while Southern Democrats and

Table 5-1 House of Representatives Votes on Balanced Budget Amendment and Overturning Reagan Veto on Appropriations Bill, 1982*

	Conservative	Hypocritical	Liberal	(n)
Republicans	54.8%	35.0	10.2	(177)
Southern Democrats	16.0	57.3	26.7	(75)
Northern Democrats	0.0	7.7	92.3	(156)
Total	26.7	28.7	44.6	(408)

*Source: Votes are tabulated from Congressional Quarterly Weekly Report., Sept. 11, 1982, pp. 2282–2284; Oct. 9, 1982, pp. 2664–2666.

Republicans, those expected to make up the backbone of an anti-spending coalition, exhibit the greatest degree of hypocrisy, as operationally defined here. With such voting patterns, there is little hope that legislatures will find ways to correct the spending policies that they have adopted in pursuit of private benefits at collective cost.

A Revised Election Model

In the normal course of telling the story concerning the reconstructed view of political processes in representative democracies, there is much to say about the impact of bureaucratic (Aranson, Gellhorn, and Robinson, 1982; Aranson and Ordeshook, 1981b; Borcherding, 1977; Fiorina, 1977, 1982; Niskanen, 1971; Tullock, 1965; Von Mises, 1944;) and judicial (Landes and Posner, 1975) decisionmaking. However, in the interest of brevity I omit this discussion here. The positive effect of these institutions on public spending and deficits seems obvious though sometimes complicated, and it is not in dispute. What disagreement does remain concerns whether or not the Congress or the bureaucracy is more nearly responsible for prevailing patterns of public policy (Moran and Weingast, 1982). At best, these institutions seem neutral concerning the level of public spending and deficits. More commonly, they reinforce and facilitate the patterns already described.

The possibility remains, nevertheless, that the electoral process itself may restrain the political processes identified. An election model in private goods—one in which candidates compete by granting, or by deleting, or by leaving unchanged the private benefits flowing from the public sector to each individual group—has been developed to get at this possibility (Aranson and Ordeshook, 1977a). Incorporating the notion of a fiscal illusion, but one in

Table 5-2. Summary of Decision Procedure and Threshold Effects on Public Sector Growth*

| | | Threshold Distribution | |
		Near Zero	Far From Zero
	Global	Net Growth	Qualified Net Reduction
Decision Procedure			
	Incremental	Net Reduction	Net Growth

*Source: Aranson and Ordeshook, 1977a.

which benefits and costs are symmetrically perceived, perhaps as a function of their net levels and perhaps as a function of the opportunity costs of securing political information, we have been able to isolate the conditions under which net growth or contraction in public sector size might occur.

Very generally, if voters are insensitive to small changes in their welfare and if politicians consider programs one at a time (incrementally)—the condition that surrounds most public policy decision making—then net growth in public sector size will occur. Following majoritarian principles, but under conditions far less likely to prevail, incremental decision making by candidates in the presence of voters who are very sensitive about net changes in their welfare will produce a net reduction in public sector size. This condition might have characterized the early months of the Reagan administration. Surprisingly, under global decision procedures, with citizens who are sensitive to small changes in their welfare, a net growth occurs, perhaps reflecting a redistributionist tendency in representative democracies. But if decision procedures are global and citizens are insensitive to small changes in their welfare, then a net reduction may occur, depending upon the distribution of individual perception thresholds. Table 5-2 summarizes these results.

We refer briefly to some of these findings in the next section, particularly with regard to macroeconomic policymaking. Here, we simply observe that most people, most of the time, seem insensitive to small changes in their welfare, so they fail to notice, and do not invest in information about, public policies that convey divisible benefits to specialized groups. Even the bailout of a Lockheed or a Chrysler Corporation could not generate sufficient resistance to matter.[13] Similarly, candidates or incumbents seeking reelection through their legislative acts, or elected chief executives in the same position, usually make public policy decisions incrementally. The result is a net growth in public sector size with an occasional contraction, depending upon parameters whose values we have not yet tried to estimate. In sum, there is little hope that the electoral process will provide more than a fleeting brake on increases in public sector size, based on an expansion in the number of private benefits programs, collectively supplied. One very likely result is an increase in the size of the deficit compared to what it would have been in the absence of such a process.

Public Sector Deficits in the Reconstructed View

The normative and reconstructed views as applied to the causes and consequences of deficits do resemble each other in certain respects. First, in both interpretations deficit size is a dependent, not an independent variable, because it results from decisions that do not immediately contemplate its size as a consequence of those decisions. Second, in both interpretations we can make sense out of deficit size by referring to the rational decisionmaking processes of the people who determine that size. Third, and as a consequence, both views resemble decisions about the acquisition of deficits in the private sector.

But there the resemblance ends. In the normative view, the deficit's size ebbs and flows as public sector decisionmakers choose benevolently to undertake public regarding programs. But in the reconstructed view, the deficit's size increases most of the time as a function of the public pursuit of private benefits. In the normative view, the costs of incurring public debt may fall legitimately and efficiently on future generations. But in the reconstructed view, future generations do not vote, have not organized, and therefore go unrepresented, the questions of legitimacy and efficiency remaining largely irrelevant.[14] And, in the normative view, the decisionmakers were those who had to bear the election and reelection related costs of correct and incorrect decisions. But in the reconstructed view, the effects of inappropriate and nonoptimal policies, as judged by their purpose, and of overly large deficits come to rest on future generations of citizens. In sum, our interpretation of deficits varies greatly, depending on whether we view the public sector as a benign agent or as a not so benign generator of external diseconomies (Aranson, 1981a). Therefore, to the extent that public debt is allowed to increase, it facilitates this interest group process. Even if public goods are supplied, they are supplied at levels that private groups prefer. Thus, they may be overproduced or not produced at all, depending on the relevant structures of groups and on the vagaries of the situation at hand.

Outlines of a Political Model of Macroeconomic Policy

We have yet to come to grips with the problem of the macroeconomy and its manipulation. We have assumed that independent decisions about individual programs determine the level of government spending, without regard for the level of spending or deficit thus created. Certainly, our discussion of a reconstructed election model does contemplate the possibility of restricting federal spending under very limited conditions (for example, with low citizen thresholds and incremental candidate decisionmaking), but a neglect of the aggregate economy itself as a political issue seems unacceptable. There are macroeconomic policies and variables, politicians do talk about them, and there is doubtless some attempt to manipulate them in and of themselves.

Hence, there is an apparent confrontation of two models, one at the micro level concerning the pursuit of individual public sector programs, and the other at the macro level, concerning such variables as unemployment, interest rates, and taxes, whose values politicians obviously do try to influence. At some point, the political imperatives easily discernible out of these two models may conflict. For example, politicians dislike (explicitly) voting for higher taxes, even though they prefer to vote for the programs that compel their imposition. Similarly, higher interest rates are to be avoided, even though legislators seem not to mind monetizing the public debt that creates higher interest rates. How are we to reconcile these all too apparent conflicts? Here, I suggest one such manner of reconciliation that fits comfortably within the reconstructed view of the political process, but it is certainly not a final or even a seasoned interpretation.

Politicians begin their terms in office with a given history of relevant macroeconomic variables and their trajectories, such as the rate of unemployment and its recent changes, the interest rate and its recent changes, and the tax schedule and GNP and their recent changes. Politicians appear to focus on the variable that has changed most dramatically in the recent time period, although certainly the parameters and elasticites of this process would be difficult to estimate.[15] This is merely an overly complicated way of saying that politicians pay attention to that variable that people complain about the most. They would then concentrate on changing that variable until people started complaining about something else.

Private Program Responses
to Macroeconomic Problems

While this prediction is neither terribly surprising nor sophisticated, what is different about it is the manner in which the reconstructed view would predict that politicians would respond. Very generally, they would do so as they do in most other instances. That is, they would listen to and respond to organized groups. And, in particular, they would fashion their programs to ameliorate the perceived macroeconomic problem as it affects those particular groups. Three examples come to mind.

Unemployment. The extant Keynesian theory about macroeconomic cures for unemployment is highly disputed. Nevertheless, to my knowledge a pure Keynesian fiscal stimulus has seldom been tried. What has occurred instead is that the federal government has targeted money and public policies to help organized groups whose members tend to be unemployed at the time of the perceived "crisis."[16] These groups, principally well established labor unions, have sought and received divisible benefits to solve their particular manifestations of macroeconomic problems. For example, workers in certain industries have received government relief from the untoward effects (unemployment) of foreign competition. Rather than locate these workers in other industries, such policies perpetuate a continued disdain for the law of comparative advantage. Industrial workers have developed an elaborate unemployment compensation system, which does little or nothing for those who have never been employed or who have worked for uninsured (principally unorganized) firms. Finally, programs for the hard core unemployed have been fashioned not by the hard core unemployed themselves, but rather by those people who service them: The "welfare establishment," whose members enjoy a superior degree of job security, compared with that of their "clients."

Public sector attacks on unemployment are thus responsive to group demands, but if an unemployed person does not belong to a group, then he is likely to go unserved in the sense of getting a first job or a new job. Policies such as unemployment compensation and government payments to defray the effects of foreign competition tend to increase periods of unemployment and to sustain the inefficient allocation of workers to various firms (Feldstein, 1982). Such particularized policies have doubtless contributed to an increase in the estimated long-term unemployment rate from four percent to six percent in recent years.

Interest rates. To some extent interest rates are in the control of the Federal Reserve Board. But we need not settle here the matter of how much control the Fed exerts. What is more important is that increases in interest rates affect various groups differently, and the public sector tends to respond to such increases not according to a well conceived national and public economic policy, but instead according to the demands of the group that makes its voice heard most stridently and most effectively. The end result of this process becomes apparent, for example, in various bail-outs for banking institutions locked into low interest mortgage loans and in subsidies to the construction industry, and especially to those firms involved in federal, state, and local government construction projects.

Taxes.   As taxes increase, the immediately apparent reaction is to pass new tax legislation. But, that legislation is highly susceptible to the demands of various groups pursuing their particularized tax breaks. Revenue statutes occasionally have even been rewritten under the rubric of "tax reform," or "tax reduction," to provide a benefit to a particular firm or family. More commonly, well organized groups can exact from the members of Congress a number of concessions each time that the tax code is revised.[17]

This kind of political decisionmaking concerning problems such as unemployment, inflation, and taxes does not add up to a coherent macroeconomic policy. Obviously, this characterization of incoherence also extends to the size of the deficit and to the degree to which it is divided between monetizing and bond sales.[18] But the group based generation of public policy leads us to no other conclusion than that the goal of public policy, insofar as macroeconomic effects are concerned, is first to ameliorate conditions for individual groups, probably avoiding or making impossible long-term solutions to the problem at hand, as well as suppressing the possibility of desirable change.

This group based response is only a first level reaction to these macroeconomic problems, however, and it is doubtless possible that the response would be insufficient for the targeted groups themselves. For example, surely the banks and the housing industry would not be satisfied with individual bail outs, because these are unlikely to solve their problems and certainly not at reasonable cost and without promoting a major and politically unacceptable disruption of federal fiscal policy. At that point, public sector decisionmakers probably engage a second level reaction involving larger macroeconomic engines. For instance, they promote rapid increases in the money supply, especially shortly before an election. Once again, though, the animus for such policies remains the demands of organized groups in the population with whom the political decisionmakers have had substantial interaction in the past. The average citizen continues to go unrepresented in this legislative matrix. And, once again, the resulting macroeconomic policy continues to lack coherence or principle. (Hence, in the example cited, the Fed may overstimulate.)

On the Deficit

The Reagan administration estimates the deficit for fiscal year 1982 through fiscal year 1985 as $108.9, $115.0, $92.6, and $73.6 billion, respectively. The Congressional Budget Office, in what I regard as a more realistic assessment, estimates these numbers at $116.0, $146.0, $152.1, and $150.2 billion, respectively. Various spokesmen for the Reagan administration have sought mightily to diminish the impact of these numbers but, I believe, without success. And, as noted earlier (Table 5–1), the administration has the strength neither to impose a constitutional constraint on federal spending, and therefore deficits, nor to limit particular spending in the face of a skillfully crafted congressional coalition.[19]

The Reagan administration, of course, is not really interested in reducing federal spending per se. Rather, it is more interested in servicing its own interest groups, instead of those that have traditionally been serviced by Democratic administrations in the past. These groups most notably include firms engaged in defense manufacturing and foreign construction. In that sense, the deficit is bothersome to the Reagan administration, because it requires debt servicing. Thus, like all deficits, this one represents a prior "tax" on public spending for subsequent programatic activities: it reduces the administration's ability to serve its client groups. Then, too, we can see in this and previous administrations' spending decisions an approach to reducing spending (deficits) that accords well with the interest group view of the political process. For instance, at the margin, cuts are made in future Social Security payments to relatively unorganized sets of recipients. And, Social Security tax increases (in base and rate) are voted to occur in the future, not immediately (Campbell, 1982).

What is more, we can see in the Reagan administration's programs an incremental approach of reducing the macroeconomic measure most complained of. First it was inflation, then interest rates, and finally unemployment. The relevant planning horizon (at the time of this writing) appears to be the 1982 elections, after which it is difficult to predict the administration's next policy change, because we cannot predict whether the interest rate or the inflation rate will increase first, and most dramatically, and most painfully. The deficit, with which we began this discussion, will only become important as changes in its level affect these other macroeconomic measures: inflation, unemployment, and the interest rate. But the bottom line remains that we cannot as yet discern a compelling purpose for sustaining these deficits. They finance (1) large numbers of inappropriate programs; or (2) appropriate programs inappropriately fashioned; or (3) appropriate programs supplied at inappropriately high levels, or else we would not be worried about the deficit, whatever its size or recent growth.

Correctives

I have in the past publicly endorsed the balanced budget amendment as a step in the right direction for controlling the undesirable practices and tendencies outlined here (Aranson, 1981a, 1982a). If such an amendment were well constructed, it would be binding, constrain spending to a specified maximum percentage of GNP, and require that all revenues and expenditures be balanced over a relevant time period. At the very least, such an amendment would place a maximum on the amount of money used to finance private benefits at collective cost. At the very worst, groups would have to compete with each other at the margin for the last dollar, and possibly a large portion of the structure that Fiorina (1977) calls "the Washington Establishment" would fall apart.

I am not satisfied with the amendment that the members of Congress just rejected, nor am I blind to the many criticisms that have been leveled at it and at others like it. And, while I am not ready entirely to repudiate my support of a well constructed amendment, nevertheless my exploration into macroeconomic theory and practice, occasioned by writing this essay, has further eroded the confidence that I place in such a measure. It may not create further damage, but I do not believe that it will be quite as effective as I had once hoped.

The problem with a balanced budget amendment and with other restrictions on particular macroeconomic measures is that they are what I like to call "accounting solutions to economic problems." In this regard the amendment is like a price control, because it tries to ameliorate a symptom without affecting its cause. Of course, the underlying incentives that created the problem will quickly reappear, as people respond on other, unconstrained margins. For example, price controls lead to shortages, queues, black markets, and nonmonetary considerations in lieu of cash payment. Dare we impose a constitutional control on federal taxing and spending while the Federal Reserve Board, a "creature of the Congress," controls the money supply?[20]

Were the lawmaking process differently constructed, and were lawmakers' and citizens' incentives differently arranged, we might approve of the deficit size, because it reflected opportunities for improving the human condition that federal lawmakers had seized upon. I suspect that our concern for the deficit is not that we expect the debt thus accumulated eventually to redound to our collective benefit, but that we expect the deficit to finance continued reductions in GNP and human welfare. Accordingly, rather than placing a governor on the machine and hope that the machine's undesirable tendencies might not be made manifest in other, perhaps worse forms, we might try to find some way to rearrange the institutions themselves, thus changing the incentives that maintain the actions that we deplore.

Recently, I have argued that we need to find the political equivalent of the Pigouvian emissions charge and impose it upon the members of Congress who use the fisc as a common resource for their and their clients' own purpose (Aranson, 1982a). Richard McKenzie (1982) has independently argued that a salary structure for members of Congress, inversely related to the size of the deficit, might be appropriate. While these proposals are somewhat more sophisticated than a simple balanced budget amendment, nevertheless they are also more outlandish, and therefore less likely to be enacted. But, rather than issue a counsel of despair, we must recognize that proposals to restructure incentive systems and institutions, to the extent that they are more radical than the simpler (and probably less effective) methods of controlling accounting measures, are also more likely to succeed. The problem with outlawing further increases in deficits, of course, is that after we have paid our political leaders to be fiscally virtuous, or deterred them from being fiscally reckless, we might want them to incur deficits for our benefit.

Notes

1. Of course, there remains the unlikely possibility that the economic behavior of economic aggregates may gain stability from political decisionmaking. But such a possibility would contradict over three decades of recent research, arguing that the outcomes of political processes are far less stable than the outcomes of economic ones (Riker, 1980).

2. Such a divergence is not a sufficient condition for public sector action, because voluntary action may improve on the situation, because parallel markets may emerge that resolve it satisfactorily, and because the cost of such action may exceed the benefit. For a review of such limitations and others, see Aranson (1982b).

3. The new learning on antitrust challenges nearly every proposition of the description of conventional wisdom about monopoly that follows in this paragraph. For instance, market-like arrangements might foster a more efficient allocation of resources in traditional public utility regulation (Demsetz, 1973). Vertical integration may reduce several costs that consumers otherwise might have to bear (Klein, Crawford, and Alchian, 1978). Practices such as base point pricing, rather than providing clear examples of collusion, occur naturally in certain geographically relevant settings (Haddock, 1982). And, the entire structure of antitrust

economics may wildly exaggerate the extent of market power, because it does not adequately account for the threat of entry (Baumol, 1982).

4. For instance, many of the B-52 bombers now in service are older than their crews.

5. This proposition applies especially to the problem of natural monopolies if legislators decide to incorporate them into the public sector. The benefits of a public transit system, say, might flow over many years, so the cost of the plant ought to be borne over that period of time, just as it would be by its owners in the private sector.

6. The desirability of the resulting redistribution may vary from the short run to the long run. For example, some low income persons may gain in the short run but lose in the long run, as the result of (lagged) inflation. By contrast, those on fixed incomes might lose consistently.

7. James M. Buchanan, though seldom befuddled, is the most articulate exponent of the view that Laffer-like thinking is seriously misplaced.

8. For a recently developed dynamic view of this process as applied to deficits, see Buchanan, 1982.

9. The underlying game model in these situations is usually a prisoners' dilemma.

10. We use the term "group" very inclusively. For example, individual congressional constituencies may be viewed as groups, and the resulting analysis of the constituency based model carries through impressively in substantiating this analysis. See particularly Weingast, Shepsle, and Johnsen, 1981.

11. Mayhew (1974, pp. 92–93 n.32) describes the solitary, poor, nasty, brutish, and short existence of a legislator committed to "principled" (in the sense indicated) public policy by reporting that "Senator James L. Buckley (R., N.Y.) . . . tried to delete forty-four public works projects at the committee stage in the Senate. The members voted down all his amendments except the ones cutting out projects in New York; these latter they adopted."

12. Only one House member, Jack Kemp (R., N.Y.), voted against both motions.

13. Of course, public opinion might have constrained the nature and size of each bail-out.

14. If future generations could vote and could form associations, it is not apparent that public policy would be improved upon. They, presumably, might undertake the same varieties of political action as do present generations. Happily, we need not work through the implications of such fantasy based suggestions.

15. While the description here is of a behavioral model, not a deductive one, my guess is that we could deduce the behavioral postulates from a more rigorously deductive framework. See, for example, Fiorina (1981) and Aranson (1981b).

16. Roger Meiners has suggested to me that this strategy is especially useful for workers in (and owners of) firms in cyclical industries.

17. Of course, the groups may not be doing the exacting. I lean toward the view that the members of Congress are exploiting their positions to exact payments from these groups.

18. Alan Meltzer has suggested to me that the political process also affects the maturity of bonds, as evidenced by a recent sale of long-term bonds at a ridiculously high interest rate, whose purpose was to bail out certain securities dealers and bond salesmen.

19. One good test of the balanced budget amendment might be for President Reagan to announce that he would veto every single appropriations measure until the budget was in balance. Since it would require a two thirds vote of each house of Congress to overturn the veto, this strategy would impose something very close to a natural experiment of the present amendment, because it entails a sixty percent majority to "unbalance" the budget. If the President were serious about balancing the budget or about the amendment, then he would use this strategy to demonstrate the amendment's benevolent effects.

20. This may be an argument for privately issued money, if we were to require budget balance.

References

Aranson, P. H. "Public Sector Budgets as Measures of External Diseconomies." Paper prepared for delivery at a Conference on Constraining Federal Taxing and Spending, the Hoover Institution, Palo Alto, 1981a.

Aranson, P. H. "Risk, Uncertainty, and Retrospective Voting." Paper prepared for delivery at the Annual Meeting of the American Political Science Association, New York City, 1981b.

Aranson, P. H. "Can Democratic Societies Reform Themselves?" Law and Economics Center Working Paper 82–2, 1982a.

Aranson, P. H. "Pollution Control: The Case for Competition." In *Instead of Regulation.* Ed. R. Poole. Lexington: D.C. Heath, 1982b, pp. 339–393.

Aranson, P. H., E. Gellhorn, and G. O. Robinson. "A Theory of Delegation." *Cornell Law Review* (1982, forthcoming).

Aranson, P. H. and P. C. Ordeshook. "Incrementalism, The Fiscal Illusion, and The Growth of Government in Representative Democracies." Paper prepared for delivery at the Annual Meeting of the Southern Economic Association, New Orleans, 1977a.

Aranson, P. H. and P. C. Ordeshook. "A Prolegomenon to a Theory of the Failure of Representative Democracy." In *America Re-evolution: Papers and Proceedings.* R. Auster and B. Sears (Eds.). Tucson: University of Arizona Department of Economics, 1977b, pp. 23–46.

Aranson, P.H. and P.C. Ordeshook. "The Political Bases of Public Sector Growth in a Representative Democracy." Paper prepared for delivery at the 1978 Annual Meeting of the American Political Science Association, New York City.

Aranson, P. H. and P. C. Ordeshook. "Alternative Theories of the Growth of Government and Their Implications for Constitutional Tax and Spending Limits." In *Tax and Expenditure Limitations.* H. Ladd and N. Tideman (Eds.). Washington, DC: Urban Institute Press, 1981a, pp. 143–176.

Aranson, P. H. and P. C. Ordeshook. "Regulation, Redistribution, and Public Choice." *Public Choice* 37 (1981b), 69–100.

Baumol, W. J. *Welfare Economics and the Theory of the State,* 2nd ed. Cambridge: Harvard University Press, 1965.

Baumol, W. J. "Contestable Markets: An Uprising in the Theory of Industry Structure." *American Economic Review* 72 (March 1982), 1–15.

Borcherding, T. E. (ed.). *Budgets and Bureaucrats: The Sources of Government Growth.* Durham: Duke University Press, 1977.

Brennan, G. "Pareto Desirable Redistribution: The Non-Altruistic Dimension." *Public Choice* 14 (Spring 1973), 43–67.

Buchanan, J. M. *Public Principles of Public Debt.* Homewood: Irwin, 1958.

Buchanan, J. M. *The Bases of Collective Action.* New York: General Learning Press, 1971.

Buchanan, J. M. "Debt, Demos, and the Welfare State." Paper prepared for delivery at the Annual Meeting of the Southern Economic Association, Atlanta, 1982.

Campbell, C.D. "Where is the U.S. Social Security System Headed?" Paper prepared for delivery at the 1982 Biennial Meeting of the Mont Pelerin Society, Berlin.

Clarkson, K. E. and R. Tollison. "Toward a Theory of Government Advertising." *Research in Law and Economics* 1 (1979), 131–143.

Coase, R. H. "The Federal Communications Commission." *Journal of Law and Economics* 2 (October 1959), 1–40.

Coase, R. H. "The Lighthouse in Economics." *Journal of Law and Economics* 17 (October 1974), 357–376.

Dahl, R. A. *Who Governs?* New Haven: Yale University Press, 1961.

Demsetz, H. "Why Regulate Utilities?" *Journal of Law and Economics* 11 (April 1968), 55–65.

Downs, A. *An Economic Theory of Democracy.* New York: Harper and Row, 1957.

Downs, A. "Why the Government Budget is too Small in a Democracy." *World Politics* (July 1960), 541–563.

Feldstein, M. "Inflation and the American Economy." *The Public Interest* 67 (Spring 1982), 63–76.

Fiorina, M. P. *Congress: Keystone of the Washington Establishment.* New Haven: Yale University Press, 1977.

Fiorina, M. P. *Retrospective Voting in American National Elections.* New Haven: Yale University Press, 1981.

Fiorina, M. P. "Legislative Choice of Regulatory Forms: Legal Process or Administrative Process." *Public Choice* 39 (1982), 33–66.

Frydman, R., G. P. O'Driscoll, Jr. and A. Schotter. "Rational Expectations of Government Policy: An Application of Newcomb's Problem," *Southern Economic Journal* 49 (October 1982), 311–319.

Galbraith, J. K. *The Affluent Society.* New York: New American Library, 1969.

Goetz, CC. J. "Fiscal Illusion in State-Local Finance." In *Budgets and Bureaucrats: The Sources of Government Growth.* T.E. Borcherding (Ed.). Durham: Duke University Press, 1977, 176–187.

Haddock, D. D. "Base-Point Pricing: Competition vs. Collusive Theories." *American Economic Review* 72 (June 1982), 289–306.

Hochman, H. D. and J. D. Rogers. "Pareto Optimal Redistribution." *American Economic Review* 59 (September 1969), 542–557.

Klein, B., R. G. Crawford, and A. A. Alchian. "Vertical Integration, Appropriable Rents, and the Competitive Contracting Process." *Journal of Law and Economics* 21 (October 1978), 297–326.

Landes, W. and R.A. Posner. "The Independent Judiciary From an Interest-Group Perspective." *Journal of Law and Economics* 18 (December 1975), 875–901.

Lerner, A. P. "Conflicting Principles of Public Utility Price Regulation." *Journal of Law and Economics* 7 (October 1964), 61–70.

Martin, D. L. "The Economics of Employment Termination Rights." *Journal of Law and Economics* 20 (April 1977), 187–204.

Mayhew, D. R. *Congress: The Electoral Connection.* New Haven: Yale University Press, 1974.

McKelvey, R. D. "General Conditions for Global Intransitivities in Formal Voting Models" *Econometrica* 47 (September 1979), 1085–1112.

McKenzie, R. D. "Incentives for a Balanced Budget." The Heritage Foundation, Mimeo, 1982.

Moran, M. J. and B. R. Weingast. "Congress as the Source of Regulatory Decisions: The Case of the Federal Trade Commission." *American Economic Review* 72 (May, 1982), 109–113.

Niskanen, W. A. Jr. *Bureaucracy and Representative Government.* New York: Aldine-Atherton, 1971.

Plott, C. R. "A Notion of Equilibrium and its Possibility Under Majority Rule." *American Economic Review* 57 (September 1967), 787–806.

Riker, W. H. "Implications from the Disequilibrium of Majority Rule for the Study of Institutions." *American Political Science Review* 74 (April 1980), 432–446.

Samuelson, P. A. "The Pure Theory of Public Expenditure." *Review of Economics and Statistics* 36 (1954), 387–390.

Smith, V. L. "On Models of Commercial Fishing." *Journal of Political Economy* 77 (March/April 1969), 181–198.

Steiner, P. "Public Expenditure Budgeting." In *The Economics of Public Finance.* A. Blinder, *et al.* (Eds.) Washington, DC: The Brookings Institution, 1974, 271–357.

Tullock, G. *The Politics of Bureaucracy.* Washington, DC: Public Affairs Press, 1965.

Von Mises, L. *Bureaucracy.* New Haven: Yale University Press, 1944.

Wagner, R. E. "Revenue Structure, Fiscal Illusion, and Budgetary Choice." *Public Choice* 25 (Spring 1976), 45–61.

Weingast, B. R., K. A. Shepsle and C. Johnsen. "The Political Economy of Benefits and Costs: A Neoclassical Approach to Distributive Politics." *Journal of Political Economy* 89 (August 1981), 642–664.

6 A CONSTITUTIONAL CURE FOR DEFICITS

Alvin Rabushka

There would be little point in advocating a constitutional ban on deficits unless there was broad agreement that chronic deficits were undesirable. A second implication in the title I have chosen is that moral exhortations, further congressional reform of the budget process, electing good men and women to office, or passing laws prohibiting deficits are all ineffective: nothing short of a constitutional amendment can curtail federal budget deficits. On August 4, 1982, the United States Senate, having arrived at the same conclusion, approved by a vote of 69 to 31 Senate Joint Resolution 58 (S.J. Res. 58). This proposed amendment to the Constitution would require a balanced federal budget and limit the growth in federal receipts to the rate of growth in national income, unless Congress voted explicitly for deficits or higher taxes. In the summer of 1982, for the first time in American history, a chamber of Congress debated and approved such a limitation. The object of my paper is to explain and defend S.J. Res. 58, although we are still a long way from its incorporation in the Constitution as the 27th amendment.

Seven-for-Granteds

My task in this conference is made easier by the inclusion of papers that attempt to show the impact of federal budget deficits on monetary growth, inflation, interest rates, and capital formation. I would be shocked to discover no adverse effects whatsoever. Doubtless, monetary and other economic policies interact with deficits to attenuate or intensify any adverse effects they have. Still, I take as given that chronically large deficits are, like the plague, to be shunned. Moreover, lecturing members of Congress on the evils of deficit financing is akin to stopping an epidemic of plague by lecturing rats on the benefits of proper hygiene.

Deficits are Undesirable

One of my discussants, Kenneth A. Shepsle (1982a) has written that "A crisis atmosphere exists today in the nation's conduct of fiscal affairs. The reason is clear: There *is* a fiscal crisis." Shepsle points to Congressional Budget Office estimates of a 1985 deficit equal to five percent of Gross National Product. As a result of this fiscal mismanagement, he reports that the President's popularity has eroded and the Congress has become an object of scorn. Case rests.

Those who support the principle of balanced budgets do not insist that Congress do so on a strict annual timetable, but rather over a period of time taking one year with another. The government cannot operate with a large chronic deficit without serious adverse consequences to the economy and the society. Such a deficit means that part of the government debt will never be repaid, and if the public perceives that irresponsibility, it will be increasingly reluctant to hold government debt. A functioning government debt market means the public believes that ultimately the budget will come into balance.

The Reality of Deficits

Numbers document my second "for-granted." The federal budget has been in deficit in forty-one of the past fifty years, and in nineteen of the past twenty. Since 1960, deficits have become the accepted practice of federal budgeting. Apart from one modest surplus of $3 billion in 1969, the Congress has imposed a regime of persistent deficits. The national debt of $300 billion in FY 1962 rose to $437 billion in FY 1972 and surpassed $1 trillion in October 1981. Eight deficits in the 1970s exceeded $40 billion. The first half of the 1980s witnesses $100 billion deficits. Interest payments on the debt, which absorbed approximately six percent of the national budget twenty years ago, consumed about twelve percent in FY 1981.

Virtually unlimited access to deficit spending by the Congress has fueled federal spending from ten percent of GNP in 1930 to 23 percent by 1982. Had the federal government been compelled to balance its budget during the past half century, it is likely that current spending would take a smaller share of GNP.

Deficit spending is not a unique feature of American democracy. It is the fiscal norm of virtually all Western industrial democracies. In 1981, for example, our federal deficit ranged between two to three percent of GNP, similar to that of Canada, France, and West Germany. In Japan and Italy, the deficits ranged from eight to twelve percent of GNP. Smaller nations such as Holland, Belgium, Denmark, Sweden, and Norway currently run deficits approaching one-tenth of GNP. Ireland has the astonishing share of seventeen percent. So we may be less guilty on this score than our Japanese and European friends, but that is small consolation indeed.

A Bias Toward Deficits

Shepsle (1982) has made a convincing case for my third given. In his analysis of "The Failure of Congressional Budgeting," he points to the two territorial imperatives of jurisdiction and geography that he states cause both a deficit in the functioning of our democratic system and our budgetary process. Shepsle identifies the conflict between the need in Congress for centralized control, if budgeting is to be coordinated and constrained, and the reality of decentralized legislative collegiality that gives full play to the uncontrollable pressures of committees and constituencies. The conflict engenders in us a love-hate relationship. We love our individual members of Congress, who sustain us with private benefits, but we hate the system, which punishes us with taxes, deficits, inflation, high interest rates, and so on. I accept Shepsle's diagnosis of the problem, but not his remedy. Suggestions to strengthen the executive, the appropriations committee and the budget committee are weak palliatives that afford only modest relief.

Before moving on, I want to draw one very important inference from Shepsle's analysis: rules matter. Shepsle himself has noted that adaptive behavior can undermine regulatory objectives. But I doubt that he would go so far as to charge that no set of rules can constrain budgetary behavior, lest his own favored remedies fall on pain of self-contradiction. Our disagreement will revolve around the choice of rules: institutional versus constitutional.

I sometimes think that our founding fathers were overly captives of their day. Had they not taken for granted the concept of limited government, they might have inserted a balanced budget requirement into the original

Constitution. A decade after the Constitution had been in operation, Thomas Jefferson wrote to John Taylor: "I wish it were possible to obtain a single amendment to our Constitution. I would be willing to depend on that alone for the reduction of the administration of our government to the genuine principles of its Constitution; I mean an additional article, taking from the federal government the power of borrowing." (Ford, 1896) Jefferson's "single amendment" is a balanced budget amendment. One can, however, Jefferson's reflections aside, make a convincing case that the founding fathers had taken adequate steps to protect future generations of Americans from oppressive government.

The founding fathers adopted two explicit constitutional provisions and assumed a third which served to restrain spending and deficits. One reserved powers not expressly delegated to the federal government to the states and to the people. The second provided for per capita distribution among the states of taxes on income. The third, implicit, assumed that federal spending would not exceed federal revenues except in times of war or recession. All three have been abrogated or eroded by time and events, especially by the adoption of the Sixteenth Amendment (income tax) in 1913.

Someone born in the post-depression era would regard deficit financing as normal budget practice. Yet until the Great Depression, the balanced budget, save in wartime or recession, was considered part of our "unwritten constitution." Thomas Jefferson warned that "the public debt is the greatest of dangers to be feared by a republican government" and proposed the idea of a balanced budget amendment as early as September 6, 1789. Alexander Hamilton strongly urged the repayment of national debt. Presidents John Adams, James Madison, James Monroe, John Quincy Adams, and Andrew Jackson all urged avoiding public debt. A balanced budget was synonymous with sound political economy.

Until the Great Depression of the 1930s, budget deficits occurred only in times of war and recession. The budget surpluses generated in good times were invariably used to reduce the national debt these deficits produced. Historical deficits of large proportions arose during the Revolutionary War, the War of 1812, the Mexican War of 1846, and during brief recessions in the late 1830s and 1850s. In each instance, the debts were immediately reduced at the onset of peace or prosperity. Between 1795 and 1811, Congress cut the national debt nearly in half from $84 million to just over $45 million. After the War of 1812, eighteen surpluses (of twenty-one budgets) between 1815 and 1836 virtually eliminated the national debt. A run of twenty-eight consecutive surpluses following the Civil War lowered the national debt from $2.7 billion to $960 million. Finally, throughout the

1920s, consecutive surpluses reduced the national debt from $24 billion to $16 billion, at the very time that major tax rate reductions were approved.

Sustained deficits first arose during the depression years of the 1930s and the war years of the early 1940s, leaving in their wake a national debt of about $170 billion. These deficits were consistent with the national experience of wartime and recession. When peace returned, deficits again disappeared. Between 1949 and 1960, seven surpluses of $31 billion roughly offset seven deficits of $32 billion. However, for the first time in American history, no effort was made to reduce the national debt.

Due to the operation of the unwritten norm of budget balance, the federal government was rarely troubled by budget deficits through almost 200 years of our history. Indeed, revenues and expenditures were not incorporated into an overall official budget until 1921.

But today federal budgets are wildly out of balance. Why? The answer lies in the political reality that budget objectives and the budget process are in direct conflict. The Congress, as a whole, is concerned with stable prices, low interest rates, and full employment, which require some check on the scope of government spending. As individuals, however, each congressman confronts pressures to increase spending. The reality of our system has shown convincingly that the collective need to control spending is no match for the pressures each individual member faces to increase it. With virtually unlimited access to deficit spending, the pressures to increase spending prevail.

This bias toward more spending is due, first, to what analysts of government call the phenomenon of "concentrated benefits versus dispersed costs." This describes the fact that the benefits of any given spending program normally are concentrated among a small number of persons, while the costs of such a program are dispersed throughout a much larger class, the general taxpayer.

The competition between tax spenders and tax payers is highly unequal: it is simply not as worthwhile for an individual taxpayer to spend much time and effort to save a few dollars in taxes as it is for the spending interests to secure millions or billions of dollars for themselves. Thus, whenever government programs are considered one by one, as they are in our budgetary system, there is a bias toward government growth, which of late has brought twelve digit deficits.

The explosion in federal spending is not due to the failure to elect the "right" people, it is an institutional defect. The federal budget process is inherently biased toward deficits, higher taxes, and greater government spending. The trends toward bigger government and economic instability reflect the decisions of reasonable men and women in Congress who, as individuals, cannot successfully resist the pressures they face to increase spending.

A second source of bias toward greater spending and deficits is the separation of benefits, which are short run, from costs which are typically more long run. The benefits of spending programs are immediate, both to the recipients and the sitting congressmen who supported them. The costs of spending programs—in the form of potentially higher future taxes, higher future inflation, higher future unemployment or higher future interest rates— will be evident only at some future time, to be borne, perhaps, by future congressmen. Since the electoral time horizon of all house members and one third of the senators is never more than a year or two away, short-term benefits invariably take precedence over potentially long-run adverse economic effects due to higher government spending.

Shepsle has aptly identified a third bias toward spending and deficits— the committee system within the structure of Congress itself. Reelection rewards those members who successfully serve their constituencies, even if the actions of Congress as a whole damage the growth rate of the economy. Asking the Congress to restrain overall spending and eliminate deficits is tantamount to giving the same American Express card number to 535 people, with a polite request that they consider the impact of their individual purchase on the total bill as each person embarks on his or her shopping spree. You can guess the result. It will not be in the interest of any one person to curtail spending since his purchases will have an imperceptible effect on the total bill. Also, any one cardholder's prudence can be offset by any other cardholder's improvidence. Spending under this system will stop only when the company imposes an overall credit limit on these 535 "good" men and women. Pity the federal government has no such credit limit!

Recent Budget Process Reforms Have Failed

Reforming the federal budget process has been and remains a popular topic with politicians, scholars and taxpayers. The most cited example of major reform is the Budget and Impoundment Control Act of 1974, which reflected Congressional concern over executive impoundment of appropriated funds and that little overall control over the federal budget existed. The 1974 Act established budget committees within each house, created the nonpartisan Congressional Budget Office to supply timely information and analysis, and set forth a budgetary timetable. An ostensible purpose of the Act was to better enable Congress to consider individual spending measures in light of overall budget objectives.

And what have been the results? Control over the budget has steadily declined. Despite adherence to the budget timetable, deficits have reached record proportions. Seven deficits exceeded $40 billion in the 1970s. A regime of $100 billion deficits has taken hold in the early 1980s. Control over off-budget outlays has eroded even more sharply: off-budget outlays have increased from less than $1 billion in FY 1973 to surpass $20 billion in FY 1982. Finally, those items in the budget known as "uncontrollables" have increased from 72 percent in FY 1973 to 77 percent in FY 1983. Despite the Act, Congress has been wholly unable to impose its own priorities on the budget.

The 1974 Act has failed to control deficits because it does not allow members of Congress to cope with spending pressures that Shepsle and I have described. I find little solace in the claim that deficits would have been greater without the Act—a strange defense of budget reform indeed.

Statutory Reform is Inherently Flawed

We have thus arrived at my fifth "for-granted:" statutory reform is inherently flawed. In the famous Humphrey-Hawkins Full Employment Act, a balanced budget was declared to be a national public policy priority. An amendment offered by Representative (now Senator) Charles Grassley and Senator Harry Byrd, Jr. to an IMF loan program measure was enacted into law and requires that, beginning with FY 1981, total budget outlays of the federal government "shall not" exceed its receipts (P.L. 95–435). In 1979, a provision in a measure to increase the public debt limit stated that "Congress shall balance the federal budget" (P.L. 96–5). It required the congressional budget committees to propose balanced budgets for FY 1981 and beyond.

None of these measures has reduced or eliminated deficits. The most general reason is that no Congress can bind a succeeding Congress by a simple statute. A balanced budget or tax limitation statute can itself be repealed by the simple expedient of adopting a new statute or new budget which is in conflict with the earlier measure. The Byrd-Grassley amendment, which required a balanced budget for FY 1981, provided no deterrent whatsoever to the adoption of a $50 billion deficit budget for that year.

Rules Matter

That rules matter is my sixth "for-granted." This point is so uncontroversial that I am tempted to say no more on it. After all, it is the purpose of a constitution to limit government. Laws and regulations govern behavior among persons. Committee assignments in the Congress influence legislative outcomes. And so on.

A new branch of public choice dubbed "constitutional economics" asserts that the constitution affords a means for constraining the activities of government in the economic marketplace. For most of our history, the restriction against direct taxation of income restrained the size of government receipts. Similarly, the constitution limited the regulatory power of the federal government until the Supreme Court's interpretation of the commerce clause allowed the government to encroach on a greater range of economic activities crossing state lines.

Would anyone argue today that we should repeal the First Amendment and trust our future right to free speech to the Congress of public opinion at large? How many of you believe we would retain our political and civil rights if we abolished the entire Bill of Rights?

Just because a rule is written on a sacred piece of paper does not mean that it will insure total adherence. For example, the Tax Equity and Fiscal Responsibility Act of 1982 originated in the Senate despite the constitutional requirement that all revenue measures originate in the House of Representatives. But for the most part, the Constitution constrains the actions of government. As far as the budgetary process is concerned, the key question is whether a constitutional amendment could eliminate the persistent bias towards chronic deficits that past statutory reforms have failed to remedy.

The Balanced Budget/Tax Limitation Amendment

This brings me to my final "for-granted." S.J. Res. 58 is the current candidate for a constitutional amendment to prohibit deficits. It would also limit the rise in federal receipts. Before reviewing each section of the amendment, it is useful to provide some historical background on how it came to be known as the consensus amendment.

Article V of the Constitution provides two methods of proposing amendments. The first method, by which all 26 amendments have thus far been adopted, requires the proposal of an amendment by two thirds of each House of Congress, and ratification by three fourths of the states. The second method allows for an amendment drawn by a constitutional convention, which must be called by Congress in response to the application of two thirds of the states. Whichever method is invoked, the proposed amendment must be approved by three-fourths of the states (38) before it becomes part of the Constitution.

Since 1975, the National Taxpayers Union has worked with the state legislatures to pass resolutions—of which thirty one have thus far been approved—calling upon the Congress to invoke Article V of the Constitution and convene a constitutional convention for the purpose of writing a balanced budget amendment.

In early 1979, largely because of pressure being exerted by the states to convene a constitutional convention, the Senate Judiciary Subcommittee on the Constitution also began efforts to develop its own constitutional proposal to prohibit budget deficits. Proponents of constitutional restraint offered two competing proposals. One would require a balanced budget and the other would limit government spending. Critics of the balanced budget approach argued that under such an amendment the budget might be balanced at higher levels of taxes, since inflation fueled automatic unvoted increases in receipts through tax bracket creep. Critics of the major spending limit proposal, a measure drafted by the National Tax Limitation Committee and introduced by Senators John Heinz and Richard Stone, charged that the Heinz-Stone measure was too complex for the public to understand, that it failed to take advantage of public support for the concept of a balanced budget, and that it inappropriately read substance, not procedure, into the Constitution.

Senate Joint Resolution 58, a combined balanced budget tax limitation amendment, was reported out of the full Senate Committee on the Judiciary on May 19, 1981. Its companion in the House of Representatives is House Joint Resolution 350. On August 4, 1982, the Senate passed S.J. Res. 58 by a vote of 69 to 31, two more than the required two thirds majority. Support was clearly bipartisan, though more Democrats were in opposition than Republicans. However, the House Judiciary Committee did not report the counterpart measure, H.J. Res. 350, to the floor for consideration. Supporters of the amendment circulated a discharge petition to circumvent Peter Rodino's committee. Through clever political strategy, supporters garnered the necessary 218 signatures by September 29, 1982. Although House rules require that a discharge petition must wait seven business days for action, the Democratic leadership permitted a vote on October 1, 1982, lest the Republicans use the issue to their advantage in the congressional elections, charging the Democrats with fiscal irresponsibility. The vote in the House was 236 yes to 187 no, a 56 percent majority that fell clearly short of the needed two-thirds constitutional requirement.

At the end of 1982, discussion of the amendment remained largely academic. It is unlikely that the tenuous coalition which produced a two thirds Senate vote in August 1982 would hold together when the 98th Congress convened. Nor is the House likely to have a change of heart. To move consideration of the amendment to the front burner in 1983 will require that several state legislatures pass resolutions calling on the Congress to convene a constitutional convention. Here the odds are better, but not high enough that I dare risk a guess. I am certain, though, that passage of a resolution by the thirty second and thirty third states would bring overnight approval of S.J. Res. 58/H.J. Res. 350. The one thing worse than a Congressionally-initiated balanced budget-tax limitation amendment is one drafted by a constitutional convention beyond the control of members of Congress.

Senate Joint Resolution 58: A Balanced Budget-Tax Limitation Constitutional Amendment

Let us examine the proposed amendment to see how it would redress the present imbalance in our budgetary process.

Balanced Budget

Section 1.   Prior to each fiscal year, the Congress shall adopt a statement of receipts and outlays for that year in which total outlays are no greater than total receipts. The Congress may amend such statement provided revised outlays are no greater than revised receipts. Whenever three-fifths of the whole number of both houses shall deem it necessary, Congress in such statement may provide for a specific excess of outlays over receipts by a vote directed solely to that subject. The Congress and the President shall, pursuant to legislation or through exercise of their powers under the first and second articles, ensure that actual outlays do not exceed the outlays set forth in such statement.

The purpose of Section 1 is two-fold. First, Congress would be required to plan to balance its budget every year. It would do so by adopting a statement or budget prior to the start of each fiscal year, in which planned outlays (spending) do not exceed planned receipts (revenue). Congress could violate this rule and plan for a deficit only by a three-fifths vote of the whole number of each House of Congress, not just three-fifths of those present and voting. In contrast, a simple majority could approve a budget surplus. Second, Section 1 also mandates that actual outlays do not exceed the spending levels set forth in the approved statement or budget.

It is important to point out that the amendment establishes the basis for a planned balanced budget. It does not require that the budget be in actual balance during the course of the fiscal year. In some circumstances, actual outlays may exceed actual receipts. For example, a recession might reduce actual receipts below the level of receipts set forth in the planned statement. This is permissible under the amendment, but actual outlays could not exceed statement outlays. Deficits caused by increased spending would also not be permitted.

If circumstances warrant, the Congress may adopt an amended statement of receipts and outlays for the fiscal year (provided again that outlays do not exceed receipts) at any time during the fiscal year. An amended statement containing a deficit would require a three-fifths vote only if such deficit was greater than the deficit in the previous statement. Thus the budget would not be "locked in" and could be changed by an explicit vote of Congress in response to changing economic conditions.

An important feature of Section 1 is that it imposes upon the Congress and the President a mandate to prevent total actual outlays, which includes both on- and off-budget items, from exceeding statement outlays. For example, should the economy perform below expectations, leading to increased spending on entitlements or on debt service due to higher interest rates, the Congress would be called upon either to increase statement outlays and approve a deficit (by a three-fifths vote), or to postpone spending programs and/or to reduce eligibility for entitlements. To guard against the possibility that actual outlays might exceed statement outlays through unintentional and presumably modest error, an obvious remedy would be for Congress to plan a surplus of equivalent size for the next fiscal year.

The Congress is expected to adopt the most accurate estimates of receipts and outlays that it can in drafting its budget, but in all cases a congressional majority will be the final arbiter among the choice of estimates. As the fiscal year unfolds, actual receipts may or may not meet expectations. An unexpectedly more robust economy may yield receipts above statement receipts; an unexpectedly weaker economy may yield receipts below statement receipts. Either result is permissible. The amendment imposes no obligation upon the Congress to react to the flow of actual receipts during the fiscal year, only to the flow of actual outlays.

Recent years have witnessed congressional failure to adopt a budget by the October 1 date on which a new fiscal year begins. Congress has funded government operations in such instances by adopting continuing resolutions. Under the amendment, this practice would be banned. Failure to adopt a statement of receipts and outlays by the October 1 deadline would be construed as an implied adoption of a statement in which both receipts and outlays are zero. In that event, the Congress and the President would be mandated constitutionally to ensure that fiscal year outlays also would be zero. In short, the government would shut down on October 1 without prior passage of a budget by September 30.

Loans for which the federal government guarantees in whole or in part the repayment of principal and/or interest impose no funding obligation on the treasury unless and until such loans come into default and the treasury must discharge the guarantee obligation. Such a discharge is intended to be construed as an outlay in the fiscal year of discharge.

A large portion of federal spending is currently on automatic pilot. That is, spending for entitlements grows every year as a share of federal spending. An amendment prohibiting deficits would create a strong incentive to bring these "uncontrollables" under control, since they would compete directly with discretionary programs. At present, the automatic growth of spending on "uncontrollables" erodes the ability of Congress to impose its own priorities on the budget, which is tantamount to passing the congressional buck.

Section 1 does not propose to read any specific level of spending or taxing forever into the Constitution, nor does it intrude into the day to day decisions of the government as to how the federal dollar is allocated. It merely restores the balance between taxspenders and taxpayers by constraining spending totals to available revenues.

Tax Limitation

Section 2. Total receipts for any fiscal year set forth in the statement adopted pursuant to this article shall not increase by a rate greater than the rate of increase in national income in the year or years ending not less than six months nor more than twelve months before such fiscal year, unless a majority of the whole number of both Houses of Congress shall have passed a bill directed solely to approving specific additional receipts and such bill has become law.

The purpose of Section 2 is to prevent tax receipts from growing more rapidly than the general economy, as occurs with our graduated rate tax code. Under the amendment, a whole majority of the membership of both Houses would have to vote to permit receipts to outpace general economic growth. In particular, Congress would be required to enact a bill expanding a specified tax base and/or increasing specified tax rates.

Put another way, Section 2 states that the balanced budget requirement in Section 1 should not occur at levels of receipts and outlays that consume an increasing proportion of the national economy. It attempts to achieve this result by limiting the increase in receipts for a new fiscal year to the percentage increase in the national income during a prior congressionally chosen time period. If present tax laws are likely to yield revenues in excess of this limit, the Congress must modify the revenue laws to reduce anticipated receipts.

The relationship between the growth of national income during the prior period and the growth of receipts during the following fiscal year provides the Congress with reasonably precise guideposts in its budgeting process. Quite accurate estimates of the growth in national income are available by mid-July prior to the beginning of the fiscal year.

Take fiscal year 1981, for example, which began October 1, 1980. The rate of increase in statement receipts for fiscal year 1981 would have been limited to the rate of increase of national income for calendar year 1979, assuming Congress chose calendar 1979 as the base period. Since national income rose 11.4 percent in 1979, statement receipts for fiscal 1981 could not have exceeded fiscal 1980 statement receipts by more than 11.4 percent. The planned increase for FY 1981 with no changes in the current tax law was set at 14.5 percent. Had the amendment been in effect, the tax law would not have produced this automatic tax increase. Taxes would have been about $16 billion lower. To increase taxes, Congress would have had to explicitly vote for a tax increase for FY 1981.

Statement receipts may also rise by less than the proportionate increase in national income. In that event, the new lower level of receipts would then become the base for statement receipts in subsequent fiscal years, until the Congress voted a rise in allowable receipts.

It is important to recapitulate how the budget process would work under the amendment. The Congress would determine the increase in national income during the prior defined period in accord with Section 2. That percentage rise, in turn, would determine the maximum increase in receipts the government could collect for the coming fiscal year. If, say, national income rose ten percent during the prior period, then receipts could rise by no more than 10 percent for the new fiscal year. Since outlays cannot exceed receipts (the budget must be balanced or in surplus), government spending could not rise by more than ten percent. Sections 1 and 2, in conjunction, establish a *de facto* spending limit. Thus neither taxes nor spending can grow more rapidly than the economy.

The amendment permits federal spending to grow more rapidly than the economy only if Congress explicitly votes to allow receipts to rise more rapidly than the growth of the economy. It takes a direct vote of a constitutional majority of both Houses of Congress to permit the growth of federal spending to outpace the growth of the economy. Or, federal spending may outpace economic growth if Congress approves, by a three-fifths majority vote, a deficit in which outlays from year to year exceed economic growth rates. Thus the federal government is not hamstrung; it can meet what may be regarded as increased genuine needs of the people, if it also were prepared to vote on the record for higher taxes or deficits to finance higher spending.

Wartime Waiver

> *Section 3.* The Congress may waive the provisions of this article for any fiscal year in which a declaration of war is in effect.

In the event of a declaration of war, Congress has the discretionary authority to operate outside of the provisions of the amendment. Such a waiver would be on a year to year basis by concurrent resolution of Congress, as defined under Article 1, Section 8, of the Constitution. Congress would have to adopt annually a separate waiver for each fiscal year at issue.

Borrowing and Repayment of Debt

> *Section 4.* Total receipts shall include all receipts of the United States except those derived from borrowing and total outlays shall include all outlays of the United States except those for repayment of debt principal.

The purpose of Section 4 is to exclude the proceeds of debt issuance from receipts. Thus, treasury notes and bonds would not count as receipts, but as the proceeds of selling debt. Similarly, the term outlays is intended to include all disbursements from the Treasury of the United States, both on-budget and off-budget, either directly or indirectly through federal or quasi-federal agencies created under the authority of acts of Congress. Section 4 states that funds used to repurchase or retire Federal debt would not count as outlays. Interest accrued or paid in conjunction with the debt obligation would, however, be included in outlays.

The amendment permits Congress to plan for a budgetary surplus. Those surplus receipts, subject to the increase limit of Section 2, used to repay principal—that is, retire national debt—would not be counted as outlays. Should the government fully retire the national debt, the amendment would still allow the government to plan for an annual surplus, and even accumulate reserves. Interest earned on these reserves, however, would be subject to the revenue limit. (Admittedly, it would take generations for this scenario to develop.)

Implementing Legislation

Section 5.   The Congress shall enforce and implement this article by appropriate legislation.

S.J. Res. 58 is in accord with a federal constitutional tradition that favors the expression of broad, fundamental principles but leaves further specification and the elaboration of detail to later usage and experience (Scalia, 1982). The amendment does not define in detail such terms as "receipts," "outlays," or "national income," which clutter the text of some state constitutions. It relies on the Committee Report and legislative history to flesh out details, leaving the specifics of implementation to future Congressional legislation.

Some critics contend that the proposed amendment would not be enforceable, either because the courts would not hear suits based upon it, or because Congress could easily comply with it technically as required in Section 5, while evading its purpose and intent. Note first that several current provisions in the constitution are not actionable in the court. For example, if someone asserts that the constitutionally prescribed manner of election has not been complied with, the Constitution leaves it to the respective houses of Congress, rather than the courts, to resolve the dispute (Article I, Section 5, clause 1). Second, the doctrine of standing renders other provisions, one distinctly budgetary, of the Constitution unenforceable: the requirement that "A regular Statement and Account of the Receipts and Expenditures of all public Money shall be published from time to time" (Art. I, Sec. 9, cl. 7).

The supposition that prohibitions which can be observed to the letter but violated in spirit and intent do not belong in the Constitution should be disspelled by the Supreme Court's use of the commerce clause to disregard the careful enumeration of federal powers (Art. I, Sec. 8) and the Tenth Amendment. Thus neither judicial enforceability nor practical inevadability has in the past been a criterion for constitutional guarantees.

Section 5 instructs the Congress to enforce the amendment, but does not say how. By whatever means it selects, in the final determination, the Congress and the President are expected to act in accord with their constitutional duties of office, exercising the trust reposed in them by the people. The amendment is also self-enforcing through the political process. By establishing a focus upon two or three critical votes each year relating to the level of taxation or the size of the deficits, in place of the present piecemeal focus on hundreds of separate spending measures, the amendment will enable the electorate to better identify those members of Congress most responsible for higher levels of spending, taxing, and deficits.

Nor is it costless to circumvent an amendment. There is a world of difference between an ordinary statute and a constitutional provision. Without the protection of the Constitution, it is quite likely that many of our individual freedoms would have been eroded over time by successive acts of Congress. Similarly, members of Congress will find it more difficult to flout the constitutional requirement of budget balance and tax limitation.

Debt Ceiling

Section 6.   On and after the date this article takes effect, the amount of Federal public debt limit as of such date shall become permanent and there shall be no increase in such amount unless three-fifths of the whole number of both Houses of Congress shall have passed a bill approving such increase and such bill has become law.

Section 6 was added to the proposed amendment during floor debate in the Senate. It drew support from strange bedfellows—conservatives, who abhor public debt, and liberals, who would like to encumber the amendment with provisions that make House passage more difficult and ratification in 38 states less likely. Under Section 6, three-fifths of the whole membership would have to authorize a federal debt limit beyond $400 billion. Failure to do so would halt the government's power to borrow, literally shutting down the federal government.

Supporters of the original amendment hope to delete Section 6 in any final version that emerges from both chambers. H.J. Res. 350 does not include this section. Nothing can be said in support of this section, other than that a few well meaning Senators were conned into an unwise move.

Section 7.   This article shall take effect for the second fiscal year beginning after its ratification.

Section 7 stipulates when the amendment would take effect. If ratification were completed before September 30, 1983, the amendment would require Congress to adopt its first balanced budget statement before September 30, 1984; if ratification were completed between October 1, 1983, and before September 30, 1984, the first balanced budget adoption would be required by September 30, 1985, and so on. Realistically, the amendment could not take effect until 1985 or 1986 at the earliest, which assumes early passage in the 98th Congress, and quick ratification in 38 states.

To complete the story on S.J. Res. 58, it should be noted that one section in the original version had been dropped. Section 4 in the prior version stated that "The Congress may not require that the States engage in additional activities without compensation equal to the additional costs." This section was intended to prevent the Congress from shifting a portion of its fiscal responsibilities to the states and their local units of government through mandates imposed upon these governments. The section was deleted from the final version of the Senate resolution out of concern that such a clause had no place in the Constitution. Its deletion creates a loophole by which the Congress can adhere to the letter, but not the spirit and intent, of the amendment.

References

"Balanced Budget-Tax Limitation Constitutional Amendment," *Report to the Committee on the Judiciary,* United States Senate, 97th Congress, 1st Session, Report No. 97–151, Washington, DC: US Government Printing Office, 1981.

Ford, P. L. ed. *The Writings of Thomas Jefferson.* New York and London: G. P. Putnam's Sons, 1904–05. 1896, Vol. 7, p. 310.

Rabushka, A. "A Compelling Case for a Constitutional Amendment to Balance the Budget and Limit Taxes." A paper prepared for the Taxpayers' Foundation, Washington, DC, 1982.

Scalia, A. "Constitutional Aspects of SJR 58/HJR 350, The Tax Limitation/ Balanced Budget Amendment." A paper prepared for the Tax Limitation Research Foundation, Washington, DC, 1982.

Shepsle, K.A. "Constitutional Regulation of the U.S. Budget." Contemporary Issues Series 1, Center for the Study of American Business, Washington University, St. Louis, May, 1982a.

Shepsle, K. A. "The Failure of Congressional Budgeting." Formal paper no. 46. March, 1982b.

DISCUSSION
Roger G. Noll

The Case Against the Balanced Budget Amendment: Comments on Aranson and Rabushka

Since the publication of Arrow's classic work, *Social Choice and Individual Values,* a hardy, growing band of scholars has attempted to use social choice theory to build a positive theory of government. Alternatively called social choice theory, public choice and formal positive political theory, this work investigates methods of collective decisionmaking in terms of their efficiency, their distributional effects and the existence and uniqueness of equilibrium. Applications have been made to small group decisionmaking, the structure of legislatures, and procedures for electing political leaders as well as undertaking referenda on policy issues. A sampling of this literature is contained in the bibliography of this paper.

The most fundamental level at which this theory can be applied is to the question of designing a constitution. A constitution establishes the rules of the political game. It defines the rights and obligations of citizens acting in various capacities as voters, owners of private property, candidates for public office and government officials. It describes the process for organizing the government, establishes the range of actions that government can take, defines the powers and responsibilities of various parts of government in the policymaking process, and even sets forth rules for changing the rules themselves. Moreover, the constitution is preeminent in the hierarchy of rules and procedures established by all organizations in society, private and public: constitutional principles always take precedence, by definition.

The papers by Aranson and Rabushka attempt to undertake a theoretical analysis of an issue of constitutional design: namely, what is the effect, normatively and positively, of adopting a constitutional rule requiring a balanced federal budget? I have phrased the question in a somewhat altered form than can be found in either paper, but the change is intentional—to emphasize that the problem is one in comparative equilibrium analysis, and that it has both positive and normative aspects. These distinctions are not always clearly made in the two papers. I have also been rather more comprehensive in defining the point of a constitution. To state, as does Rabushka, that the purpose of a constitution is to limit government is, in my opinion, narrow, confused and loaded. A view that I find more useful is that a constitution is a contract among citizens defining their rights, their mutual obligations, and the procedures they will follow to make collective decisions.

Both papers attack the issue of the balanced budget limitation in the following way. Both examine the formal theory of the political process to determine whether (a) it has a systematic tendency to produce a public sector that is too large; (b) it has a systematic tendency to produce lower tax revenues than expenditures; and (c) if the first two are true, an amendment to balance the budget will cure these problems. The two papers reach different conclusions: Aranson believes that one should answer the questions, respectively, as "probably," "probably," and "maybe," whereas Rabushka gives a confident "YES" on all parts.

In these brief remarks I simply want to dissent on all three points. I do so as a matter of political theory; my answers to the three questions would be: "Who knows," "probably not," and "probably not." But I wish to emphasize one central point: the economic theory of politics applied to the American system of government yields no firm results on any of these issues. Indeed, like most of rational choice theory, including microeconomics, it is far too general to produce definitive qualitative results. It is not even intended to do so. Instead, its purposes are to help one organize one's thoughts about how political processes work and, especially, to guide empirical research to explain and predict changes in political outcomes. It is not designed to tell us whether we need or want a constitutional amendment to balance the budget any more than it is designed to tell us whether women should have the franchise or citizens should be guaranteed freedom of speech.

First, rational choice models of the political system do not tell us that government is too big. At best, some parts of formal political theory tell us that some aspects of the political process work in this direction, under some conditions. The most famous body of theory in this field is the Arrow paradox and its ramifications. It says that in general majority-rule elections do not have a unique equilibrium and, moreover, that with appropriate selection of the agenda for voting on alternatives one generally can produce a final outcome that is strictly Pareto dominated by others. Interpreted in the context of the size of government, this theory implies that to err on one side is as likely as to err on the other. Government, *a priori,* cannot be said to have a systematic tendency to be either too big or too small.

Other theories that are richer in institutional details, while costly in making more assumptions, pay off in clearer results. But the effect of the American system of representative democracy on the size of government is still ambiguous. The primary results of these models deal with the mix and efficiency of government provision of goods and services. They state that certain kinds of policies will tend to be favored over others, and that certain methods of producing government services will be preferred over others. The foundation of these results is in the fact that the act of participation in the political process is itself a public good. Effective political participation has spillover effects because the resulting policy will affect everyone. Consequently, people will be moved to participate only when they have large enough stakes in an issue to make it worth their while to pay the costs of participation and when for some reason they do not elect to free ride. The conclusion derived from this is that narrow issues pertaining to well organized groups will receive relatively more attention than more diffuse issues spread over unorganized citizens, even if the aggregate stake of the latter exceeds that of the former. Using this conceptual model, it is not hard to think of situations in which public goods are undersupplied rather than oversupplied. For example, nuclear waste facilities provide diffuse public benefits of great value, but concentrate the risks on people who would live near them. Hence, attempts to build them tend to meet with such organized, vehement opposition that government is afraid to undertake them. The result is a hazardous condition of improperly managed nuclear wastes and an undersupply of waste management facilities. The general point is this: there is a tendency in a democratic form of government for the concentrated effects of a political action to be given greater weight than the diffuse effects. Consequently, some types of public goods will be in relatively too large a supply compared to others.

It is natural for journalists to observe that part of government tends to be a gigantic pork barrel machine, and therefore to conclude that government is too big. The problem with this conclusion is that it is based upon a fallacy that ought to be well known to social scientists: sampling on the dependent variable. Obviously, relatively little government activity will take the form of programs that are too small or even nonexistent, whereas much of it will be programs that are too big. It is correct to say that we probably spend relatively too much on public works; it is not at all correct to conclude, therefore, that government is too large because some programs are too large.

Another line of political theory investigates how the political process affects the design of government programs. The single member congressional district is the focus of this analysis, and the point is to explain and predict the consequences of the observation that representatives from such districts spend a great deal of time working as ombudsmen for constituents, as contrasted to making public policy. The result of this theory is that in order to preserve the possibility of responding effectively to citizen requests for help, a representative has an incentive to use bureaucratic means of providing public policies: regulations rather than emissions taxes or marketable emissions permits, project grants and contracts rather than block grants, etc. The result is inefficiency in the cost of providing public services. Costs of public goods are not minimized because it is worth it to legislators to use higher cost means of supply that enable them to intervene on behalf of constituents and thereby score points that will redound to their benefit on election day.

This theory says that government programs will cost too much per unit of output. Whether this means that total expenditures in the public sector are too high depends on the elasticity of demand for public goods. If demand is inelastic, expenditures are higher than they otherwise would be; but if demand is elastic, expenditures are too low. Whatever the expenditure effect, of course, the quantity effect is unambiguous if demand curves have negative slopes—higher price means less quantity. Hence, the effect of facilitation activities is almost certain to be to reduce the real output of the public sector.

So much for government being clearly too large. But what if, as an empirical matter, it is? This brings the second issue: is there a persistent tendency for deficits to be too large? Worth noting is the obvious: this is the only argument that supporters of the balanced budget need. The discussion of the actual versus optimal size of government is necessary only for an argument to limit expenditures.

The basic argument advanced in support of the notion that government is too prone to run deficits is that expenditures and taxes are more visible to individual citizens than are debts and money creation. A secondary argument is that deficits represent an intergenerational transfer from the future to the present. I will ignore the latter; it confuses the means of finance with the political selection of a division between consumption (private and public) versus investment (private and public). The less said about this argument the politer.

Certainly the question of the politics of tax policy is one of the most interesting—and least developed—components of formal political theory. Thus, we can speak less confidently about it than we can about the question of the size of government. Nevertheless, theory in this domain is developing quite similarly to theory about expenditures. Specifically, the most important results are about the form of taxation, rather than its level relative to expenditures.

Recall that the theory of expenditures relied upon two phenomena: the relative responsiveness of the public sector to well organized, narrow interests in relation to more diffuse, broader interests, and the activities of legislators as ombudsmen. Suppose in this milieu that citizens wish tax relief. Each citizen will have two types of avenues available: as a member of a diffuse group of voters who, *ceteris paribus,* can vote for politicians who favor lower taxes, and as a member of various particularistic interests, who will, among other things, favor particularistic tax preferences for themselves. The part of political theory that deals with the greater relative influence of narrow interests says that the latter avenue will tend to be more successful than the former. It also says that when a legislature raises taxes, it will tend to increase taxes that have an effect on more diffuse groups. The ombudsmen feature of representatives reinforces this tendency. Each legislator will try to provide specialized tax breaks for complaining constituents. Senator Russell Long, commenting on one of Congress' annual "Christmas Tree" tax bills, put the matter rather pointedly: "Don't tax you, don't tax me; tax that guy behind the tree."

The key point about formal political theory is that it imagines voters to be in a prisoner's dilemma on election day. They know that their representatives in the House and Senate have little chance of affecting the winning position in Congress on major issues of public policy, such as the level of taxation or, indeed, the overall size of any program or of the government itself. They do know, however, that as government grows, it is increasingly important to have a legislative facilitator, someone who can provide favors to constituents. And Congress, by fractioning itself into myriad specialized subcommittees for programmatic oversight activities, has created an ideal device for providing small favors through a timely phone call to an agency, or a personalized break in the annual tax "reform" bill. The structure of Congress not only gives stability to the otherwise unstable majority rule process in Congress, but by encouraging specialization, it creates an environment for mutually beneficial trades among members who have different committee assignments. Hence, it makes sense for voters to give weight to facilitation as well as to public policy in voting for legislators. Applied to the taxation case, this means relatively less attention will be given to the overall level of taxation.

Of course, the prisoner's dilemma can be overcome if the general state of policy becomes so bad that even after accounting for diffuseness, it becomes important in an election. This places a check on legislators. There is no reason for them to run the risk of widespread voter revolt when, by being good ombudsmen, legislators can remain incumbents almost as long as they wish. And, historically, one of the two diffuse issues that more or less regularly raises the specter of defeat for an incumbent (the other is international affairs) is the state of the economy. Hence, to the extent that running big deficits undermines the economy, there is a good reason for a legislator not to vote for them, especially in light of the ongoing opportunity to defuse the outrage of some unhappy constituents in the annual tax bill.

Thus, formal political theory probably does have something to say about the structure of the tax system and about why tax reform and simplification are so difficult to accomplish. But it probably has little or nothing to say about the question of deficits, for much the same reasons it has nothing definitive to say about the direction of distortion, if any, in the size of government.

As a practical matter, the argument that government is biased in favor of deficits has more severe problems than are encountered by the argument about size. The first question is why are deficits so small? What checks them at all? The empirical observation in support of the position that there is a bias in favor of deficits is that, since fiscal 1961, the federal budget has been in deficit every year except 1969. But in most years the economic significance of the deficit has been small. During the first ten years of this period (1961–1970), in only two years did the deficit exceed five percent of federal expenditures, and in only one did it reach two percent of GNP. In the next ten years, the deficits averaged ten percent of expenditures and two percent of GNP; however, the economy was weaker in the 1970s than in the 1960s, and one would expect that automatic stabilization would have caused higher deficits during this period in the absence of any political action to encourage them.

The second question about the bias toward deficits is why it is so recent a phenomenon? No explicit constitutional change altered the incentive structure of legislators. Rabushka argues that there was an implicit balanced budget amendment before the New Deal; however, the question remains why legislators, facing no explicit requirement, failed to respond to the incentives inherent in the political system for the first 150 years of the republic.

Indeed, to look at only the sign and not the magnitude of the bottom line of the budget is to overlook two very important facts. The first is that by far the most important predictors of the degree of imbalance in the budget are (a) the state of the economy; and (b) whether the country is at war. If neither of the above is straining the system, budgets are normally very close to balancing. The most important factor explaining the fact that the budget has been in the red for twenty two of the past twenty three years is that we have spent most of that period in either recession or the war in Vietnam. Second, the budgets of the past two years set new indoor records. Fiscal 1983 will be the highest deficit in relation to federal expenditures and GNP since World War II. The contest is not even close: in 1983, the deficit will be five or six percent of GNP, whereas the previous postwar record was around three percent. There is something incongruous about a President who speaks of the need to have a constitutional amendment to restrain him from responding to political incentives that other presidents have been substantially more successful in resisting. Perhaps he simply wants to assure the permanence of his entry in the Guinness Book of World Records.

Unlike the argument about the size of government, the argument about deficits can be subjected to empirical scrutiny. When it is, the validity of the argument is cast in even greater doubt. There simply is no reason to believe that the political system is biased in favor of deficits for the reasons given.

Nevertheless, a third question still must be addressed: will the balanced budget amendment as proposed be a binding constraint? The answer here is quite simple: it is substantially less binding a constraint than the veto power of the President. Presidential vetos require a two thirds vote to be overridden, whereas the proposed balanced budget amendment requires sixty percent. A President who wanted to balance the budget would have an easier time of it than erstwhile balancers in Congress would have under the amendment.

Even above this detail, there is a more important element of political reality to contend with. The problem is the enforceability of such an amendment. A deficit can be proven to be a reality after a fiscal year draws to a close. Prior to that, revenues and expenditures are based on estimates and forecasts. To enforce a balanced budget requirement necessitates estimating a deficit in a politically meaningful way—within the executive and/or congressional branches of the government. If the political incentives were present for a majority in Congress to enact a deficit and the President to sign it, they will also be present to employ the services of that mythological forecaster of recent years, Rosy Scenario.

Even if Rosy fails, the form of enforcement is a shut down of government. Grandma's social security check will not be in the mail, etc. This is an extraordinarily high political price for a legislator to pay. Moreover, if the deficit is too large for even Rosy to paper over, most likely the country will be in a recession, so that legislators will be equally dissatisfied with the alternative of raising taxes or cutting expenditures—assuming either could be enacted and implemented quickly enough to affect the overall budget balance. The easy path will surely always be to override the balanced budget amendment.

The preceding conclusion seems to be verified by the experience of states that have balanced budget requirements. A recent study by the Congressional Budget Office found that "states faced with statutory and constitutional limitations on debt appear to have avoided the limitations successfully by creating various authorities that are allowed to issue 'moral obligation' bonds." Moral obligation bonds pledge the coercive taxation powers of the state as collateral for the bond, thereby permitting a quasi-governmental entity outside the budget to finance itself by floating loans at the state bond rate. What this phenomenon illustrates is the ingeniousness of political entrepreneurs at "inventing around" institutional constraints. If there were a political bias in favor of a government that is too large and too much in deficit, a constitutional amendment to deal with these problems would face the difficulty of preventing ways to get around it by engaging in off budget activities that have the same overall effect on the economy. An obvious example is greater use of tax incentives and loan guarantees to channel private expenditures into areas the government would abandon if the budget had to be smaller. Another example is the use of regulation to require certain kinds of private expenditures as a condition for doing business, or Richard Posner's idea of "taxation by regulation."

On all three counts, then, the case for the balanced budget amendment is insubstantial. But suppose each of the three subissues had gone the other way: suppose we could prove that the government is too large, too prone to deficit, and susceptible to effective control in both regards. Would it naturally follow that the constitutional approach is the appropriate one?

Here the answer must be more speculative. It depends upon philosophical questions about the nature of the social contract, which inevitably turn on questions of individual values. Nevertheless, there is a compelling argument for thinking twice about limiting expenditures and deficits.

The guts of the question about the performance of government have to do with the way it allocates resources among groups, between public and private goods, and between consumption and investment. To limit the size of the federal government, subject to a requirement that a substantial majority (not a bare majority) approve a proposal to do otherwise, is to constrain future citizens in their attempts to find an optimal allocation of resources. It is also to give more voting power to those who favor private goods in comparison to those who favor public ones. Additionally, it is to build an institution that works against a precept that is generally regarded as desirable in government, namely positive responsiveness: i.e., the direction of a change in government policy should be the same as the direction of shift in the tastes of citizens. Finally, it is to set in concrete a current macrotheoretic wisdom, shared only by some, about how deficits and the size of government affect the overall economy. Rabushka, quoting Jefferson, elevates a particular macroeconomic theory to the status of universal truth. But it is a good thing lots of other universal truths of Jefferson's time—bleeding as a treatment of fever, for example—were kept out of the Constitution.

The American Constitution has proved to be remarkably resilient, and has served as the foundation for a remarkably durable system of government. One plausible reason this is so is that it stands for the most part above matters of day to day politics. It deals with how we should govern ourselves and what individual rights the government should protect, but leaves to the political process the problem of deciding the amount of public goods to be provided and the method of paying for them. The proposed budget amendment upsets this feature of the political system. It elevates to the status of enduring, universal value the concept of a fixed size of the federal budget as well as whether the bottom line is written in red or black. And by so doing, it inhibits the responsiveness of government in ways that cannot be justified to losers on the ground that to do so protects some democratic principle related to fairness, justice and the rights of individuals. Unlike most of the Constitution, the proposed amendment appears to losers as the work of one faction to enhance their control of the policy outcomes of the government. It strikes me that this is the stuff of which political instability is made.

References

Arrow, K. J. *Social Choice and Individual Values.* New York: John Wiley and Sons, 1951.

Davis, L. E. and D. C. North. *Institutional Change and American Economic Growth.* London: Cambridge University Press, 1971.

Fenno, R. *Home Style.* Boston: Little, Brown, 1978.

Fiorina, M. P. "Universalism, Reciprocity, and Distributive Policymaking in Majority Rule Institutions." In *Research in Public Analysis and Management* 1, J. P. Crecine (Ed). Greenwich: JAI Press, 1981.

Fiorina, M. P. and R. G. Noll. "Majority Rule Models of Legislative Elections." *Journal of Politics* 41, No. 2 (November 1979), 1081–1004.

Fiorina, M. P. "Voters, Bureaucrats and Legislators: A Rational Choice Perspective on the Growth of Bureaucracy." *Journal of Public Economics* 9 (1978), 239–254.

McKelvey, R. D. "General Conditions for Global Intransitivities in Formal Voting Models." *Econometrica* 47 (1979), 1085–1111.

Olson, M. *The Logic of Collective Action.* Cambridge: Harvard University Press, 1965.

Plott, C. R. and M. E. Levine. "A Model of Agenda Influence on Committee Decisions." *American Economic Review* 68, No. 1 (March 1978), 146–160.

Posner, R. "Taxation by Regulation." *Bell Journal of Economics* 2, No. 1 (Spring 1971), 22–60.

Shepsle, K. "Institutional Arrangements and Equilibrium in Multidimensional Voting Models." *American Journal of Political Science* 23 (1979), 27–59.

US Congressional Budget Office, *Balancing the Federal Budget and Limiting Federal Spending: Constitutional and Statutory Approaches.* Washington: Government Printing Office, September 1982.

Weingast, B., K. Shepsle and C. Johnsen. "The Political Economy of Benefits and Costs: A Neoclassical Approach to the Politics of Distribution." *Journal of Political Economy* 89 (August 1981), 642–664.

DISCUSSION
Kenneth A. Shepsle

Overgrazing the Budgetary Commons: Incentive—Compatible Solutions to the Problem of Deficits

In these brief remarks I assume that nominal deficits are a problem. This may be somewhat controversial: for some macroeconomic theories, real deficits, deficits as a proportion of GNP, or full employment equivalent deficits are more appropriate measures of fiscal distress and, in turn, are less problematic than the nominal level would suggest. This qualification aside, however, current nominal deficits and, *a fortiori,* those that are forecast for the next few years are a political (if not an economic) problem of major proportions. The reason they have become a serious problem, I suggest, is that governmental revenues and debt-financing opportunities, like the proverbial commons, are a common pool (McKenzie, 1982). The benefits from grazing on the budgetary commons are detached from the costs of grazing. Absent user fees, a better specification of property rights, or regulation, each special

The author acknowledges gratefully the research support of the National Science Foundation (SES-8112016) and the constructive comments of Barry Weingast.

interest, geographic constituency, and government bureau may graze at a fraction of its cost. Legislators, in turn, serve as agents for interests, constituents, and bureaus, facilitating their grazing rights and opportunities. There is little incentive to economize on the use of this common resource, since no political actor has to fear being held responsible for the problem. The common pool is a common(s) problem. As Alvin Rabushka cleverly puts in his paper it is as though the American public has provided its 535 legislators each with an American Express card carrying the same account number (Don't leave the House—or the Senate—without it!). Moral restraint is a weak reed with which to discourage a spending spree.

In the papers of this section, each author has implicitly adopted the budgetary commons metaphor. Aranson presents an ingenious argument about the ways politicians, Lombardiesque in their belief that "winning [elections] isn't everything, its the only thing," consume at the common pool. He provides a story, an adaptation of a theory of public choice of which he has been one of the main architects (Aranson and Ordeshook, 1977a,b, 1978, 1981), emphasizing differential monitoring and sanctioning of elected politicians by organized groups. Deficits happen, and particular kinds of political adaptations emerge as myriad policy decisions are made by politicians energized by the electoral connection and their relationships to these groups.

Rabushka, too, takes the overgrazing phenomenon as a political given. His essay is a piece of advocacy for a specific solution to the commons problem—command and control regulation. In the remainder of my remarks I will also take the problem of deficits as a manifestation of a common pool problem. I shall briefly examine three general solutions to such problems—the establishment of property rights, user fees, and regulation. The overriding question for me is whether or not a proposed solution lays down proper incentives for political actors to behave in a more generally appropriate manner than they now do.

Solutions to Budgetary Overgrazing: User Fees

The central feature of grazing on the commons, and expending public funds, is the attenuation of benefits and costs. A congressional district benefits from public expenditure in several ways (this discussion is drawn from Weingast, Shepsle, and Johnsen, 1981). First, such spending often results in local public goods—a floodwall, dam, levy, post office, federal building, and so on—the enjoyment of which is disproportionately (if not exclusively) allocated to district residents. Second, spending in the district to purchase inputs for "government goods" entails a shift in the local demand curve for these inputs. While entry and competition on the supply side may ultimately drive rates of return back to normal, for a period super normal rates may be enjoyed. Moreover, the level of economic activity after equilibration will be higher, thereby generating additional local benefits, e.g., a larger local property tax base, larger payroll volume, etc. These benefits are undeniable and legislators (at the urging of potential beneficiaries) go after them with a vengeance.

What makes them even more attractive is that these benefits may be enjoyed at a fraction of the total cost. While a district enjoys benefits from public expenditures, its tax share to finance those expenditures is normally but a small proportion of the total. To abstract from reality, but not to do any serious injustice to my concerns here, suppose that district j pays tax share t_j ($0 \leq t_j \leq 1$, $\Sigma\, t_j = 1$), that a public project costs T, and that tax revenues are sufficient to cover project costs. Then district j's tax bill is $t_j T$ and it is a net beneficiary of a project if benefits exceed this bill ($b - t_j T > 0$). When all legislators and districts engage in this practice, thereby producing an array of projects (a pork barrel?), every district may be a net loser. Nevertheless, for legislators such behavior constitutes a "dominant strategy" as long as the system is given. And legislators have little incentive to alter a system that allows them to "claim credit" for district projects while "ducking blame" for the aggregate consequences (Mayhew, 1974).

The attenuation of benefits from costs (tax burdens) encourages a preference for bigger, more extensive or intrusive, projects and greater inefficiencies. *A fortiori,* if taxes need not cover costs (if budgets need not be balanced), then the size, extent, and inefficiency of public projects are accentuated (especially if the incidence of debt-financing is subject to illusion or effects a shift of the burden to other citizens or other generations).

Suppose there were a way to charge individuals (or congressional districts) for the benefits they enjoy. Two things follow (assuming costs are fully chargeable, that joint costs can be unpacked and allocated, and so on). First, deficits would be driven to zero (so, too, would surpluses if no charges/taxes applied when no benefits were enjoyed). Second, preferences for public activity would diminish since only those projects that could pass the muster of economic efficiency would win public support (in contrast to a much weaker benefit/cost test when beneficiaries bear only a fraction of the tax burden).

I suspect that both increased efficiency and a preference for a reduced scale of public activity accompany an improved match between benefit incidence and tax burden incidence. I believe further that preferences for public activity are better rationalized in those policy areas where user-charge-like vehicles are employed—proportional charges to, and cost-sharing by, localities for water and reclamation projects, highway funds, and some formula grants; co-payments by individuals for food stamps, medical and hazard insurance.

But user charges are not altogether practical and are unlikely to dampen enthusiasm for public spending sufficiently to make a major dent in deficits. To name three problems (and these may not even be the most important): (i) the difficulty of writing intertemporal contracts that require (allow) an individual to bear a tax burden (enjoy a benefit) at t_1, in exchange for the enjoyment of a benefit (bearing of a burden) at t_2; (ii) the general problems posed by redistributive schemes; and (iii) the difficulty of allocating joint costs and joint benefits. Incentive-compatability problems arise in each of these areas. Even if these difficulties were minimized, there is every reason to believe that legislative agents would seek alternative means by which to bestow benefits on their constituents (the burdens from which were more widely distributed). Cartelization of an industry to preserve cartel profits does not remove incentives to cheat and compete (e.g., in airlines, if not on price than on service, flight frequency, etc.). So, too, with congressional districts. The bottom line, then, is to employ user fees where practical, but not to count on them to reduce budgetary overgrazing or substitute activity by any substantial amount.

Solutions to Budgetary Overgrazing: Regulation

A constitutional amendment to balance the budget is a form of command and control regulation (of politicians)—a set of standards and a mechanism to enforce them. Given this close resemblance of a constitutional amendment to command and control regulation, I find it ironic that some of its leading proponents are in the vanguard of the movement to deregulate America. In particular, they seem to have applied few of the lessons they taught us about economic regulation to constitutional regulation. So, without reviewing Senate Joint Resolution 58, the version of the balanced budget amendment which was endorsed by President Reagan and passed by the Senate (see Rabushka, this volume), let me see if I cannot raise some flags of caution about the general approach.

First, regulation encourages adaptive behavior. The adaptations may accomplish the purposes of the regulation, but then again they may not. And even if the purposes are accomplished, *ex post* it is not always evident that the post-regulation/post-adaptation circumstance has resulted in an improvement of social welfare. In this regard, I am fond of the pedagogical philosophy articulated by my colleague, Lee Benham: "The one thing I try to teach students is that you can't do just one thing." Regulation leaves margins of behavior unregulated, margins on which adaptations take place (the CAB and the airlines come to mind again). In the present context, the most important implication is that a constitutional amendment to balance the budget leaves political ingenuity free to operate.

How might political ingenuity operate in a post-amendment environment? Let me answer this, first, by confessing that my imagination pales in comparison to those of professional politicans for whom billions of dollars ride on their ingenuity and imaginative adaptation. In short, I could not begin to do justice to this question. I can, however, look at how politicans have adapted to previous fiscal constraints and draw some conclusions. I have done this elsewhere (Shepsle, 1982a,b; Hardin, Shepsle and Weingast, 1982), so let me be brief.

Congress, almost from the beginning and except for a brief period in the late nineteenth and early twentieth century, separates authorization from appropriation. Program advocates, sitting on substantive legislative committees, produce bills which create authority to engage in some particular government activity. Programs, however, require both authority and funds, the latter determined by an appropriation produced by the Appropriations Committee in each house. The Appropriations Committee (especially in the House) throughout most of this century has been an extremely conservative force, seeing itself as the last bastion between the federal treasury and hordes of claimants (Fenno, 1966; Schick, 1980). When an irresistible force meets an immovable object, the former finds some way to get around the latter! Between 1880 and 1920, the authorizing committees ganged up and forced the disbanding of the Appropriations Committee in the House, essentially seizing the appropriations function for themselves. In the post-New Deal period, after the Appropriations Committee had been reconstituted, authorizing committees began inventing entitlement programs (reaching their height in the 1960s) which end-ran around Appropriations; they presented the latter with *faits accomplis*. In the 1970s, after the Budget Act proscribed entitlements unless Appropriations approved, loan guarantees, credit programs, and other off-budget schemes were invented. By decade's end well under half of all federal outlays passed through the normal appropriations process. As well, the 1960s and 1970s saw a tremendous growth in regulation—a nonfiscal mechanism for accomplishing public purposes. In short, every effort to constraint programmatic activism was met by ingenious adaptation. Should we really expect a constitutional amendment to work any differently? History says no.

The reason, I maintain—and this is my second flag of caution to the enthusiastic advocates of constitutional regulation—is that regulation does not change incentives. Nothing changes the legislator's natural political predilection to deliver bright shiny objects to the district at as little cost to the district as possible. True, an amendment raises the cost of pursuing that incentive by current practices. But which do you think will change, the incentive or current practices? I suspect the latter.

In sum, advocates of constitutional amendments, like their pro-regulation fellow travelers (politics makes strange bedfellows), have not done their general equilibrium homework. Problems of enforcement, adaptive behavior, and undisturbed incentives do not bode well for regulatory solutions to the problem of overgrazing the budgetary commons.

Rabushka's False Dichotomy

Rabushka (this volume), in his articulate piece of advocacy in behalf of the balanced budget amendment, poses what is to me a false dichotomy (or, if not false, irrelevant). Given the legislative tendency to overgraze, Rabushka suggests there are two modes by which this behavior may be regulated— either institutionally or constitutionally. The former, he claims, is inherently flawed since future Congresses, unless proscribed, may undo whatever a previous Congress has done. A current Congress cannot constrain future Congresses. Hence, no permanent overgrazing prohibition can take the form of an ordinary statute or institutional practice. It must be extraordinary, i.e., a constitutional provision.

This argument conveys the sense that a constitutional provision provides an exogenous enforcement mechanism that both describes what must be enforced and commands enforcement as well. It begs the entire enforcement issue by assuming it is unproblematic. I am not denying that there is a difference between constitutional and statutory provisions. But I believe the difference derives not from its name, but from the different political commitments and intentions that produce the one or the other. In this particular instance, it is the political commitment to balance the budget and the political intention to sanction those whose behavior leads to violations that provide incentives for compliance and enforcement.

Political commitments and incentives are not peculiarly constitutional. Their absence at either the constitutional or institutional level produces failures in governance (witness the Volstead Act). The appropriate dichotomy is incentive-compatible vs. nonincentive compatible. The issue is whether rules—be they constitutional, statutory, or institutional—induce the desired behavior. A constitutional instruction commanding foxes to alter their taste for henhouse residents does not change their fowl preferences. It is not incentive-compatible. And this is precisely the difficulty with attempts to limit legislative overgrazing by command and control regulation.

Solutions to Budgetary Overgrazing: Property Rights

Rights in a common pool may be established in a variety of ways. One, already discussed, is user fees in which a beneficiary is entitled to whatever he pays for. Alternatively, imagine a sort of residual claimant (normally called the owner) empowered to limit or proscribe consumption from the common pool. Such an arrangement, I claim, actually existed up until the very recent past in the Congress. "Institutional regulators"—specifically, the Speaker of the House, the Appropriations Committees, and the Rules Committee—"owned" the budgetary commons. The authorizing committees of Congress dreamed up various schemes for grazing these pastures, but the institutional regulators—the surrogate owners—could say yea or nay. And, with considerable frequency, they said nay.

Rabushka notes that up until 1960 deficits were common only during wars and recessions. It has only been in the last twenty years that deficit financing has become a standard operating procedure. These same twenty years have witnessed a continuing erosion in the power of party and institutional leaders, the destruction of the House Rules Committee, and endruns around the normal appropriations process. The incentives on the part of congressmen to spend public monies for constituency benefits had been and continued to be omnipresent. The means by which to do this in a relatively unconstrained fashion, however, came into being only recently as the power of those who could say no was restricted.

The Congresses of the 1960s and 1970s were consumed by reform (see, e.g., Ornstein, 1976). A by-product of these reforms (some cynics would argue it was their main purpose) was the destruction of the surrogate owners of the budgetary commons. The Rules Committee, in the early 1960s, was expanded and packed in order to "grease the skids" for a new Democratic administration's program. With this, the authorizing committees were freer to act affirmatively on administration initiatives. When the appropriations process remained a constraint—especially in the nondefense area—its wings were clipped with the invention of entitlement, credit, and regulatory tools over which the Appropriations Committees had limited authority. In short, the owners of the budgetary commons had their property expropriated!

The process is reversible. It is my belief that expropriation was the intent of only a small minority in Congress and that, with the deficit problem growing in severity, there is (or would be) considerable sentiment in Congress for reestablishing some institutional regulation of the budgetary commons. If the (re)establishment of property rights is regarded as an appropriate analytical solution to the problem of budgetary overgrazing, then it is preferable to exogenous constraints (like constitutional amendments) because it embodies individuals and institutional entities with the proper incentives to regulate the commons as owners would.

Conclusion

I shall not dwell on the particulars of the case for reestablishing property rights (see Shepsle, 1982a,b). I think, however, that most economists will not, in the abstract, find it a particularly odd solution to a commons problem. Nor will many political scientists be unduly disturbed by the idea of institutional solutions to these problems inasmuch as they echo the very familiar message of Madison and his *Federalist Papers* collaborators, who wrote approvingly of "pitting ambition against ambition" both within and between institutions of government. A corollary of this argument is that a belief in exogenous constraints is misguided and wishful unless there are both the means of enforcement and the incentive, embodied somewhere, to employ them. In the end, it comes down to the question of how best to exploit private interest to preserve the commons. The reader must decide for himself which of the variety of solutions to common pool problems makes best use of the motive force of ambition and interest.

References

Aranson, P. H. and P. C. Ordeshook. "A Prolegomenon to a Theory of the Failure of Representative Democracy." In *American Re-evolution: Papers and Proceedings.* R. Auster and B. Sears (Eds.). Tucson: University of Arizona, Department of Economics, 1977a, 23–46.

Aranson, P. H. "Incrementalism, the Fiscal Illusion, and the Growth of Government in Representative Democracies." Prepared for delivery at the Annual Meeting of the Southern Economic Association, New Orleans, 1977b.

Aranson, P. H. "The Political Bases of Public Sector Growth in a Representative Democracy." Paper prepared for delivery at the Annual Meeting of the American Political Science Association, New York City, 1978.

Aranson, P. H. "Regulation, Redistribution, and Public Choice." *Public Choice* 37 (1981), 69–100.

Fenno, R. F. *The Power of the Purse.* Boston: Little-Brown, 1966.

Hardin, C. M., K. A. Shepsle, and B. R. Weingast. "Public Policy Excesses: Government by Congressional Subcommittee." Formal Publication No. 50. Center for the Study of American Business. Washington University, St. Louis, 1982.

Mayhew, D. Congress: *The Electoral Connection.* New Haven: Yale University Press, 1974.

McKenzie, R. B. "Incentives for a Balanced Budget." Heritage Foundation Backgrounder No. 207. Washington, DC, 1982.

Ornstein, N. J. *Congress in Change: Evolution and Reform.* New York: Praeger, 1976.

Schick, A. 1980. *Congress and Money.* Washington: Urban Institute.

Shepsle, K. A. "The Failure of Congressional Budgeting." Formal Publication   No. 46. Center for the Study of American Business. Washington University, St. Louis, 1982a.

Shepsle, K. A. "Geography, Jurisdiction, and the Congressional Budget Process." Working Paper No. 73. Center for the Study of American Business. Washington University, St. Louis, 1982b.

IV KEYNOTE ADDRESS

7 DEALING WITH DEFICITS AND THE RISE IN FEDERAL SPENDING

Murray L. Weidenbaum

At a time when, alas, economist jokes are in vogue, I would like to add my favorite wisecrack about our profession: If all the economists in the world were laid end to end, it might be a good thing. This sour remark is instigated by my having to listen to, and occasionally participate in, what seems to be endless debates on whether budget deficits really matter, and, if so, on what arcane basis of measurement. I finally have found a short cut that reconciles the great intellectual wisdom of our profession with the practical concerns of participants in and observers of financial markets. Thus, I conclude that deficits do not matter—but that Treasury borrowing and money creation surely do!

Having disposed of this weighty subject so quickly, let me go on to examine several current policy questions relating to federal finance. First, let us consider the nature of the changes made in federal outlays by the Reagan Administration and second, let us analyze some of the economic implications, covering both military and civilian programs. This task, it turns out, is a bit more complicated than one might expect.

The author is indebted to Lee Benham, Kenneth Chilton, Arthur Denzau, Ronald Penoyer, Kenneth Shepsle, and Barry Weingast for numerous helpful comments on an earlier draft.

How Much Has the Budget Been Cut?

To begin, it is difficult to directly compare the current estimates of outlays under the Reagan program with those contained in President Carter's last budget message, presented in January, 1981. Since then, the publications of the Office of Management and Budget have generally "adjusted" the Carter numbers for a change that it believes President Carter should have made— providing for what is now considered to be an adequate national defense.[1] That procedure does have its advantages. That is, by assigning the present Administration's increases in national defense to the numbers associated with the previous Administration, OMB can take credit for its cuts in civilian outlays while ignoring the increases in military outlays. It should be noted that this unusual procedure is an OMB practice. The White House Office of Policy Information, in at least two of its recent publications, uses the more straightforward approach of comparing Carter's numbers with Reagan's numbers, assigning to the present Administration all of the changes it made in the budget, both up and down.[2] However, these latter publications lack the detail contained in the budget statements.

What all this means in practice is that, if we want to compare Reagan with Carter, we must dig the Carter reports out of our archives and compare the data in them with the figures in the most current Reagan budget publications. I will note in passing that this is a chore that the average journalist working under a tight deadline may forego. In any event, I find such statistical explorations useful for those engaged in more leisurely scholarly pursuits.

Table 7–1 contains a first effort to make such a comparison. It compares total outlays for fiscal years 1982–1984 as estimated in the last Carter Budget report with those shown in the most recent Reagan Administration budget report. Clearly, the Reagan spending totals in current dollars (unadjusted for inflation) are lower in each year than the Carter figures. The current Administration's much slower growth in civilian spending more than offsets its increases in defense outlays, but by about one half of the 1981 tax cuts—about $350 billion versus over $700 billion for the five year period 1982–86.

More sophisticated comparisons can be made. For example, the comparison can be restated in terms of constant dollars, using in each case the inflation assumptions that accompanied the respective current dollar estimates. The results based on the GNP deflators are contained in table 7–2. The differences between the two sets of projected outlays are very much smaller than in table 7–1, about $23 billion when viewed in real (deflated) terms over the period 1982–86.

Table 7–1. Reagan and Carter Budget Estimates
In billions of current dollars

Fiscal Year	Defense Carter	Defense Reagan	All Other Carter	All Other Reagan	Total Carter	Total Reagan	Difference
1982	$184.4	$187.7	$554.9	$543.3	739.3	$731.0	$ −8.3
1983	210.4	221.5	606.9	540.0	817.3	761.5	−55.8
1984	237.8	253.4	652.5	559.1	890.3	812.5	−77.8
1985	267.8	292.5	700.1	582.2	967.9	874.7	−93.2
1986	299.5	332.0	750.8	600.7	1050.3	932.7	−117.6

Source: Federal Budget for Fiscal Year 1982; Mid-Session Review of the 1983 Budget

Table 7–2. Reagan and Carter Budget Estimates In billions of constant
1972 dollars (Using GNP deflators in respective documents)

Fiscal Year	Amount Carter	Reagan	Difference
1982	$345.0	$354.9	$ +9.9
1983	351.7	347.1	−4.6
1984	355.4	347.7	−7.7
1985	361.2	353.0	−8.2
1986	368.8	356.1	−12.7

Source: Federal Budget for Fiscal Year 1982; Mid-Session Review of the 1983 Budget

A variation of this theme is contained in table 7–3, where the CPI assumptions are used to adjust both sets of outlay projections. In this case, the results are more ambiguous. That is, using the CPI as a deflator, the aggregate estimates for fiscal years 1982–1986 under the Reagan programs are shown on balance to be a bit higher than the Carter estimates—by about $7 billion.

It does seem clear that, especially in relation to the 1981 tax cuts, the net spending reductions in the past twenty months seem to be quite modest. It is not surprising, therefore, that current estimates of the budget deficit for the next several years are unusually high (see table 7–4).

Table 7–3.   Reagan and Carter Budget Estimates in Billions of Constant Dollars (Using CPI Deflators in Respective Documents)

| Fiscal Year | Amount | | Difference |
	Carter	Reagan	
1982	$241.0	$253.5	$+12.5
1983	245.0	247.4	+2.4
1984	247.6	247.0	−.6
1985	251.7	250.0	−1.7
1986	257.0	251.5	−5.5

Source: Federal Budget for Fiscal Year 1982; Mid-Session Review of the 1983 Budget

Table 7–4.   Projections of the Federal Budget
(Fiscal Years, In billions of dollars)

| | 1982 | | 1983 | | 1984 | | 1985 | |
	OMB	CBO	OMB	CBO	OMB	CBO	OMB	CBO
Outlays	$731	$733	$762	$788	$812	$844	$875	$910
Revenues	622	621	647	633	720	692	801	757
Deficit	109	112	115	155	92	152	74	153

Source: Office of Management and Budget, *Mid-Session Review of the 1983 Budget,* July 15, 1982; Congressional Budget Office, *The Economic Outlook: An Update,* September 1982.

The Problem of Entitlements

When we probe beneath the aggregate spending levels, we find that entitlements or payments to individuals constitute the largest category of the budget. In recent years, entitlement payments also have been the most rapidly growing budget category. It therefore is quite appropriate that increasing attention is being given to this area.[3] I have little to add to the extensive public debate. I am, however, struck by the vast amount of ignorance attached to the largest entitlement, social security benefit payments.

Given the current focus on the desire to reduce those outsized budget deficits, any discussion of possible change in social security outlays is immediately attacked as an effort to balance the budget on the backs of social security pensioners. It is true that facing the problem of social security financing would likely result in smaller budget deficits. But—and this is the fundamental point that is usually ignored—even if the federal budget were in such great shape that we could declare dividends out of the surplus, we would still have to face the basic problem that the social security system is not adequately financed.

Over the years, Congress has been more aggressive in voting benefit increases than in enacting the social security tax increases to pay for them. Also, demographic and economic trends have turned out in recent years to be more adverse than assumed in the system's actuarial calculations. Thus the public debate on social security seems to have the issue backwards: our attention is needed on the question of social security finance, not because of the budget deficits but to ensure that the program fully meets the disbursements to which it is committed. But we must recognize that, although it is the largest single item, social security is only one of the many entitlement programs. A comprehensive budget restraint effort must take a hard look at the other components in this category, including veterans' pensions and government employees' retirement benefits.

The Question of National Defense Spending

Let us turn to the second largest category of budget outlays, national defense. Here we should acknowledge at the outset that there is a broad based agreement on the need to expand US national defense spending. Both the Carter and Reagan budgets projected significant growth in defense spending in real terms for each of the five fiscal years 1982–1986. As would be expected, there has been considerable discussion and disagreement over the specifics of the buildup, including the question of how rapid an expansion in military spending is desirable. But it should be recognized that none of this is a debate between hawks and doves.

Among the specific questions raised is the economic feasibility of the currently contemplated schedule of military outlays. As the Council of Economic Advisers (CEA) stated in its annual report accompanying the President's Economic Report of February 10, 1982, "any economic effects ... must be assessed in the context of the overriding need for maintaining the level of defense spending necessary for national security."[5] Moreover, the 1981–82 recession has resulted in such substantial amounts of excess capacity in American industry that, at least for the next year or two, there is likely to be adequate industrial capacity to meet military and civilian needs. But it is useful to look beyond, to the middle of the decade when significant economic growth may coincide with the peak of the military buildup. In such circumstances, capacity questions would arise. The CEA annual report deals with that eventuality, pointing out three results of the defense buildup that can be anticipated:

1. The substantial transfer of resources in the durables sector to defense production may increase relative prices in at least some of the affected industries. Both the Department of Defense and private purchasers may have to pay more for goods from these industries. This premium is likely to increase with the size of the defense budget.

2. Increased demand may produce delays in the delivery of military goods. Delivery timetables that seem realistic today may, in some cases, become obsolete as producers try to accommodate both the defense buildup and rigorous expansion in civilian investment at the same time.

3. Some temporary crowding out of private investment may occur. Defense procurement uses many of the same physical resources needed for private investment in civilian producer durables and the Defense Production Act gives defense priority in the market place. Some private firms may turn to foreign sources for materials while others may cancel or postpone plans for expansion.[6]

Along similar lines, a private economic consulting organization—Data Resources, Inc. (DRI), of Cambridge, Massachusetts—has stated that the concentration of the planned military increases within the procurement and research and development accounts implies weapon production growth rates more rapid than those which occurred at the peak of the Vietnam buildup.[7] Moreover, the present expansion occurs after a decade of steady reductions in the defense industrial base.

DRI also pointed out:

... the combination of the increasing defense shares and the acceleration in growth rates raises concerns about industrial capabilities and spillover impacts on the economy.[8]

DRI goes on to note that, with the implementation of significant investment programs in both plant and equipment and skilled labor forces, the problems of price pressures, bottlenecks and crowding out of civilian demand "could be constrained to isolated instances." See table 7–5 for some examples of extremely rapid growth rates in future defense industry requirements. Over the six year period 1982–87, double digit increases in annual output are shown for many industries, ranging from semiconductors to computers. The DRI conclusion is that the uncertainties about the capabilities of the defense industrial base and its linkages to other critical economic variables "will continue to cloud decisions regarding the defense

Table 7–5. Projected Increases in Output in Major Defense Supplying
Industries, 1982–1987

Average annual real percentage growth in projected output

Industry	Annual Increase In Total Output, 1982–87	Annual Increase In Defense Output, 1982–87
Radio & TV Communication Equipment	11.2%	15.7%
Aircraft	12.8	18.6
Aircraft engines and engine parts	13.0	16.3
Aircraft parts & equipment, n.e.c.	11.2	14.7
Complete guided missiles	11.5	15.2
Electronic components, n.e.c.	11.2	17.2
Tanks and tank components	22.6	27.1
Ammunition, excluding small arms, n.e.c.	15.0	15.2
Motor vehicles parts and accessories	6.3	20.5
Motor vehicles	6.7	27.8
Other ordnance and accessories	13.5	14.4
Communciations, excluding radio and TV	6.9	10.3
Semiconductors	13.7	20.2
Miscellaneous machinery	6.9	15.3
Electronic computing equipment	12.6	16.8
Aluminum rolling and drawing	7.9	17.9
Miscellaneous plastic products	8.5	17.3
Primary aluminum	7.3	17.1
Plastic materials and resins	8.8	17.8
Special dies, tools and accessories	8.2	15.8
Telephone and telegraph equipment	11.5	16.4
Metal stampings	7.0	18.6
Industrial trucks and tractors	9.9	14.1
Machine tools, metal cutting	9.2	15.7
Iron and steel foundries	4.3	13.2

Source: Compiled from Data Resources, Inc., *Defense Economics Research Report*, August 1982.

budget."[9] This point is enhanced when we consider that the author of the paper just cited heads up the ongoing analysis, commissioned by the Pentagon, of the economic impacts of the defense program.

A more recent Data Resources report is even less sanguine, pointing out that, since 1948, there has never before been a period of sustained growth in real defense spending such as that now planned. This more recent study concludes that the projected requirements for such large increases in defense output raise obvious questions about the ability of industry to meet them without adverse implications in terms of costs and leadtimes.[10] A variation of that theme appears in a recently released study by the US Department of Commerce which reminds us that defense expenditures do not affect all industries equally, but have "highly concentrated industrial impacts."[11]

The Commerce Department examined a somewhat different time period than did DRI, but the conclusions are fairly similar. For most of the 58 major defense supplying industries which it studied, the Department of Commerce reported that existing capacity is sufficient to supply the projected military and civilian demands through 1985. However, the Department said that, should further capacity expansion not take place in some of these industries, meeting projected 1985 requirements would mean using outmoded, economically inefficient capacity, which would increase costs and prices.[12] For example, requirements for lead smelting and refining are projected to rise by 12 percent from 1979 to 1985, but economically efficient capacity is estimated to decline by 4 percent. Likewise, requirements for brass, bronze, and copper foundries are shown to increase by 32 percent, but economically efficient capacity is expected to rise by 25 percent (see table 7–6).

The Commerce study reported that some of our basic metal processing industries will likely need to increase their dependence on foreign sources of supply in order to meet the stepped-up military demands. For example, the electrometallurgical products industry (which was specifically noted because of its "qualitative importance to defense") met 27.6 percent of its needs with imports in 1979, and is expected to increase that dependency to 45 percent in 1985. Likewise, zinc smelting and refining is anticipated to increase its import dependency from 33.4 percent in 1979 to 45 percent in 1985. Imports of miscellaneous refined nonferrous metals are estimated to comprise 66 percent of the industry in 1985, compared to 55.7 percent in 1979 (see table 7–7). It is ironic to note the matter-of-fact way in which the Commerce Department reports such increased foreign dependence for some of the key defense producing industries when on many other occasions, the hoary national security argument is trotted out to justify a host of subsidies to sectors of the economy far less closely related to defense output.

Table 7–6. Demand and Supply Balance of Selected Defense-Intensive
Industries, 1979–1988

Industry	Growth in Output Requirements 1979–1985	Potential Increase in Supply	
		Economically Efficient[a]	Maximum Attainable[b]
Guided missiles and space vehicles	86%	86%	98%
Ammunition, except for small arms, n.e.c.	50	119	133
Tanks and tank components	83	83	107
Small arms	7	40	50
Small arms ammunition	82	72	89
Ordinance & accessories, n.e.c.	33	112	128
Iron and steel forgings	19	33	39
Lead smelting and refining	12	−4	11
Aluminum production and refining	15	16	16
Nonferrous rolling and drawing, n.e.c.	33	33	37
Brass, bronze and copper foundries	32	25	37
Electronic computing equipment	83	106	122
Semiconductors and related devices	76	106	116

[a]Based on concept of preferred capacity, defined as the level of operations plant managers
prefer not to exceed because of considerations of cost and economic efficiency.
[b]Based on concept of practical capacity. Assumes no material, utility, or labor shortage and
no consideration of increased pay or other input costs as limiting factors.
Source: US Department of Commerce, Bureau of Industrial Economics.

The point of these data should not be misunderstood. Drawing attention to
the economic impacts of the contemplated expansion of military outlays does
not call in question the desirablity of the expansion but, rather, its feasibility
and cost in the period contemplated. An implicit assumption arises from
these concerns: any adjustment of scheduled defense outlays to conform
more closely with expected domestic production capabilities would result in
slowing down the rate of increase in defense spending in the next few years
and thus lower the projected deficits.

Table 7–7. Changing Import Dependence of Selected
Defense Industries

Industry	Imports as Percent of Total Supply	
	1979	1985 estimated
Iron and ferroalloy ores mining	25.0	28.1
Small arms	9.4	10.6
Blast furnaces and steel mills	10.1	13.0
Electrometallurgical products	27.6	45.0
Lead smelting and refining	8.8	11.0
Zinc smelting and refining	33.4	45.0
Aluminum production and refining	8.9	10.0
Refining of nonferrous metals, n.e.c.	55.7	66.0
Machine tools, metal-cutting types	17.2	23.0
Machine tools, metal-forming types	9.2	13.6
Ball and roller bearings	10.5	14.0
Instruments to measure electricity	8.9	13.0
Semiconductors and related devices	20.6	30.0
Electronic components, n.e.c.	8.0	11.5
Optical instruments and lenses	14.1	19.5

Source: US Department of Commerce, Bureau of Industrial Economics

Conclusions

In responding to the concerns over the continuing large federal deficits projected for the next several years, I have emphasized the desirability of another hard look at the spending side of the budget. Unlike another round of tax increases, restraining government expenditures is entirely consistent with the efforts of President Reagan to strengthen the private sector by reducing the size of the federal government.

Three major areas of the budget appear to be promising candidates for further pruning of outlays—above and beyond the Reagan Administration's important existing efforts to ferret out low priority and postponable items and to curb waste, fraud, and abuse:

The So-called Entitlements. These open-ended commitments on the budget range from social security and medicare to medicaid, welfare, veterans' pensions, and the retirement systems for federal employees, military and civilian. In the short run, reductions could be made in the generous formulas for computing annual cost-of-living increases (the COLA clauses) contained in many of these programs. More fundamental changes could be made by recognizing the great extent to which many of these "social insurance" programs have taken on a subsidy or welfare aspect—e.g., providing benefit payments far more generous than those that would result from basing the benefits solely on employee/employer contributions plus earnings on those contributions. Making benefits subject to income taxes—as is now done with private retirement benefits—would reduce the net subsidy payment, especially to those taxpayers with substantial amounts of other income.

The Defense Budget.   Official projections of future military outlays, in real terms, have risen successively during the last two years from five percent to seven percent to nine percent or more per annum. There seems to be little justification offered of the economic feasibility of this sharply upward movement. Without prejudging the results, intensive analysis should be given to the military budget, comparable to the tough minded attitude quite properly taken toward many civilian spending activities of the federal government. Surely, reducing the extent of cost overruns and bottlenecks in defense production will help to maintain the necessary support for the strengthened national defense that is needed in the dangerous world in which we live.

Because of the potential capacity problems, a given cutback in nominal militlary spending would actually result in less than a proportional reduction in real procurement outlays. This would come about because of reduced price pressures on military purchasing generally.

Imbedded Subsidies.   Advocates of smaller federal budgets typically focus on entitlements and/or defense spending because these are the two largest categories. However, it does not take a great deal of research to discover a third category of the budget, "all other." Contrary to widespread belief, not all of the items in this part of the budget are social programs, nor have they been cut to the bone. Generous and expanding programs such as subsidies to dairy and tobacco farmers and sugar producers quickly come to mind. There is no serious justification for these subsidies, and many others like them in other departments of the federal government. Such special benefits to specific segments of the society are in the budget simply because of the political muscle of the producer or other special interest groups supporting them. The Congressional Budget Office has presented several comprehensive listings of potential budget cuts that could be made. There is no shortage of information. All that is lacking is the will to cut more.

On reflection, we need to realize that at times—such as earlier this year—the failure to curtail federal spending leads to pressures for tax increases. Given the outlook for rising deficit financing, if we are to avoid further reversals of the Administration's most welcome tax cuts, more of the existing sacred cows in the federal budget should be taken out of pasture and led to slaughter.

Notes

1. See, for example, US Office of Management and Budget, *Fiscal Year 1983 Budget Revisions,* March 1981, p. 3.
2. White House Office of Policy Information, *Real Growth in the U.S. Defense Budget,* September 22, 1982, and *Non-Defense Budget Growth Reductions,* September 23, 1982.
3. See, for example, C. M. Hardin and K. W. Chilton, *Budget Control and Indexed Entitlements: Are They Compatible?,* 1981.
4. White House Office of Policy Information, *op. cit.*
5. *Economic Report of the President,* February 1982, together with the Annual Report of the Council of Economic Advisers.
6. *Ibid.,* p. 86.
7. G. F. Brown, Jr., "Defense and the Economy: An Analysis of the Reagan Administration's Programs," *Data Resources U.S. Review* (May 1982), p. 1.17.
8. *Ibid.,* p. 1.24.
9. *Ibid.*
10. Data Resources, Inc., *Defense Economics Research Report,* August 1982, p. 7.
11. US Department of Commerce, Bureau of Industrial Economics, *Sectoral Implications of Defense Expenditures,* August 1982, p. 4.
12. *Ibid.,* p. 8.

References

Brown, F., Jr. "Defense and the Economy: An Analysis of the Reagan Administration Programs." *Data Resources U.S. Review* (May 1982).

Data Resources, Inc. *Defense Economic Research Report,* August 1982.

Economic Report of the President. February 1982, Washington, DC: Government Printing Office, 1982.

Hardin, C. M. and K. W. Chilton, *Budget Control and Indexed Entitlements: Are They Compatible?* St. Louis: Center for the Study of American Business, Washington University, 1981.

US Department of Commerce, Bureau of Industrial Economics. *Sectoral Implications of Defense Expenditures.* Washington, DC: Government Printing Office. August, 1982.

US Office of Management and Budget. *Fiscal Year 1982 Budget Revisions.* Washington, DC: Government Printing Office, March 1981.

White House Office of Policy Information, *Real Growth in the U.S. Defense Budget,* September 22, 1982.

White House Office of Policy Information, *Non-Defense Budget Growth Reductions,* September 23, 1982.

Contributing Authors

Peter H. Aranson, Emory University, Atlanta

Alan H. Auerbach, Harvard University and National Bureau of Economic Research

Alan S. Blinder, Princeton University

Scott E. Hein, Federal Reserve Bank of St. Louis

Laurence J. Kotlikoff, Yale University and National Bureau of Economic Research

Preston J. Miller, Federal Reserve Bank of Minneapolis

Frederic S. Mishkin, Northwestern University, National Bureau of Economic Research, and University of Chicago

Franco Modigliani, M.I.T. Sloan School of Management

Roger G. Noll, California Institute of Technology

Alvin Rabushka, Hoover Institution, Stanford University

V. Vance Roley, Federal Reserve Bank of Kansas City

Kenneth A. Shepsle, Professor of Political Science and Research Associate at the Center for the Study of American Business, Washington University, St. Louis

Jerome L. Stein, Brown University

Murray L. Weidenbaum, Mallinckrodt Distinguished University Professor, Washington University, St. Louis

237

List of Conference Participants

Bai Akridge, Washington University

James Alt, Washington University

Peter Aranson, Emory University

Alan Auerbach, Harvard University

Tom August, McDonnell Douglas Corp.

Rachel Balbach, Centerre Bank

Anatol B. Balbach, Federal Reserve Bank of St. Louis

Sandy Batten, Federal Reserve Bank of St. Louis

Arbi Ben Abdallah, Washington University

Lee Benham, Center for the Study of American Business

John Biggs, Washington University

Jerre Birdsong, Union Electric Company

Bob Blanchard, St. Louis Globe Democrat

Alan Blinder, Princeton University

Norman N. Bowsher, Federal Reserve Bank of St. Louis

David Brown, Washington University

James Brzyski, Northwestern Mutual Life Insurance

Randy Calvert, Washington University

Claudia Campbell, Washington University

Keith Carlson, Federal Reserve Bank of St. Louis

239

Kenneth Chilton, Center for the Study of American Business
Dan Clark, Centerre Bank
Norman Coats, Ralston Purina Co.
Don Cox, Washington University
Christian de Boissieu, University of Paris
Art Denzau, CSAB
Lou Ederington, Washington University
Steve Fazzari, Washington University
A. Nicholas Filippello, Monsanto Company
Mark Flannery, The Wharton School
Joel Fried, Federal Reserve Bank of St. Louis
Thomas Gettings, Federal Reserve Bank of Chicago
Tom Gilligan, Council of Economic Advisors
Kevin Grier, Washington University
Joe Golec, Washington University
Clifford M. Hardin, CSAB
Ronald Harris, Washington University
Scott Hein, Federal Reserve Bank of St. Louis
Dean Hiebert, Illinois State University
Richard Henken, Harris Trust and Savings Bank
Jerome Hollenhorst, Southern Illinois University
Brian Horrigan, Federal Reserve Bank of Philadelphia
Raymond Jean, Washington University
Homer Jones
Edward Kane, Ohio State University
Bill Kester, St. Louis Post Dispatch
Robert W. King, Lindenwood College
Laurence Kotlikoff, Yale University
Michael Krassa, Washington University
Kenneth Lehn, Washington University
Michael Levy, Conference Board
Jim Little, Washington University
Clifton Luttrell, Federal Reserve Bank of St. Louis

Kevin Maloney, Washington University
Paul E. Merz, St. Louis University
Laurence Meyer, Washington University
Preston Miller, Federal Reserve Bank of Minneapolis
Hyman Minsky, Washington University
Fredric Mishkin, Visiting Prof., Northwestern University
William Mitchell, University of Missouri
Franco Modigliani, MIT
Cornelia Motheral, House Budget Committee
Mike Munger, Washington University
Greg Neihaus, Washington University
Howard Neiman, Washington University
Roger Noll, California Institute of Technology
Randolph Ollom, Washington University
Seymour Patterson, Northeast Missouri State
. Howard Perez, May Company Dept. Stores
Joel Prakken, IBM
John H. Qualls, Monsanto Company
Alvin Rabushka, Stanford University
Fred Raines, Washington University
David Ramsey, Illinois State University
Fred Ribe, Congressional Budget Office
Brian Roberts, Washington University
V. Vance Roley, Federal Reserve Bank of Kansas City
Karl Scheld, Federal Reserve Bank of Chicago
Kenneth Shepsle, Center for the Study of American Business
Donald Simonson, University of Oklahoma
Michael Smirlock, The Wharton School
Jerome Stein, Brown University
Courtenay Stone, Federal Reserve Bank of St. Louis
Werner Sublette, Northeast Missouri State
John Sylvia, Harris Trust and Savings Bank
Jack Tatom, Federal Reserve Bank of St. Louis

Dan Thornton, Federal Reserve Bank of St. Louis
David Tsadka, Washington University
Chris Varvares, Washington University
Robert Virgil, Washington University
Eric Webber, Federal Reserve Bank of St. Louis
Murray Weidenbaum, Center for the Study of American Business
Barry Weingast, Center for the Study of American Business
Dee Wilson, Bond Week
Rick Wilson, Washington University
John Wooley, Washington University
Jess Yawitz, Washington University
Burton Zwick, Prudential Insurance Company